Faulkner's Sexualities
FAULKNER AND YOKNAPATAWPHA
2007

Faulkner's Sexualities

FAULKNER AND YOKNAPATAWPHA, 2007

EDITED BY
ANNETTE TREFZER
AND
ANN J. ABADIE

UNIVERSITY PRESS OF MISSISSIPPI
JACKSON

www.upress.state.ms.us

The University Press of Mississippi is a member of the Association of
American University Presses.

Manufactured in the United States of America

First printing 2010
∞
Library of Congress Cataloging-in-Publication Data

Faulkner and Yoknapatawpha Conference (34th : 2007 : University
of Mississippi)
Faulkner's sexualities : Faulkner and Yoknapatawpha, 2007 / edited
by Annette Trefzer and Ann J. Abadie.
p. cm.
Includes bibliographical references and index.
ISBN 978-1-60473-560-4 (alk. paper)
1. Faulkner, William, 1897–1962—Criticism and
interpretation—Congresses. 2. Faulkner, William,
1897–1962—Sexual behavior—Congresses. 3. Faulkner, William,
1897–1962—Aesthetics—Congresses. 4. Sex in literature—Congresses. 5. Sex (Psychology) in literature—Congresses. 6. Gender
identity in literature—Congresses. I. Trefzer, Annette, 1960– II.
Abadie, Ann J. III. Title.
PS3511.A86Z7832113 2007
813'.52—dc22   2009034639

British Library Cataloging-in-Publication Data available

In Memoriam,

Martha Glenn Stephens Cofield
November 23, 1935–September 29, 2008

Charles E. "Chuck" Noyes
July 19, 1917–August 30, 2008

Jill Faulkner Summers
June 14, 1933–April 21, 2008

Contents

Introduction

Every decade scholarship on William Faulkner concentrates with renewed energy on the topic of sex and gender in his work, and every time, the conversation shifts. At the twelfth annual Faulkner and Yoknapatawpha Conference in 1985 on "Faulkner and Women," critics heatedly debated whether or not Faulkner portrayed his female characters with sympathy or misogyny.[1] What, they wondered, did Faulkner think and say about women, and where in Faulkner's fiction do we find a woman who is feminine *and* smart? In the 1994 volume *Faulkner and Gender*, the discussion shifted from feminism to gender studies.[2] At stake were the difference between sex and gender and the extent to which gender is socially and historically constructed. Faulkner, scholars observed, presents us with a plurality of gender performances and a wide "network of gender enactments."

The title of this current volume—*Faulkner's Sexualities*—directs our attention away from the conjunction that customarily binds Faulkner to various topics perceived as external to him. In the preceding volumes *Faulkner and Women* and *Faulkner and Gender* the conjunction leaves the integrity of the "master" intact and bound in oppositional relation to the subject. *Faulkner's Sexualities* promises instead a more intimate implication of Faulkner in the subject at hand. The reference to *Faulkner's* sexualities is intentionally ambiguous—his own? his works?—and blurs the lines between the author's body and the body of his work in addressing the dynamics of sex, sexuality, and sexual desire. To speak of Faulkner's sexualities, therefore, means to address the sexuality of the author *and* the sexuality of his texts. The reference to *sexualities*, in the title's plural form, opens a field of signification that gestures beyond the binary relations of the terms "heterosexual" and "homosexual." In *The History of Sexuality* Michel Foucault points out that these terms are inventions of the nineteenth century, with the term "homosexuality" (1870) predating the term "heterosexuality." The plural form of sexualities refutes these binaries and includes the terms bisexual, lesbian, gay, and straight. But even these terms, many critics believe, no longer signify with any certainty or consistency. Many recent studies on sexuality propose that "all identity categories have been, or should be, or must be, disrupted, questioned, and queered."[3]

For the essays collected in this volume, the theoretical foundations by Sigmund Freud, Jacques Lacan, Michel Foucault, Judith Butler, and Eve Sedgwick remain relevant for a discussion of gender and sexuality today. When Faulkner was writing in the early half of the twentieth century, the presence and influence of Freud's psychoanalytic theories would have still been prevalent. Freud's *Three Essays on the Theory of Sexuality* (1905) attempted to relate the body, sex, and pleasure.[4] Freud believed that all subjects are "sexualized" and that it is essentially an inner drive (Trieb) or disposition that produces sexual pleasure. By contrast, for Foucault, sexuality is not simply the natural expression of some personal drive or desire, but a discourse written in or on the body. Sexuality, Foucault argues, is produced in culture and discourse itself. In the modern era, sexualities multiplied in "an explosion of distinct discursivities which took form in demography, biology, medicine, psychiatry, psychology, ethics, pedagogy, and political criticism" (33), and, we might add, art and literature.[5] In other words, sexuality is closely linked to textuality. Based on the idea that sexuality is essentially linguistic, Cristina Garrigós suggests a number of interesting propositions:

a) Literary texts have a sex, not only that of the author reflected in the text, but an independent voice with its own desire.
b) Literary texts have a relationship with other texts, including literary and non-literary ones.
c) These relationships take place at the same level, that is there exists neither a temporal nor a hierarchical difference between them that should condition their relationship.[6]

Taking into consideration these propositions, she coins the term "sextuality," which implies an acknowledgement on the part of the literary critic of "writing as the site where desires, fears, and *jouissance* . . . come to existence."[7] Thus, she concludes, "the term *sextuality* includes both the idea of *sexuality*, that is, of a particular sexual attitude or appetite, while at the same time making it clear that we are referring to texts, and that we have to bear in mind their *textuality*."[8] It would follow that Faulkner's texts have bodies with their own desires and erotic dynamics, and the inquiries in *Faulkner's Sexualities* attempt to address these.

What, then, is the status of sex and sexuality in Faulkner? What are the major texts that address this question? The authors in this volume raise provocative questions about how Faulkner's writing offers ways of thinking about sexual subjectivities in relation to the dynamics of the body, language, and culture. How, they ask, does he narrate sexual identities, how does he construct them in and around the dynamics of speech? How does he relate to the cultural and material conditions of sex in the South in the first half of the twentieth century? How does he understand the political dimensions of modern sexual economies? How does he imagine sexuality and the possibility of love in a racially bifurcated South? What medical and scientific texts on the subject did he read? How did he understand the sexed subject of early twentieth-century sexology and medicine, a subject that was typically understood as either hetero- or homosexual, normal or aberrant, healthy or pathological? What we find is that at the same time as science was trying to figure out what was "normal" and healthy, Faulkner was experimenting with the pluralities of sexuality and sexual desire. From his early work in the 1920s to the postwar period, Faulkner's examination of sex and his writing of sexualities reveal that daily life in Yoknapatawpha was part of the modernist climate of sexual experimentation.

The essays in this volume form a dialogue around particular questions and topics. The first three contributions by Catherine Gunter Kodat, Gary Richards, and Jaime Harker probe Faulkner's sexual experimentation through the framework of queer theory. These readings of Faulkner's work yield a rich understanding of complicated homoerotic desires and fears. Starting from the premise that any discussion of sexuality bears the impressions of the particular social and economic conditions of its emergence, the next two essays, by Michael Zeitlin and Peter Lurie, examine the erotic as part of a modern political economy. Both essays link Faulkner's depiction of sexuality to the rising mass culture industry and to an urban economic modernity that threatens to extinguish erotic passion. The idea that the sexual subject is always materially and discursively constructed is important in the essays by Deborah McDowell, Kristin Fujie, and John Duvall, who take up the topic of racialized sexuality in the South. Against the background of slavery and racial segregation, these scholars ask, how does race impact the workings of erotic desire? What, for instance, was the status of black women as love objects for white men? Or, of white women as erotic subjects for men, black and white? Or, of white heterosexual men, like Faulkner? Following these questions about racial and sexual interrelations in Faulkner's work, the closing contributions by Michael Wainwright and Caroline Garnier both focus on the sexual politics of Faulkner's 1931 novel *Sanctuary*.

We begin, however, with the recent shift to a queer framework for Faulkner studies. In "Unhistoricizing Faulkner" Catherine Kodat asks about the questions queer theory poses for the popular mode of historicist literary analysis. To answer these questions, she looks back to the New Historicism that came to dominate the academy for the last twenty-five years in the wake of Fredric Jameson's famous 1981 injunction:

always historicize! She argues that Faulkner scholarship—beginning with Eric Sunquist's *Faulkner: The House Divided*—eagerly responded to Jameson's call by reconstructing the social and historical contexts of his fiction. The recent move to queer theory, however, "which gives us the queer Faulkner," seems to press "against many assumptions governing historicist literary analysis." What these pressure points are, and how the study of sexualities intersects with new historicism, is the subject of the first part of Kodat's essay. Here she surveys the interface of sexuality with history in Foucault's work, with biology and rhetoric in Judith Butler's theory, and with psychoanalysis in Tim Dean's work. All of these theorists share a suspicion of the idea that sexual identity is ever knowable, and for many of them, the question of sexuality best remains a question. How Faulkner approaches this question is the subject of the second part of Kodat's essay, which turns to Faulkner's short story "The Leg," one of six stories from the "Beyond" section in his *Collected Stories*. This story, located "beyond" immediate historical concerns, as Kodat argues, traces "multiplying circuits of sexual fantasy and action" involving an amputated limb—the leg—that stands in for a loss and functions much like Lacan's "objet petit a" in the homoerotic plot of the story.

The homoerotic plot of Faulkner's fiction and life is also the topic of Gary Richards's "The Artful and Crafty Ones of the French Quarter: Male Homosexuality and Faulkner's Early Prose Writings." Richards suggests that Faulkner's literary apprenticeship in New Orleans and his friendship with the painter William Spratling made him anxious about "cultural conflations of male artistry and male homosexuality." For Richards, it is not Sherwood Anderson who stands at the center of a circle of artists during Faulkner's time in New Orleans, as critics claim, but rather the openly gay William Spratling. Faulkner lived with Spratling for several months, the two traveled to Europe together, and they shared many similarities and interests, including their collaborative 1926 book, *Sherwood Anderson and Other Famous Creoles*. Faulkner's early sketches, written for the New Orleans *Times-Picayune* and the literary magazine the *Double Dealer*, as well as some of the scenes and portrayals in his novel *Mosquitoes*, have strong homoerotic currents. Drawing on previous work by John Duvall and Minrose Gwin, Richards reads many of these early sketches to find in them "a near constant anxiety about heterosexuality" and a "constellation of homoerotic images." Richards concludes that in Faulkner's fiction of the 1920s, Spratling was a "significant source of inspiration"—in fact, he may have been so significant that Faulkner grew increasingly anxious about links between art and homosexuality, including his own writing and sexual orientation.

Modeled after Eve Sedgwick's famously provocative questions, Richards poses the question of a gay legibility—"has there ever been a gay Faulkner?"—and Jaime Harker asks "has there ever been a lesbian Faulkner?" The answer to both questions is a resounding "yes." Harker's essay, "'And You, Too, Sister, Sister?': Lesbian Sexuality, *Absalom Absalom!*, and the Reconstruction of the Southern Family," opens an intertextual conversation between Faulkner's novel and Southern lesbian literature. Harker points out textual similarities that allow her to posit Faulkner's novel as a "foremother" to contemporary lesbian writing in the South. She puts Faulkner into a trajectory of lesbian writing beginning with Florence King's *Confessions of a Failed Southern Lady* and probes the ways characterization and space are mapped out in Faulkner's *Absalom, Absalom!* to correspond with novels that articulate lesbian desire such as Alice Walker's *The Color Purple* and Dorothy Allison's *Bastard Out of Carolina*. Drawing on scholarship by Michel Frann, who first posited "William Faulkner as a Lesbian Author" in 1989, Harker sketches the transformation of Supten's Hundred into Judith's Hundred, in a reading that takes us from a patriarchal plantation to a "queer contact zone." She argues that, whereas the homosocial bond between Bon and Henry has been noticed and articulated by critics, the bond between Clytie and Judith, a relationship illuminated by Rosa, has been so far unrecognized. Together, the first three essays by Harker, Richards, and Kodat explore models of sexuality that tend to cohere around the assumed stability of heterosexuality and break open the patriarchal linkages in the body of Faulkner's work.

Shifting from the homoerotic politics of Faulkner's texts to the politics of his time, the next two essays examine the political and economic dimensions of Faulkner's erotic imagination. Michael Zeitlin in "Faulkner, Marcuse, and Erotic Power" proposes that Faulkner's public discourses of the decade following the publication of *The Portable Faulkner* in 1946 might be read alongside the ideas of the Frankfurt school. Like Herbert Marcuse, Faulkner believed that personal and political categories were closely related and that, in the 1950s, the idea of sexual privacy was in danger of being eroded and creative resistance to this erosion was needed. In this context, Zeitlin reads Faulkner's speech to the cadets of the military academy at West Point as offering a dangerous transgression when Faulkner publicly admits to his imaginary desire to be a "beautiful woman." Zeitlin argues that the suggestion of a transgender desire at this time might be read not only as nonheteronormative, but dangerously un-American. In an era that rigidly distinguished between first-world capitalism and second-world communism, definitions of masculinity and femininity were thought of as stable and were used to prop up the political systems. Yet, a look at Faulkner's fiction shows that his characters' sexualities are "invariably misaligned and uncertain." In fact, the sexuality of early Faulknerian characters is "polymorphous" and often "perverse." Zeitlin enumerates Freud's "perverted human types" and invites us to match these descriptions with their Faulknerian analogues. He concludes that Faulkner tolerates a full range of sexualities in individuals whose identity is often multiple and excessive.

Like Zeitlin, Peter Lurie also addresses the role and function of the erotic in Faulkner's work. In "Faulkner's Sexualized City: Modernism, Commerce, and the (Textual) Body," Lurie traces Faulkner's treatment of the erotic in urban settings from his early work—including *Mosquitoes*, *Pylon*, and *Sanctuary*—to his later writings. Against the background of the economic modernity of Southern cities like New Orleans, the erotic ambitions of Faulkner's characters in *Mosquitoes* are highly thematized but largely unrealized. In *Pylon*, too, urban economic interests prevail that make the spectacular in-air lovemaking scene an entertainment spectacle for the crowd and the newspaper. *Pylon* shares with *Sanctuary* Faulkner's interest in "the voyeuristic and objectifying habits of primarily male characters who act as substitutions for genuine erotic life." Such objectification, Lurie argues, "serves well the workings of a modern, abstract money economy" in cities such as New Orleans or Memphis. Faulkner's city dwellers suffer from the loss of personal relations, the loss of intimacy, and its replacement by a culture of entertainment and consumption. *Sanctuary*'s concern with voyeurism and prostitution, for instance, suggests a "modern urban malaise" indicative of modern capitalism. Moving from urban to rural environments, Lurie argues that even in the pastoral neighborhoods of Faulkner's fiction, like Frenchman's Bend in *The Hamlet*, the urban and mercantile world has already intruded. Although Faulkner does find a degree of erotic "bliss" in the pastoral environments of a premodern era, it is primarily in the language itself—in Faulkner's sexuality, so to speak—where the erotic truly lives. Lurie asks us to consider, for example, the eroticized style of Rosa Coldfield's language in *Absalom, Absalom!* and the passage in *The Hamlet* describing Ike's love for the cow. Lurie concludes that Faulkner's writing is deeply and "provocatively pleasurable"—his stylistic refinement and baroque expressions are the most truly erotic spaces in his work.

In "Must Have Been Love: Sexualities' Attachments in Faulkner," Deborah McDowell argues that the topic of sexuality in Faulkner "must inevitably confront the sordid details of the brutal history of slavery and segregation at the heart of his entire Southern cycle." But, she suggests, we should also consider the presences and possibilities of love, "the reciprocal affective bonds, the emotional intimacies this history engendered simultaneously." Her essay focuses on the "intimacy effect" of interracial sex in Faulkner and his search for a language of love and a "grammar of emotion." McDowell begins by establishing that Faulkner's "old verities and truths of the heart" are not eternal, but historical and social. Given this history of slavery in the South, McDowell asks, is love possible between white men and black women of Faulkner's time? This is a question brought into sharp focus recently by revelations about the relationship between Thomas Jefferson and Sally Hemings: was it love, or was it coerced sex? In answering this question, McDowell suggests, we first have to address the cultural assumptions and discursive constructions of what we understand by love and "emotion." Turning to Faulkner's texts for evidence, McDowell interrogates the possibility of the black woman as love object in figures such as Hightower's "cook" in *Light in August*, Uncle Hubert's black female "cook" in "The Bear," and also Eunice's relationship to Old Carothers and the function and meaning of her suicide. Ultimately, in interracial relationships in Faulkner's culture, black women could not attain "true womanhood," but white men, by contrast, could attain "true manhood."

The interrelationship between race and sex is also at the center of Kristin Fujie's essay "All Mixed Up: Female Sexuality and Race in *The Sound and the Fury*," which shifts the framework from Faulkner's social culture to his canon and career. In response to Eric Sundquist's critical assessment of *The Sound and the Fury* as a flawed text in need of support from his other work to make sense, Fujie reads the 1929 novel as a pivotal text in Faulkner's career. What makes it central is Faulkner's treatment of female sexuality, "a problem that proves at once too troubling and not indeterminate enough to be read as symptomatic of a deeper, unspeakable anxiety centered on race." Fujie points out that Faulkner's novels before *The Sound and the Fury* all "cultivate a virgin ideal" without any threat of contamination, sexual or racial. In early novels, like *Elmer, Mosquitoes*, and *Flags in the Dust*, this virgin ideal is deeply anchored in the core of the male psyche of characters who attempt to deny the sexuality of the menstruating female body. Beginning with *The Sound and the Fury* and through the character of Caddy, however, Faulkner exposes the "impurities which the virgin ideal seeks to deny, impurities rooted not in sex or female sexuality but in the very condition of being." Fujie shows that although the novel seems more focused on menstruation than miscegenation or racial transgression, Faulkner returns in later novels to the racial impurities of female sexuality, captured in the famous image of Caddy's muddy drawers. Why, she asks, is Quentin obsessed with his sister's virginity? The answer is provided in the later novels, particularly in *Absalom, Absalom!*, where Quentin's meditation on female sexuality is explicitly bound up with miscegenation and where sexual and racial panic coincide. For Fujie, this is hinted at already in *The Sound and the Fury* in the tension surrounding Caddy. Although critics have often argued menstruation seems to be what troubles Quentin's mind, Fujie argues that it is really the "specter of contaminated blood," of miscegenation that creates the anxiety that materializes at the heart of the drama.

The next essay also addresses the role of Faulkner's racialized sexualities. In "Faulkner's Black Sexuality," John Duvall provocatively claims that Faulkner's racial signifying games with characters who appear white while they perform cultural blackness makes him "America's first black Nobel Laureate." Faulkner's blackness, he argues "emerges . . . from his imagining a realm of sexual identity that serves ultimately to detach blackness from the southern concept of the Negro." From the characters in Faulkner's earliest work, *The Marionettes*, through the novels of his major period, Faulkner develops a whiteface minstrelsy that blackens white male sexuality. Although Faulkner's representations of blackness rely in part on racial stereotyping of the oversexed African American male, he "unhinges blackness as a form of unlicensed sexuality from a biological or essentialist notion of race." Among white men, artists in particular, including Faulkner himself, are good candidates whose whiteness hides a figurative queer blackness. Duvall touches on the artist figure in Faulkner's second novel, *Mosquitoes*, and then provides an in-depth reading of Popeye's race changes in *Sanctuary*. Popeye, he argues, is (mis)identified as black; his whiteness and his heterosexuality are questioned by Faulkner's deployment of a cultural and figurative "blackness" that queers the heterosexual gender performances of his characters.

Sanctuary, and its representations of sexuality, remains the focus of the last two essays by Michael Wainwright and Caroline Garnier, who examine, respectively, the biological and patriarchal contexts in which sexual subjects are constructed in Faulkner's culture and fiction. Wainwright, in "Popeye's Impersonal Temple," suggests that questions of reproduction may have been on Faulkner's mind when he married Estelle—a divorcee with two children—and willingly became a stepfather, thereby subordinating his own "reproductive interests." Inquiring into the processes of sexual selection, Wainwright asks, what is the biological basis for the sexual economy of the early twentieth-century South? *Sanctuary*, he argues, explores a case of "biologically fostered and culturally conditioned behavior." Based in Darwin's study of reproductive cell size, Wainwright maps the courtship behaviors of Faulkner's characters onto biological principles. When read in light of Darwin's evolutionary strategies of selection, Temple's and Gowan's courtship behavior becomes more accessible, and Temple's relation to Popeye can be explained. Wainwright argues that

Popeye's biological inheritance results in deformities that place him "outside the patriarchal norm." However, it is precisely these deformities that appeal to Temple who reads the "seemingly disadvantaged" Popeye as conveying a "singular kind of evolutionary fitness." What motivates Popeye is a strategy of impersonal gratification. But, Popeye's impotency does not correspond to Temple's procreative state; therefore, Popeye finds a substitute, the vigorous Red, who satisfies Temple's needs for physical contact. This arrangement, while initially satisfying Popeye's sexual economy of voyeurism, creates tension. Wainwright argues that the murder of Red and Popeye's suicide can all be explained within the framework of the Darwinian sexual politics of the novel and the evolutionary strategies of the characters.

Whereas Wainwright focuses on Popeye's sexual desire for "impersonal gratification," Caroline Garnier reads Popeye's sexual practices as "a powerful tool" to subdue, silence, and objectify Temple. In "Temple Drake's Rape and the Myth of the Willing Victim," Garnier explores *Sanctuary* (1931) and *As I Lay Dying* (1930) as "different aspects of a Southern sexual culture." Both novels, Garnier argues, highlight various forms of sexual abuse and the female characters' resulting experience of psychic trauma. In Garnier's reading of *Sanctuary*, Temple emerges as a "privileged Southern college girl," but a "girl" no less who is framed, literally and figuratively, by patriarchal environments. Temple's home is a male space, a patriarchal "sanctuary" in which her father and brothers seek to control her awakening sexuality. This environment is structurally similar first to Frenchmen's Bend, a place inhabited by men who seek to take advantage of Temple, second to Miss Reba's, a male sanctuary of prostitution, and finally to the courtroom, "a male space made up of fathers and husbands." Garnier's essay challenges those readings of Temple that characterize her as the instigator of her own demise by readers who may have "failed to unmask the patriarchal structures" of the novel. Supported by psychiatric studies on sexual trauma and trauma neurosis, Garnier explains Temple's most puzzling behavior in the courtroom, where her accusation of Lee Goodwin as the perpetrator of the crime, instead of Popeye, points away from the insane criminal to the structure of white male paternalism as the underlying cause of evil. Turning to *As I Lay Dying*, Garnier also addresses Addie's experience of sex in terms of violation and forced pregnancies, and Dewey Dell's pregnancy, which she experiences as a threat to her life and sanity. Garnier suggests that "trauma theories applied to childbirth shed new light on Addie as a mother." She concludes that "through Temple, Addie, and Dewey Dell, Faulkner depicts the life of women in a culture that deprived them of a real right of refusal to have sex or to bear children." Without medical instruction, and without the right to make choices about their sexual lives, there was ultimately no "safe sanctuary" for women in Faulkner's Yoknapatawpha—except death.

If the sexual is conceived in relation to words and discourses, all writing, including Faulkner's, has a sex. Together the essays in this volume illustrate a variety of different methodologies and approaches as they attempt to answer the question, what precisely does it mean to speak of Faulkner's sexualites? Faulkner's fiction is entangled in contemporary contexts and discourses, some of which attempt to regulate and pathologize race and sexuality; it is bound up in Darwinian and Freudian thinking, in the political and economic ideologies of his time, and in the racialized history of sexuality in the South. However, as these essays powerfully demonstrate, his textual sexualities often problematize the social and sexual norms of his time by articulating both the anxieties that accrue around sexual subjects and performances and by writing into being a variety of enabling desires, straight and queer.

Annette Trefzer
University of Mississippi

NOTES

1. Doreen Fowler and Ann J. Abadie, *Faulkner and Women: Faulkner and Yoknapatawpha, 1986* (Jackson: University Press of Mississippi, 1986).

2. Donald M. Kartiganer and Ann J. Abadie, *Faulkner and Gender: Faulkner and Yoknapatawpha, 1996* (Jackson: University Press of Mississippi, 1996).

3. Tony Purvis, "Sexualities," in *Literary Theory and Criticism*, ed. Patricia Waugh (New York: Oxford University Press, 200), 428.

4. Sigmund Freud, *Three Essays on the Theory of Sexuality* (1905), trans. and ed. James Strachey (London: Hogarth Press, 1975).

5. Michel Foucault, *The History of Sexuality: An Introduction*, vol. 1, trans. Robert Hurley (New York: Random House, 1990), 33.

6. Cristina Garrigós, "On the Sexuality of Literature," in *Sexualities in American Culture*, ed. Alfred Hornung (Heidelberg: Universitäts Verlag, 2004), 178.

7. Ibid., 178.

8. Ibid., 179.

Note on the Conference

The Thirty-fourth Annual Faulkner and Yoknapatawpha Conference sponsored by the University of Mississippi in Oxford took place July 22–26, 2007, with more than a hundred and fifty of the author's admirers in attendance. Ten presentations on the theme "Faulkner's Sexualities" are collected as essays in this volume. Brief mention is made here of other conference activities.

The program began on Sunday with lectures by Dawn Trouard and Deborah McDowell. Following a buffet supper at the home of Dr. M. B. Howorth Jr. was *Mr. Twain, Meet Mr. Faulkner*, a dramatic reading written and directed by Roseanna Whitlow of Southeast Missouri State University. Whitlow's colleagues Patrick Abbott (as Faulkner) and Lester Goodin (as Twain) read passages from the authors' writings and sayings, and Oxford actor George Kehoe provided commentary. Before the readings, Mayor Richard Howorth welcomed participants to Oxford and conference director Donald M. Kartiganer introduced Jennie Joiner, a University of Kansas graduate student writing a dissertation on marriages in Faulkner's fiction, as the winner of the 2007 William Faulkner Society Fellowship. The award, which provides graduate student fellowships to the conference, is funded by the Faulkner Society and the *Faulkner Journal*, as well as donations in memory of John W. Hunt, Faulkner scholar and emeritus professor of literature at Lehigh University. Charles Reagan Wilson, director of the Center for the Study of Southern Culture, presented the twenty-first annual Eudora Welty Awards in Creative Writing. Lauren Klaskala, Emma Richardson's student at the Mississippi School of Math and Science in Columbus, won first prize, $500, for her poem "Alligators." Jonathan Hughes, William C. White's student at Madison Central High School in Madison, won second prize, $250, for his poem "The Father at the Cross." The late Frances Patterson of Tupelo, a longtime member of the Center Advisory Committee, established and endowed the awards, which are selected through a competition held in high schools throughout Mississippi.

John Duvall, Gary Richards, and Michael Zeitlin presented lectures on Monday. The day's program also included sessions during which Seth Berner, a book dealer from Portland, Maine, talked about "Collecting Faulkner," focusing on the book jackets and paperback covers that emphasize (or ignore) the sexual content of Faulkner novels; James B.

Carothers, Charles A. Peek, Terrell L. Tebbetts, and Theresa M. Towner discussed "Teaching Faulkner"; and David Madden, Michelle Moore, and Gina Patnaik made presentations for the first of three panels featuring short papers selected through an annual call for papers. Registration for panelists was funded in part through an anonymous gift made in honor of Faulkner biographer Joseph Blotner. The day's activities ended with Colby Kullman moderating the seventh Faulkner Fringe Festival, an open-mike evening at Southside Gallery on the Oxford Square.

Guided tours of North Mississippi, the Delta, and Memphis took place on Tuesday, as did an afternoon party at Tyler Place, hosted by Charles Noyes, Sarah and Allie Smith, and Colby Kullman. The day ended with Jaime Harker's lecture. Wednesday's program included lectures by Catherine Gunther Kodat, Peter Lurie, and Michael Wainwright; short papers by Joel Dinerstein, Jennie J. Joiner, and Matt Low; and a session during which Elizabeth Nichols Shiver brought together current or former Oxford residents Harter Williams Crutcher, Carl S. Downing, Dr. Byron Gathright, and Mildred Murray Douglass Hopkins to reminisce about Faulkner and his family. Attendees then gathered for the annual picnic at Faulkner's home, Rowan Oak. Program events on Thursday were "Teaching Faulkner" panels, Caroline Garnier's lecture, and presentations by Stephen D. Barnes, Kristin Fujie, and Chris Teepe. The conference ended with a party at Off Square Books.

Four exhibitions were available throughout the conference. The Department of Archives and Special Collections at the University's John Davis Williams Library sponsored *Men and Women in Faulkner's World*, an exhibition that included first editions of Faulkner's most evocative works about relationships between men and women and accompanying manuscript pages from the Rowan Oak Papers, as well as several photographs from the Southern Media Archive illustrating the actual men and women living in Lafayette Country during that time. There were also images drawn by Faulkner himself illustrating men and women from *The Marionettes, The Scream*, and the University of Mississippi yearbooks. The University Museum sponsored an exhibition entitled *Faulkner Family Artistic Endeavors*, featuring paintings by Maud Falkner and John Faulkner and drawings by William Faulkner. The works were on loan from members of the Oxford community and the Special Collections department of the John Davis Williams Library. *Terra: A Delta Tango in Time*, a collection of twenty black-and-white photographs by Mississippi photographer Lisa Bourdeaux Percy, was on exhibit at Barnard Observatory's Gammill Gallery. In these photographs, Percy captures images in the Mississippi Delta: places where "nature and its cohort time transform, if sometimes only fleetingly, what we think of as permanent. Man places, natures effaces. Man builds and perhaps abandons, and nature puts things to its own uses." Southside Gallery exhibited *Willie and Katrina: Portraits of Willie Morris in Oxford/The Aftermath of Hurricane Katrina*, photographs by David Rae Morris. The University Press of Mississippi exhibited Faulkner books published by university presses throughout the United States.

The conference planners are grateful to all the individuals and organizations that support the Faulkner and Yoknapatawpha Conference annually. In addition to those mentioned above, we wish to thank Square Books, St. Peter's Episcopal Church, Mr. and Mrs. William Lewis and the Downtown Grill, the City of Oxford, and the Oxford Tourism Council. Also, we thank the *Memphis Commercial Appeal* for use of the December 6, 1950, photograph of Faulkner to illustrate this year's conference materials.

Faulkner's Sexualities
FAULKNER AND YOKNAPATAWPHA
2007

Unhistoricizing Faulkner

Catherine Gunther Kodat

. . . all human beings are capable of making a homosexual object-choice and have in fact made one in their unconscious.
—*Sigmund Freud*[1]

For more than twenty-five years, historical modes of analysis have dominated literary study in the United States, and Faulkner studies have been no exception. Indeed, one could say that Faulkner scholars have been in the vanguard of the historicist movement, which is generally seen as having replaced excessively formalist New Criticism, hastily universalizing mythical readings, and rigidly allegorical "psychoanalytic" approaches with long-overdue attention to the economic, social, and political conditions under which authors and their texts come into being. Fredric Jameson's 1981 command to "always historicize!" was followed just two years later by Eric J. Sundquist's influential *Faulkner: The House Divided*, in which reconstructing "a context for Faulkner's fiction out of historical experience, contemporary literature, or political and sociological documents" is postulated as "the *only* way in which Faulkner's power and significance can be made to emerge."[2] As Sundquist's title hints, Faulkner scholarship since the early-to-mid-1980s has granted privileged interpretive status to U.S. Southern history and its legacies of slavery, military conquest, and *de jure* racial segregation. Yet historicist modes of reading, like the allegorical ones they sometimes still resemble, are virtually limitless; and while the road to Yoknapatawpha has for good reason proceeded mostly through this landscape of racialized sectionalism, it has not been the only historical route through the novels. The nativist Faulkner, the New Deal Faulkner, the Cold War Faulkner, the postcolonial Faulkner, and, yes, the queer Faulkner—all are historically derived interpretive constructs in one way or another.

Before going further I should make one thing clear. I am not at all opposed to historical literary and cultural analysis; I do it myself a lot of the time; one might say that there's nothing else I, or any one of us, can ever do, given our own historical boundedness. But acknowledging one's

3

own historically derived epistemological limitation as a reader is rather a different thing from delimiting an artwork's historically determined zone of meaning. Certainly both gestures are foundational to any ethical or politically aware cultural analysis; but while the first is the cornerstone of humility, the second risks hubris, even cynicism. The emergence of the last of those contextual frames that I just listed—the sexual frame, which gives us the queer Faulkner, historically inflected as that emergence is— has highlighted the difference between these two ways of reading history in literary study, raising fundamental questions about the analytic catego- ries informing most historicist modes of inquiry (for example, identity, teleology, and consciousness). We should not ignore these questions, if only because we would wish to be certain that, in our own interpretive work, we do not (to anticipate my discussion of a recent essay by Tim Dean) practice our politics at the expense of our ethics.[3] It would be fool- ish, of course, to claim that reading Faulkner's sexualities through queer theory puts to rest a generation's worth of historically informed readings, many of them brilliant and illuminating both ethically and politically. Still, if a discussion of Faulkner's sexualities is to be more than an occasion for one-liners (I am thinking here of Frederic Koeppel's question, "Who knew that the Nobel Prize winner was ambidextrous?"[4]), then we should acknowledge the questions queer theory poses for historicism. Toward that aim, here is what I plan to do in this essay: first, I will describe some fairly recent developments in queer theory, a volatile field of inquiry that has productively reopened questions long treated as closed. It will be clear how these developments press against many of the assumptions governing historicist literary analysis, but I will hone in on some of those pressure points so as to make plain the issues they raise. Since my research began with my own confusion over how to proceed through the dozen or so ways it seems to me one could approach Faulkner's sexuali- ties, I will close with a discussion of the short story "The Leg"—an early work useful for considering how one angle on Faulkner's sexualities can lead to what we might call, following Jonathan Goldberg and Madhavi Menon, a more "unhistoricist"[5] approach enabling "antihistoricist ways of formulating . . . historicity."[6]

Not unlike psychoanalysis, about which it has a good deal to say, queer theory is a *fin de siècle* development: two of its acknowledged founda- tional texts, Judith Butler's *Gender Trouble* and Eve Kosofsky Sedg- wick's *Tendencies*, were published in 1990 and 1993, respectively. If only because her prior work had been almost exclusively within the domain of gay literary and cultural analysis, Sedgwick's study more clearly marks the shift in thinking involved in moving from the post-Stonewall, strongly identitarian, antihomophobic mode of cultural inquiry to what Goldberg and Menon have called "the non- and even anti-identitarian" work of queer theory (1609), but Butler's rhetorical reading of sexuality and gender, which casts both as effects of "performative" language practices, was seen as the more radical and (as her title hopefully predicted) troubling of the two works. In postulating a hollowness at the core of any notion of sexual or gender identity, *Gender Trouble* offers one of the most strictly constructionist of the many social constructionist theses of human sexuality that arose in the wake of Michel Foucault's incomplete, multivolume *History of Sexuality*, a study often invoked as a prototype for the rigorously historicist work that has come to be associated with the constructionist thesis as such. The nature and consequences of Foucault's thought are contested to this day, but one does not have to read very far in the world of sexuality studies before bumping into the observation, widely attributed to the first of the three completed volumes of Foucault's *History*, that it was only in the mid-nineteenth century that a variety of sexual practices were named and configured as human "identities" in order to allow us to "not only seek the truth of sex, but demand from it our own truth." As Foucault sharply puts it, "We expect it [sex] to tell us who we are,"[7] and it would not be inaccurate to see much of his research as meant to demonstrate the unreasonableness of this expectation. In his analysis, homosexual and heterosexual identities emerge as effects of discourse, inventions of intellectual and emotional disciplines (in all senses of the word) that work both to incite and to police human sexual behavior. The merits of this thesis (and obviously I offer a potted summary here) lie in the degree to which it demonstrates how what was assumed to be a transhistorical biological "truth" was in fact a Victorian-era construct stitched together out of tissue immanent to long-standing Western moral, racial, and religious beliefs—prejudices, really, that became objective and convincing largely through their rearticulation in the new discursive formations of anthropology, sociology, criminology, and psychology. This is a historicist reading insofar as a particular understanding of human sexuality is shown to have been a product of a particular moment in history, bearing the impressions of the particular social, educational, and economic conditions of its emergence. The truth of human sexuality is shown to be not timeless and fixed but rather contingent and malleable; a human creation, it is a truth open to revision.

A thesis meant to diminish delusion, enhance self-understanding, and enable liberation, this forcefully constructionist view of human sexuality, as rearticulated in Butler's *Gender Trouble* (a rearticulation that laid heavier emphasis than had Foucault on deconstruction), initially faced some skepticism from feminists and advocates of lesbian and gay civil rights in the U.S. Butler's strongest early criticism came from those who felt that she gave short shrift to "the body," a shorthand way of indicating all those physical attributes held to be unalterable through discourse or rhetoric and thus not amenable to subversive rearticulation in the manner of the drag queens Butler so admired. The ship of discourse (or rhetoricalism, or constructionism—these are in some ways synonyms) can make no headway against the shoals of biology (or foundationalism, or essentialism, to again indicate like terms)—or so the criticism went, and thus in her follow-up study, *Bodies That Matter*, Butler worked harder to explain the enlightening and liberating properties of a rigorously rhetoricalist—which is to say, deconstructive—view of sexual identity.

Butler did not convince all of her critics, and this standoff between biology and rhetoric (known in its largest contours as the essentialist-constructionist debate) might have continued indefinitely were it not for a series of articles in the late 1990s that broke the impasse by drawing on concepts developed in that branch of the "human sciences" that takes the relation between flesh and language as its chief concern: psychoanalysis. Perhaps no scholar has accomplished more in this area than Tim Dean, and in what follows I draw heavily on his work.[8] As he and others have pointed out, the problem with Butler's analysis lies less in her reliance on deconstruction than in her use of several key psychoanalytic concepts. The specifics of Butler's misreadings of Jacques Lacan in particular have drawn considerable commentary,[9] but the question of Butler's prowess as a reader of Lacan is less interesting for what it says about her theoretical acumen than for what it tells us about the ongoing seductive power of widely held assumptions regarding the "universalizing" "biologist" agenda said to drive psychoanalysis—an agenda whose totalizing pretensions are seen as best kept at arm's length via proper historicism. It is worth recalling that a certain impatience with psychoanalysis informs Jameson's study as well; in *The Political Unconscious*, "Freudian interpretation" is described as "a reduction and a rewriting of the whole rich and random multiple realities of concrete everyday experience into the contained, strategically pre-limited terms of the family narrative. . . . a system of allegorical interpretation in which the data of one narrative line are radically impoverished by their rewriting according to the paradigm of another narrative, which is taken as the former's master code or Ur-narrative and proposed as the ultimate hidden or unconscious *meaning* of the first one" (21–22). Here Jameson summarizes the argument of *The Anti-Oedipus* by Gilles Deleuze and Félix Guattari,[10] which he characterizes as a "dramatic" (that is, immoderate) attack on psychoanalysis even as he indicates some sympathy with its claims. Ultimately, Jameson judges psychoanalysis to be symptomatic of capitalism, and I will return to this issue of symptomatology later in my essay.[11] For the moment let me observe that similarly narrow, if less theoretically developed, assumptions regarding what might be called the "evil genes" of psychoanalysis are held by Sedgwick as well, and while those assumptions can be traced to several sources (not least of them Freud himself), a good portion of the problem, according to Dean, lies in the unhappy transplantation of psychoanalysis to the United States, where the ideal of disinterested investigation into psychic operations was transformed into ego psychology and where probing self-scrutiny, whose aim was self-knowledge and an accompanying measure of self-acceptance, became reformist, adaptive therapy. The psychic damage inflicted by U.S. psychoanalysts seeking to enact a sexual "cure" in their lesbian and gay patients has been amply reported in both the popular and scholarly presses, and Butler and Sedgwick are right, given this, to wonder if their purposes can be served by psychoanalysis. But in moving against psychoanalysis, Butler overlooks an important aspect of Foucault's thought. Foucault did indeed view with suspicion Freud's role in creating a world in which one's sexual practices are viewed as the "expression" of one's very being ("The West" 53). However, and as Arnold I. Davidson has noted, "the Freudian discovery of the unconscious represented for [Foucault] a decisive epistemological achievement" that "allowed one to question the old [Cartesian] theory of the subject. . . . However odd it may sound, the existence of the unconscious was a decisive component in Foucault's *antipsychologism*."[12] This is because the concept of the unconscious operates in much the same way as Foucault's institutional genealogies: to accept the existence of the unconscious is to accept the achievements of consciousness as precarious and contingent. Tim Dean and Christopher Lane point out that articulating Freud and Foucault together by means of the unconscious, in a manner more dialectical than oppositional, has drawn many theorists to explore how "psychoanalytic institutions have developed in directions antithetical to psychoanalytic concepts" (5), leading to a revived interest in psychoanalysis as a philosophical and epistemological practice.

Though it was intended primarily to dispute the widely held view that Freud (like U.S.-style psychoanalysis) was homophobic, and though it appeared before the emergence of queer theory, Henry Abelove's 1985 essay "Freud, Male Homosexuality, and the Americans" can be seen, in retrospect, to have begun this practice of rereading Freud with the aim of coming to a fuller appreciation of how his theories of human sexual desire cut across and complicate the notion of sexual "identity." Abelove's essay details Freud's lifelong refusal to posit homosexuality as an illness, opening with a discussion of Freud's 1935 letter to the mother of an American homosexual seeking treatment for her son, reminding us of Freud's 1903 assertion that "homosexuals must not be treated as sick people,"[13] noting

Freud's signing of a 1930 petition urging the Austrian decriminalization of homosexuality between consenting adults, and concluding with an illuminating reading of Freud's seven-year correspondence with James Jackson Putnam, an American psychoanalyst whose moralistic view of the talking cure plainly anticipates the turn to ego psychology and just as plainly repelled Freud. In Putnam's view, patients need "more than to simply learn to know themselves"; they needed to "try to improve their moral character and temperaments." Freud's response was unequivocally hostile: "Sexual morality as society—and at its most extreme, American society—defines it, seems very despicable to me. I stand for a much freer sexual life" (386).

In describing Freud's refusal to judge homosexuality an illness, Abelove raised the question of just how Freud came to hold a position running so counter to that of most of his contemporaries. Careful readings of the 1915 footnote to the first of the 1905 *Three Essays on the Theory of Sexuality*, which provides the epigraph for my paper, have gone some distance toward supplying an answer to that question, for this footnote reveals how, in Freud's view, a proper understanding of the unconscious—filled, as it is, with wishes and drives in which gender, sex, and temporal differences and distinctions are almost totally meaningless—militates against the notion that homosexual desire is "unnatural":

> Psycho-analytic research is most decidedly opposed to any attempt at separating off homosexuals from the rest of mankind as a group of special character. By studying sexual excitations other than those that are manifestly displayed, it has found that all human beings are capable of making a homosexual object-choice and have in fact made one in their unconscious. Indeed, libidinal attachments to persons of the same sex play no less a part as factors in normal mental life . . . than do similar attachments to the opposite sex. On the contrary, psycho-analysis considers that a choice of an object independently of its sex—freedom to range equally over male and female objects . . . is the original basis from which, as a result of restriction in one direction or the other, both the normal and the inverted types develop. Thus from the point of view of psycho-analysis the exclusive sexual interest felt by men for women is also a problem that needs elucidating and is not a self-evident fact. (145–46)

A politically progressive reading of this footnote in the mid-1980s like Abelove's entailed a normalizing view of homosexuality (despite Freud's use of the conventional opposition of his time between "normal" and "invert"); indeed, a view of homosexual desire as no less normal than heterosexual desire continues to inform today's lesbian and gay civil rights movement, and for good political reasons. Contemporary queer theory, however, takes a different interpretive approach. As Dean and Lane explain, rather "than simply revealing homosexuality as a normal and natural expression of human erotic potential, Freud's connecting sexuality to the unconscious instead makes *all* sexuality perverse. . . . The idea of the unconscious dramatically changes how we can and should think about human sexuality" (4, my emphasis).[14]

How does it do this? By raising the possibility that the fundamental structuring differences of conscious life are meaningless to the unconscious. This observation has not gone unnoticed—Philip Weinstein reminds us how Freud's insight regarding the timelessness of unconscious mental processes made it possible for Faulkner, Kafka, and Proust to explore how "historical" events "remain unabsorbed, still registering their effects" in the present[15]—but only recently have we begun to add to this awareness of the unconscious refusal to recognize temporal boundedness a full appreciation of its concomitant rejection of other constraints. "To Freud's list of the characteristics of primary process thinking—the unconscious knows no negation, no contradiction, nothing of time—we now can add that the unconscious knows nothing of heterosexuality," Dean observes in *Beyond Sexuality* (86). Realizing this, we can understand why Foucault valued Freud's discovery of the unconscious even as he viewed the institutionalization of psychoanalysis with suspicion: the unconscious works in much the same manner as Foucault's genealogies to puncture the notion of a human subject who, by dint of conscious effort conducted in keeping with immutable natural laws, will come to command its capacities. To uncover the ramshackle nature of so much of the "human sciences," to recognize how the existence of the unconscious means we will never be masters in our own house: these are rhyming insights, though arising from different opening assumptions.

Freud's theory of an ungovernably desiring unconscious has had historical consequences, though, as Dean and Lane observe: "Freud's originality stems not from his treating sexuality as historical, but paradoxically from his universalizing gestures" (11). This is to say, perhaps, that the unconscious is the place where biology and rhetoric—universalism and historicism, essentialism and constructionism—touch. Viewing the unconscious as both contingent and transcendent has two consequences for the argument I am developing here. The first, and more indirect one, raises the possibility that historicist interpretations of sexuality in a text undertaken chiefly to abet judgment on an aspect of "sexual identity"—whether or not the author was "ambidextrous," whether characters are or are not recognizably lesbian or gay, whether or not a narrative is homophobic—no matter how well meant politically, unhelpfully narrow our interpretive landscape. The second, and more direct, consequence lies in grasping how a certain rigidly historicist contextualism, even if intended to expand our political understanding of how texts arise and circulate in the world, can also limit literature's purchase on that world.

Planning to develop the first point through my concluding discussion of "The Leg," I will take up the second point here. Queer theory's recognition of the unconscious as both universal and historical has consequences ranging beyond a concern with textual sexuality, and it is no surprise that two recent calls for change in literary critical practices have come from queer theory scholars. The first, Tim Dean's "Art as Symptom," shies away from a direct critique of Jamesonian Marxist historicism, but its shrewd reading of the liabilities of "the tendency to treat aesthetic artifacts as symptoms of the culture in which they were produced," centered though it is on the work of Slavoj Žižek, raises larger questions about the degree to which less avowedly psychoanalytic cultural analyses succeed in avoiding the seductions of a program of "demystification" that "elides the specificity of art" and transforms the critic into "a hermeneut with a particular relation to the world—a relation of suspicion and putative mastery" (29, 23). Dean's chief concern is the troubling ethical implications of an interpretive "conviction . . . that the work of art is duplicitous or ignorant of something, that it exhibits contradictions of which it is unaware and therefore needs the critic to help reveal. Neither artists nor their cultures are considered masters of the conflicts that produce their work; instead the role of mastery . . . falls to the demystifying critic" (30). This is not a new complaint: cultural conservatives have long derided what they see as an insufficient contemporary reverence for artistic greatness in the work of canonical "masters."[16] What *is* new in Dean's account is his proposed intervention, an "associative" reading practice that addresses the problem of overweening critical mastery not by returning authority to the text through appeals to its formal autonomy (the cultural conservatives' approach) but rather by "enabling us to appreciate how enigmas aren't always puzzles to be decoded or obstacles to be overcome, but instead represent an ineliminable condition of existence" (39). As Dean's terminology indicates, he derives this "associative" reading practice from the psychoanalytic recognition that the workings of the unconscious present us with an "otherness [that] is a property of discourse" (38). In many ways psychoanalysis is committed to making sense of that otherness, to reducing its alien character, but, through a series of moves that I will not consider here,[17] Dean reminds us that psychoanalysis "thwarts interpretation even as it prompts it" (35). Properly understood, this thwarting leads the "associative" critic to recognize how "the enigmas of otherness are exacerbated by art" (38). He continues,

To the extent that art entails a practice or experience of defamiliarization in which otherness comes to the fore, it requires an ethical rather than an epistemological approach. From this perspective the ethics of psychoanalytic criticism would consist in refusing the imperative to overcome all enigmaticity through demystification. Such an ethics would encourage us to adopt a less knowingly superior attitude toward art. . . . The hermeneutics of suspicion that characterizes interpretive practices running the gamut from psychoanalysis to materialist to historicist criticism promotes a paranoid relation to cultural forms, fueling the impulse to critically master opacity or uncertainty through rigorous interpretation. But just as psychoanalysis indubitably contributes to this project by way of its theories of a cultural unconscious and attendant cultural symptoms, so too can psychoanalysis make us less paranoid, less insistent on uncovering meaning and significance everywhere we turn. (38–39)[18]

If Dean calls us to rethink Freud, Goldberg and Menon's "Queering History" comes at the problem by a reconsideration of Foucault. For Goldberg and Menon, the rigorously constructionist approach to sexuality has proven "inadequate to housing the project of queering" (1609). Taking queer theory's critique of identity to perhaps its limit, they argue against a view of history built on the belief that "the only modes of knowing the past are either those that regard the past as wholly other or those that can assimilate it to a present assumed identical to itself" (1616). Goldberg and Menon are troubled by what they see as a tendency to cast texts as wholly one or the other: either artifacts of a time entirely alien or evidence of how we became what we are. In seeking a way around these unsatisfactory alternatives, Goldberg and Menon place Dipesh Chakrabarty's notion of the present as "not-one" next to Hayden White's call for a historical understanding of historiography in order to propose a mode of reading that would keep "alive the undecidable difference between difference and sameness [and thus] . . . refuse what we might term the compulsory heterotemporality of historicism, whether it insists on difference or produces a version of the normative same" (1616).[19]

As Dean proposes an "associative" respect for textual enigma, so Goldberg and Menon call for a historical reading practice that would pay "attention to the question of sexuality *as a question*," one that insists neither on the past's radical alterity from, nor its teleological connection to, the present, but rather is sensitive to what they term its "idemtity": "a proportionality, likeness or similarity that is more an approximation than a substantialization" (1609–10). And as Dean's critique seeks to counter the aggression that can attend a reading practice grounded in suspicion and paranoia, so Goldberg and Menon press against the conviction "that history is the discourse of answers," since such a view produces "a discourse whose commitment to determinate signification . . . provides false closure, blocking access to the multiplicity of the past and to the possibilities of different futures" (1609).[20]

So what does all this have to do with reading Faulkner generally, or Faulkner's sexualities in particular? Let me approach that question by looking at Eric Sundquist's *House Divided* and in particular its opening chapter, "The Myth of *The Sound and the Fury.*" As this title implies, Sundquist aims to trouble the conventional view of Faulkner's fourth novel as a masterpiece, and he goes at it hammer and tongs from almost the first page, asserting that "there is reason to believe that without Faulkner's work of the next ten years *The Sound and the Fury* would itself seem a literary curiosity, an eccentric masterpiece of experimental methods and 'modernist' ideas" (3). In a chapter impressive not only for its interpretive rigor but also for the elegance of its prose, Sundquist argues that the importance of *The Sound and the Fury* emerges "only . . . in the larger context of novels to which it gives rise" (9). The ingeniousness of Sundquist's argument lies in his assertion that this indispensability of *The Sound and the Fury* cuts two ways: the novel prefigures both "the many problems in Faulkner's later fiction" (4) ("the dramatic parody and philosophical nonsense . . . the bulging prose and crude, idiosyncratic symbolism" of the work after 1942 [13, 14]) and the great novels that emerge once Faulkner takes on the "social and historical context" of his Jim Crow South: *Light in August, Absalom, Absalom!*, and *Go Down, Moses* (5).

Sundquist's charge that *The Sound and the Fury* is overrated has not gone undisputed; some of our finest Faulkner scholars have picked away at his claim that the novel is best viewed as a "preparation for things to follow, a search for a way to say things that had not been said" (6).[21] For the most part, though, these critiques work by demonstrating the many ways in which the novel *does* engage with "the single most agonizing experience of [Faulkner's] region and nation: the crisis and long aftermath of American slavery" (6). I agree that Sundquist pays too little attention to the ways in which the novel dramatizes what it is "trying to say" about the Southern racial agon—but the absolute merit of this view is less interesting to me at this moment than the fact that it grants Sundquist his ground. That is, it concedes the truth of his larger claim: that only in writing explicitly about racial history did Faulkner become "great." This is a value judgment of a rather remarkable kind, postulating Faulkner's writing itself as a "house divided," torn between a virtuous engagement with historically derived literary material and an "eccentric" fascination with "experimental and 'modernist' ideas." Sundquist's highest critical praise goes to the work he sees as most clearly expressive of those social and political "dis-eases" of which it is the speaking symp-tom. *The Sound and the Fury* is flawed because it mumbles rather than speaks: its power is "determined by forces that exist even further beneath the nether reaches of consciousness . . . that only the historical depth of *Absalom, Absalom!* can reveal" (Sundquist 20). *The Sound and the Fury* is indeed opaque in many of its stylistic, formal, and structural aspects; but it seems rather a leap to claim that this opacity stems from a vaguely decadent or narcissistic "preoccupation with form rather than plot" (19). To claim that *The Sound and the Fury* is inferior work in this sense not only takes the notion of literary apprenticeship to a whole new level: it also betrays a moralizing impatience with "literariness" that, I submit, bears a family resemblance to the view that the only sex that should win our approval is heterosex, since only it has the potential to be mean-ingfully productive. Sundquist tips his hand in this moralizing direction when he characterizes "Faulkner's obsession with the unnameable [and] the inexpressible" as the author's "greatest hazard," adding that he finds it difficult "to tell why—or exactly at what point" the "poignant memories" of *The Sound and the Fury* "get transfigured into neurosis or bizarre, overbearing symbolism" and concluding that, finally, the novel's interests "remain largely unconscious" (19). This is not a good thing if one holds that the point of art is its function as symptom: its ability to translate unconscious forces into clear articulations of contextual consciousness. Thus, brilliant as much of *House Divided* remains, Sundquist's unwilling-ness to abide what Dean might term the enigmatic aspects of *The Sound and the Fury* indicates the limitations of a certain historicist criticism.

I want to insist that "unhistoricist" or "associative" reading practices are not rescue operations: revealing the previously unrecognized ways in which a text can mean does not automatically make it a more beau-tiful or sophisticated work than it was before. Such textual revelations do, however, allow for recovery efforts that are genealogical in the best Foucauldian manner, bringing to light less-traveled paths through an imaginative landscape that, in their "idemtical" relationship to other tex-tual routes, enrich our understanding. In this sense they are as useful for reading partially successful, even "bad," work as they are for analyzing masterpieces. A look at some "bad" Faulkner indicates what this sort of queer reading of Faulkner's sexualities might entail.

Most readers know "The Leg" as one of the six stories comprising the closing "Beyond" section of Faulkner's 1950 *Collected Stories*. As Theresa M. Towner and James B. Carothers have recently reminded us, most of these stories were not on the list of titles first suggested by Rob-ert Haas.[22] It is not hard to see why: all of the stories in "Beyond" are apprentice work, and most scholars view them as significantly flawed.

And flawed they are—but clearly they had some meaning for Faulkner, who not only added them to the list Haas sent him but constructed the thematic "home" that would incorporate them into the larger geography of the *Collected Stories*. Faulkner posits the world of "Beyond" as topologically connected to the world of Yoknapatawpha, in ways that other previously unpublished stories were not. In their spatial arrangement the stories contradict the temporal reality of their creation: written before Faulkner came into possession of his mythical kingdom, in *Collected Stories* they appear as stopping points on the road out of Yoknapatawpha. This arrangement hints that though the stories of "Beyond" are immature work, it would be a mistake to take them as Sundquist takes *The Sound and the Fury*: of interest *only* because of what they later enable. Rather, we might consider the possibility that these tales are compelling precisely to the degree that they go nowhere: they are not studies for later novels (though it is striking that an Everbe Corinthia both opens and closes Faulkner's writing life), nor are they sketches of Southern racial life. What these stories have in common with the others in the volume, then, is nothing so clear as theme or context, but rather something both immanent to and beyond those historical concerns: violence, mystery, and desire. We might approach the stories of "Beyond" as fantasies rather than representations—fantasies not only in the psychological sense but in the musical one. As Theodor Adorno put it in his introduction to *Quasi Una Fantasia*, "[i]n contrast to philosophy and the sciences, which impart knowledge, the elements of art which come together for the purpose of knowledge never culminate in a decision."[23] None of the stories of "Beyond" enable clear interpretive decisions, and this is particularly so of "The Leg."

Almost surrealistic in its wickedly apt linguistic slippages and decidedly canny understanding of psychoanalytic thinking, "The Leg" traces multiplying circuits of sexual fantasy and action, beginning with the implied couple of the American David and the English George, expanding to the (again implied) *ménage à trois* of David, George, and Everbe Corinthia (daughter of a lockkeeper who lives and works on a section of the Thames near Oxford), and proceeding—through the intervention of World War I, in which George is killed and David loses a leg—to the shattering concluding virtual *ménage à quatre* in which David's amputated "member,"[24] swollen into human form and imbued with a life that seems drawn in equal parts from David's flesh and George's spirit, seduces and then destroys Corinthia. Though lesser Faulkner, "The Leg" shows evidence of painstaking work on the part of the author, not only in its confident use of "Freudian symbolism" (obvious in the leg with a mind of its own) but also in its careful application of exactly the sort of elliptical narrative structure that so marks Faulkner's most famous sexual novel, *Sanctuary*.

My claim that George and David are the story's generative desiring couple is based on internal and external evidence. As other readers of the story have noted, characters named David appear in other early Faulkner in which the polymorphous aspects of sexual desire are often a subject. Faulkner's most homoerotic "David" passage, in the 1925 newspaper sketch "Out of Nazareth," describes an encounter he and his (gay) roommate, the artist William Spratling, have with a young hobo in New Orleans: "Spratling saw him first. 'My God,' he said, clutching me, 'look at that face.' And one could imagine young David looking like that. One could imagine Jonathan getting that look from David and, serving that highest function of which sorry man is capable, being the two of them beautiful in similar peace and simplicity—beautiful as gods, as no woman can ever be."[25] It seems clear the name was sexually freighted for Faulkner in ways important to our reading of "The Leg," where (turning to the internal evidence) our narrator, David, seems nearly as enamoured of George as his "mate's" (824) putative erotic interest, Everbe Corinthia. The story opens with George and David aboard a skiff in a lock on the Thames; David holds the boat in place as George flirtatiously "spouts" Milton at a "bridling" Corinthia, who, along with David, eyes with heightening anxiety a yawl awaiting its turn through the lock. The scene comes to its not-very-displaced climax when Corinthia opens her father's lock: David and the skiff are "shot through the gates" as George falls into the river (824). While George is sanguine about the mishap, David and Corinthia are deeply, and similarly, shaken: Corinthia sits on the ground, weeping, while David briefly loses consciousness (824–25). Corinthia and David take turns calling George a "damned fool" (825); for his part, George seems to enjoy the attentions of both.

A lyrical, retrospective interlude that heightens even further the romantic sense of David's attachment to George (829) links the scene on the Thames to the next in a World War I military hospital, where the wounded David, about to lose his leg, begs George to "be sure it's dead. They may cut it off in a hurry and forget about it . . . [and] that wouldn't do at all. They might bury it and it couldn't lie quiet. And then it would be lost and we couldn't find it to do anything" (830). Readers quickly realize that George is dead, but we are never given the means to decide whether we are to understand this and subsequent conversations as hallucinations or as encounters with the supernatural. Certainly there is more than conversation happening in any case: lying "there surrounding, enclosing that gaping sensation below my thigh where the nerve- and muscle-ends twitched and jerked," David describes nights when "the gap . . . would become filled with the immensity of darkness and silence despite me" (833). On one of those nights David experiences "the gap" as "the dream . . . of the corridor and the invisible corner" permeated with "a rank, animal odor . . . [that] I had never smelled before . . . but . . . knew at once, blown suddenly down the corridor from the old fetid caves where experience began" (833). When David awakens from the dream to encounter George at his bedside, he blurts out, "It isn't anything. I won't again. I swear I shan't any more" (833). George responds cryptically, "I saw you on the river. You saw me and hid, Davy. Pulled up under the bank, in the shadow. There was a girl with you" (834). Fearful of future dreams, David stays awake for several nights; when sleep unavoidably comes, he discovers with relief that he had "eluded it" and "found a sort of peace" (834). He returns to war service by training in the "Observer's School"—where he "had learned . . . to not observe what should not be observed"—his thigh "almost reconciled to the [prosthetic] new member" (834), when, without warning, he falls for a second time into the dream, experiencing "horror and dread and something unspeakable: delight" (834). The dream ends with George's silent re- and dematerialization at David's bedside, gazing down upon his friend with a look "implacable, sorrowful, but without reproach" as he slowly fades from view (835). David awakens to discover that "it" was gone and, further, that "it took George with it" (835).

"The Leg" moves to its final section by means of a visiting priest from Poperinghe whose appearance prompts a retrospective narrating of the corruption and death of Corinthia by a man who comes to her in the evenings by punt. Home on army leave, Corinthia's brother Jotham witnesses her decline and death, but never sees her seducer. All he has to go on is the sound of a laugh, heard from the shadows near the shore; after searching the entire British Expeditionary Force "for a man whose laugh he had heard one time" (840), Jotham tries to stab David in his sleep. The story ends with Jotham's execution at dawn as David muses over a photograph, left him by the priest, taken when he "was lying in the hospital talking to George" (841). David identifies the face in the photograph as his own, but yet not his: "it had a quality that was not mine: a quality vicious and outrageous and unappalled" (841–42). "The Leg" closes with David's repeated, despairing cry: "I told him to find it and kill it. . . . I told him to. I told him" (842).

While not pursuing it here, I should point out that one psychoanalytic queer reading of "The Leg" would almost certainly linger over the title item and its resemblance to Lacan's *objet petit a*, the abjected thing that constitutes the foundation of desire "by standing in for loss" (Dean *Beyond* 195). *Objet petit a* has come to bear considerable interpretive weight in recent queer theory, for "the logic of this concept . . . implies multiple, heterogeneous possibilities for desire" (Dean *Beyond* 250). For my purposes, though, I will stress that a queer reading of "The Leg" would focus not at all on finding "the homosexual" in the text (Is it the "gapped" David who loves George, who then betrays David by possessing his leg in order to possess Corinthia? Or is it George who loves David, sacrificing his spiritual self to put an end to David's pursuit of the girl?) so that one might then render judgment on the text's status as homophobic, homophilic, or closeted, but rather on acknowledging the enigmatic, uncontrollable nature of sexual desire. True, no one comes to a good end in "The Leg"—but how many sexual narratives in Faulkner do? It would be mistaken to take the story's grim conclusion as a moral about the hazards of nonnormative sexuality; rather, "The Leg" is a brief fantasia on what we would all recognize as a constant theme in Faulkner: the self-shattering force of desire. This is "associative reading" insofar as it notes certain enigmatic aspects of the story as precisely that; it is "unhistoricist" in that it bypasses the temptation to cast the leg as "a symbol of the unleashed evil forces that have created the havoc and horror of the war."[26] It is worth noting that, in refusing the consolations of historicism, we bring our textual experience closer to that of Faulkner's earliest readers, who repeatedly remarked on the perverse violence and extremism of his texts. Thus the "unhistoricist" approach gives us another entry into literary history, with the difference being that today we have revised critical tools for examining literary representations of the perverse or the extreme. Reading Faulkner's sexualities in this way gives us an "antihistoricist way of formulating . . . historicity" (Dean and Lane 30).

Further, approaching "The Leg" through queer theory allows us to see the text's merits and liabilities more clearly and dispassionately, without bending it to our will to make it do or be more (or less) than it is. This is a reading practice with obvious applications beyond the question of how to read sexuality, even as its genesis can be traced to the effort to respond to that question. To acknowledge the force of the unconscious in the author, in readers, and in the historical contexts within which works are both written and read is to acknowledge the ways in which a text eludes mastery. This necessarily is also to acknowledge that texts operate in ways both historical and unhistorical, and it obliges us to read so that we are always aware that efforts to represent the difficulties of "trying to say" or textual embodiments of the conviction that "words are no good" require more than a symptomatology that would push past the work in order to grasp what's "really" at stake.

Literature is not reducible to symptom, though we could say that Dean's call for associative reading as well as Goldberg and Menon's insistence on "idemtity" as a way of accounting for the past without being imprisoned in it are symptomatic in that they both articulate a concern to ensure that our pursuit of the many benefits of historical literary analysis does not lead us to lose sight of the unhistorical aspects of literature. Those aspects lie in the "otherness" of art itself, which is always both anchored and transcendent—a truly ambidextrous enterprise, in which one hand describes our conscious world as the other points beyond.

NOTES

1. *Three Essays on the Theory of Sexuality*, in *The Standard Edition of the Complete Psychological Works of Sigmund Freud*, James Strachey, et al., eds. and trans. (London: Hogarth Press, 1953), 7:145. Page numbers for later citations from this text will appear parenthetically within the essay.

2. Frederic Jameson, *The Political Unconscious: Narrative as a Socially Symbolic Act* (Ithaca: Cornell University Press, 1981), 9; Eric J. Sundquist, *Faulkner: The House Divided* (Baltimore: Johns Hopkins University Press, 1983), x, my emphasis. Page numbers for later citations from both of these texts will appear parenthetically within the essay.

3. Tim Dean, "Art as Symptom: Žižek and the Ethics of Psychoanalytic Criticism," *diacritics* 32:2 (Summer 2002), 22. Page numbers for later citations from this text will appear parenthetically within the essay.

4. Frederic Koeppel, "Book Folks: 'Faulkner's Sexualities,' Anyone?" Memphis *Commercial Appeal*, Sunday, 1 July 2007.

5. Jonathan Goldberg and Madhavi Menon, "Queering History," *Publications of the Modern Language Association* 120:5 (October 2005): 1609. Page numbers for later citations from this text will appear parenthetically within the essay.

6. Tim Dean and Christopher Lane, "Homosexuality and Psychoanalysis: An Introduction," in Tim Dean and Christopher Lane, eds., *Homosexuality and Psychoanalysis* (Chicago: University of Chicago Press, 2001), 30. Page numbers for later citations from this text will appear parenthetically within the essay.

7. Michel Foucault, "The West and the Truth of Sex," trans. Daniel W. Smith, in Dean and Lane, 53. Page numbers for later citations from this text will appear parenthetically within the essay.

8. See Tim Dean, *Beyond Sexuality* (Chicago: University of Chicago Press, 2000) and "Art as Symptom." Page numbers for later citations from this text will appear parenthetically within the essay.

9. See, for example, James Penney, "(Queer) Theory and the Universal Alternative," *diacritics* 32:2 (Summer 2002), 3–19, esp. 7. Dean's chapter "Bodies that Mutter" in *Beyond Sexuality* (174–214) offers a thorough analysis of Butler's use of Lacan.

10. Gilles Deleuze and Félix Guattari, *The Anti-Oedipus*, trans. Robert Hurley, Mark Seem, and Helen R. Lane (New York: Viking, 1977).

11. Jameson sees Freud's theory of unconscious wish-fulfillment mechanisms as "abstractions" derived from the capitalist abstraction of labor (66). But to claim that "we can think abstractly about the world only to the degree to which the world has itself has already become abstract" (66), and to imply that this capacity emerges first (or only) with the rise of capitalism, is to ignore realms of abstract thinking about the world (Euclidian geometry, for instance) whose appearance well predates capitalism. Though I do not have the space

here to develop this point, it seems to me that what Jameson calls the "political *unconscious*" of cultural artifacts is better understood as *conscious* knowledge, repressed. My thanks to Michael Zeitlin for pointing me towards passages in *The Political Unconscious* that helped focus my thinking about Jameson's argument.

12. Arnold I. Davidson, *The Emergence of Sexuality: Historical Epistemology and the Formation of Concepts* (Cambridge: Harvard University Press, 2001), 209–10.

13. Henry Abelove, "Freud, Male Homosexuality, and the Americans," in *The Lesbian and Gay Studies Reader*, ed. Henry Abelove, Michèle Aina Barale, and David M. Halperin (New York: Routledge, 1993), 382. Abelove's essay was first published in the Winter 1985–86 issue of *Dissent*. Page numbers for later citations from this text will appear parenthetically within the essay.

14. Arnold I. Davidson first noted that careful reading of the *Three Essays* leads to the conclusion that, from 1915 onward, "perversion is no longer a legitimate concept" within psychoanalytic thought (Davidson, "How to Do the History of Psychoanalysis: A Reading of Freud's *Three Essays on the Theory of Sexuality*," *Critical Inquiry* 13:2 [Winter 1987], 275). While Abelove emphasizes Freud's progressiveness in refusing to see homosexuality as pathological, Davidson takes a more critical view of Freud's reluctance to admit the most radical consequences of his theory.

15. Philip Weinstein, *Unknowing: The Work of Modernist Fiction* (Ithaca: Cornell University Press, 2005), 87.

16. And in 1964, long before the onset of the "culture wars," Susan Sontag articulated a similar complaint. See "Against Interpretation," in *Against Interpretations and Other Essays* (New York: Picador USA/Farrar, Straus & Giroux, 2001), 3–14.

17. Dean uses Jean LaPlanche's elaboration of Lacan's "enigmatic signifier" to demonstrate the ways in which psychoanalytic interpretation can work "against rather than toward the consolations of sense" (35).

18. For a similar view, see Leo Bersani, "Psychoanalysis and the Aesthetic Subject," *Critical Inquiry* 32:2 (Winter 2006): 161–74.

19. Dipesh Chakrabarty, *Provincializing Europe: Postcolonial Thought and Historical Difference* (Princeton: Princeton University Press, 2000), 249 (qtd. in Goldberg and Menon, 1610); Hayden White, *Tropics of Discourse: Essays in Cultural Criticism* (Baltimore: Johns Hopkins University Press, 1978), 29 (qtd. in Goldberg and Menon, 1615–16).

20. Though aspects of their critique resemble those of the self-described "New Formalists," Dean, Goldberg, and Menon are not mentioned in Marjorie Levinson's recent omnibus review of New Formalist scholarship. This is perhaps because their work remains closely tied to queer theory: for Levinson, the "mixed bag" of New Formalism lacks a theoretical anchor. See Levinson, "The Changing Profession: What Is New Formalism?," *Publications of the Modern Language Association* 122: 2 [March 2007], 558–69. My thanks to Peter Lurie for drawing my attention to this essay.

21. See John T. Matthews, "The Rhetoric of Containment in Faulkner," in Lothar Hönnighausen, ed., *Faulkner's Discourse: An International Symposium* (Tübingen: Max Niemeyer Verlag, 1989), 55–67, and Richard Godden's "Quentin Compson: Tyrrhenian Vase or Crucible of Race?," in Noel Polk, ed., *New Essays on "The Sound and the Fury"* (Cambridge: Cambridge University Press, 1993), 99–137, republished in expanded form as the first chapter of his *Fictions of Labor: William Faulkner and the South's Long Revolution* (Cambridge: Cambridge University Press, 1997), 8–48.

22. Theresa M. Towner and James B. Carothers, *Reading Faulkner: Collected Stories* (Jackson: University Press of Mississippi, 2006), 415, 423, 431, 448.

23. Theodor W. Adorno, "Music and Language: A Fragment," in *Quasi Una Fantasia: Essays on Modern Music*, trans. Rodney Livingstone (New York: Verso, 1998), 4.

24. William Faulkner, "The Leg," in *Collected Stories* (1950; New York: Vintage Books, 1977), 834. Page numbers for subsequent quotations from this text will be given parenthetically within the body of the essay.

25. Carvel Collins, ed., *William Faulkner: New Orleans Sketches* (1958; Jackson: University Press of Mississippi, 2002), 47. Widely interpreted as homosexual, the passion of Jonathan and David is described in 1 Samuel 18.

26. Edmund L. Volpe, *A Reader's Guide to William Faulkner: The Short Stories* (New York: Syracuse University Press, 2004), 57 (qtd. in Towner and Carothers, 430).

The Artful and Crafty Ones of the French Quarter: Male Homosexuality and Faulkner's Early Prose Writings

GARY RICHARDS

In literary representations as well as broader cultural understandings, no Southern city and few U.S. cities have been more closely associated with male homosexuality than New Orleans. In some cases—and especially in contemporary texts such as John Rechy's *City of Night*, John Kennedy Toole's *A Confederacy of Dunces*, Poppy Z. Brite's *Exquisite Corpse*, Christopher Rice's *A Density of Souls*, and Jim Grimsley's *Boulevard*—representations of the city's gay subcultures are overt, and these authors' stances toward these enclaves need little deciphering. In contrast, William Faulkner's early prose writings of the 1920s present a more challenging site of exploration, since here his treatment of male same-sex desire, especially as associated with New Orleans, usually includes only tentative or peripheral encodings of this desire. And yet same-sex desire and activity, even more so than men's deviant performances of gender, constantly inform this literary production. True, for all these erotic elements and Faulkner's intimacy with gay men, this work suggests that he was profoundly anxious at the beginning of his career about cultural conflations of male artistry and male homosexuality; however, these texts ultimately offer that, although he at times works diligently to minimize the sexuality of gay male artists, he repeatedly betrays his admiration of these figures and implicates himself in multiple strategies that reinforce links between artistic production and male same-sex desire.

Within this focus, perhaps the most important figure for Faulkner in the mid-1920s, the years when he spent significant time in the Vieux Carré of New Orleans, was not Sherwood Anderson, as usually offered by a critical establishment preoccupied with tracing literary genealogies, but rather William Spratling, Faulkner's roommate in the French Quarter and elsewhere, his traveling companion on his first European sojourn in 1925, his collaborator on the satiric *Sherwood Anderson and Other Famous Creoles*, and his inspiration for figures in several early prose pieces. This is not to minimize Anderson's influence on Faulkner or the men's subsequent tensions but rather to foreground the significance of Spratling, who has consistently hovered at the margins of Faulkner scholarship, and, to a lesser degree, the other gay men who prominently figured in his apprenticeship period. Although, especially of late, critics have noted the importance of this presence, they have rarely teased out the details or considered this group in its entirety. John Duvall, for instance, has noted Faulkner's presence in gay circles and offered that it "would be possible to construct an argument that Faulkner's aesthetic is a gay aesthetic," while Minrose Gwin contextualizes her discussion of same-sex desire in *Mosquitoes* by noting, "Virtually the entire year of 1925 Faulkner spent either in New Orleans—certainly an important American site of flamboyant sexual masquerade and activity of all sorts— or in Europe, mainly in Paris. Living and traveling with his homosexual friend Bill Spratling off and on for two years during this period, Faulkner mixed with male homosexuals and lesbians at various bars and houses in the Vieux Carré of New Orleans. Other homosexual friends included Ben Wasson and Stark Young."[1] Likewise, Jay Parini amplifies in his recent biography's discussion of Faulkner's living arrangements in the French Quarter that "Bill Spratling lived upstairs in the same building, and he and Faulkner got along famously. One sees that Faulkner was clearly at ease with homosexual men. As critics have pointed out, there is considerable homoerotic feeling in his work, especially in 'Elmer,' his early unfinished novel, but it would be difficult to pinpoint any 'activity' in his life that would qualify as homosexual. I suspect that he identified with homosexuals as outsiders and considered himself—as an artist—an outsider as well."[2]

Such discussions only gesture toward the pervasiveness of these gay male presences and the intimacy that Faulkner had with them. As Kenneth Holditch offers, the bohemian Vieux Carré of the 1920s was one of the few urban areas of the United States outside Harlem and Greenwich Village with a significantly open homosexual populace, and the phrase "the Quarter" often functioned—as it still does—as a euphemism for gay New Orleans. Tennessee Williams, for instance, uses this cultural shorthand in *Suddenly Last Summer* when Catherine Holly confesses that she has procured men for her gay cousin, Sebastian Venable, and offers relative to these activities, "I came out in the French Quarter years before I came out in the Garden District."[3] As in this sexual scenario, by the 1920s the Quarter had also become the key locale within the so-called Uptown marriage, "a not-uncommon union," Holditch clarifies, "in which a gay man, born into New Orleans society, marries an appropriate debutante from his own class and fathers children by her but keeps an apartment in the Quarter for liaisons with male companions."[4] It was the Vieux Carré's artists, however, with whom Faulkner most closely associated, and, although the heterosexual Anderson anchored Faulkner's circle, it also included numerous gay writers and visual artists, such as Spratling, Lyle Saxon, and William Odiorne, with whom Faulkner would later become close while in Paris. They, along with other gay protégés, such as Young, Wasson, and William Alexander Percy, often shuttled between the South and New York, and when Faulkner spent time in that city in the 1920s, it was often within this coterie of gay Southerners ensconced in Greenwich Village. In the fall of 1921, for example, while he searched for a place to rent, he stayed with the mentoring "Mr. Stark" in his Village apartment, and in the fall of 1928, Faulkner shared Wasson's "tiny Greenwich Village apartment" on MacDougal Street before moving, along with Spratling, into Saxon's more spacious rooms on Christopher Street.[5]

Within this coterie, Faulkner was perhaps most intimate with Spratling, largely because of their unique living arrangements. According to Spratling's gossipy, often unreliable 1967 autobiography, the posthumously published *File on Spratling*, he came to New Orleans, "a lively and colorful new world," to teach architecture at Tulane in September of 1922 and immediately determined for himself a provocative queerness: "in spite of discreet insinuations from older members of the faculty to the effect that it would be more respectable if I would live uptown, I had found myself a little apartment in the French Quarter overlooking the cathedral garden."[6] It was there, in the house owned by Natalie Scott at 624 Orleans Alley, that Faulkner moved in early March of 1925 when he left the Andersons' household around the corner in the Pontalba apartments. As Faulkner detailed in a letter to his mother, he shared "two rooms, a court and a kitchen" with newspaperman Louis Piper and had free run of Spratling's bathroom upstairs.[7] The relationship between Faulkner and Spratling deepened, and the two became fixtures in the bohemian Quarter. "We were a little spoiled," Spratling confesses in a late account of his friendship with Faulkner, deploying the same euphemism as Williams, "because when visitors came they had to come downtown; we rarely visited uptown."[8] In July Faulkner and Spratling set sail for Europe, arriving in Genoa on August 2. From there the two traipsed through Italy and Switzerland together, parting two months later when Spratling returned to the U.S. and Faulkner pressed on to France and England. Early in 1926, after Faulkner's December return to Oxford via New York, where Spratling was at the time, the two again took up shared residency in the Quarter, this time in an attic studio on St. Peter Street, which housed the two throughout the year except during their summer migrations.

Here, Spratling documents, as the alcohol flowed, the two men's homosocial behavior assumed elaborate rituals and on occasion shaded into the homoerotic. Perched above the narrow Quarter streets, the duo and their guests, armed with BB guns, gleefully nicked passers-by: "We also had a system of premiums, or points, which was posted to the wall. If you hit a butcher boy in the tail, you were put down for so many points. If you managed to pink a Negro nun, that rated ten points (for rarity value) and that was the highest you could go. We, of course, were popular in the neighborhood because of the game. Young Bob Anderson, Sherwood's son, could hardly be kept away. Bob would come bursting in on Bill when he was writing, usually making a nuisance of himself. The kid was so difficult to get rid of that finally, one day, we grabbed him, took his pants off, painted his peter green and pushed him out on the street, locking the door."[9] As Parini asserts, this was "a bizarre act of adolescent rowdiness, tinged with a smolder of homoeroticism," but neither his nor Spratling's account—much less Joseph Blotner's sanitized version—clarifies that the "kid," Robert Lane Anderson, born in 1907, and his newly verdigrised member were, at youngest, eighteen and, depending on when the incident occurred, more likely almost twenty, suggesting that adult sexual currents rather than those of ostensibly desexualized childhood impacted the scenario.[10]

This incident also only hints at how central same-sex activity seems to have been in the raucous Spratling's life. Although his campy autobiography, like Elizabeth Prall Anderson's memoir and Stark Young's letters, never definitively asserts Spratling's homosexuality, they record his diligent collecting of dirty jokes; his equally diligent collecting of sailors on leave in Brooklyn; his ogling of the young Mexican silversmiths who, like Bette Davis, Paulette Goddard, and Errol Flynn, routinely swam naked in the expatriate Spratling's Taxco pool; his tolerance of Hart Crane's "particular fondness for young boys" while visiting Mexico, including his troubling tryst with the son of Spratling's cleaning woman ("I have never been able to feel censorious about anyone's peccadillos as long as their acts do not create problems in other people's lives," Spratling offers of this event); and his procuring of similar boys for the aging Stark Young.[11] Although often minimizing the homoerotic material and negotiating it with anxiety and euphemism, recent biographies of Spratling by Taylor Littleton and Joan Mark clarify Spratling's homosexual activity and leave indisputable that, closeting as the previously mentioned texts are, Spratling himself was anything but circumspect about his gay identity. Even the hesitant Littleton, who first offers that Spratling's "homosexual tendencies . . . had lain discreetly latent during the New Orleans years and during the early period of his Mexican apprenticeship," ultimately affirms that "the fact that he was gay was known and mildly accepted by his associates after he moved to Taxco-el-Viejo in the mid-forties, as it must have been also in the tolerant Vieux Carré community."[12]

This homosexuality seems all the more intriguing in the context of Faulkner's relationship with Spratling when one considers the otherwise dramatic similarities between the two men. Within three years of each other in age and almost sharing a birthday (Faulkner was born 25 September 1897; Spratling was born 22 September 1900), both men, as Holditch points out, were only tangentially related by pedigree to the South's fabled plantation aristocracy and often intensified their drawls and concocted elaborate tales so as to perform the role of archetypal Southern gentleman. And yet both men also adopted in their early years a "slightly bohemian appearance" for dramatic effect.[13] Moreover, if also self-evidently, Faulkner and Spratling shared the name *William* as well as the nicknames *Bill* within social circles and *Billy* within familial circles, all of which prompts speculation about Faulkner's anxiety at maintaining as an intimate companion a man so dramatically similar to himself save for their differing object choices, especially within a culture generally marked by homophobia and homosexual panic.

The most striking parallel between the two men, however, was their artistry, especially since, in their early careers, both men gravitated toward the visual arts. As scholars have consistently noted, the youthful Faulkner was a devoted practitioner of modernist calligraphy and pen-and-ink drawing *à la* Aubrey Beardsley, as evinced by the illustrations in *The Marionettes*, the sketches in his letters, and his early cartoons. Trained as an architect at Auburn, employed as a draftsman in Montgomery before coming to New Orleans, and hired to teach architecture at Tulane, Spratling filled his time in the Quarter sketching and painting, often illustrating texts documenting southern Louisiana's historic buildings, and, after his permanent expatriation to Mexico in 1929, he extensively designed silver jewelry and other *objets d'art*. A jealous Faulkner, a poet soon to abandon the visual arts for prose fiction, rehearsed this link between the two men, noting Spratling's talents in the early sketch "Out of Nazareth," where Faulkner's textual surrogate wistfully asserts that he strolls with "Spratling, whose hand has been shaped to a brush as mine has (alas!) not."[14] The fruit of this shared preoccupation was *Sherwood Anderson and Other Famous Creoles*, a book of Spratling's caricatures edited by Faulkner, "a sort of private joke," Spratling offers, dedicated to "All the Artful and Crafty Ones of the French Quarter."[15] In both content and production, the 1926 collection documents Spratling and Faulkner's shared commitment to artistic creativity and inextricably links the two men, down to the final self-caricature in which Faulkner's face literally merges with Spratling's in an intimate shared workspace.

If the caricature's fusion of the two artists is Spratling's handiwork, biographers record that Faulkner also blurred the lines between the two Bills' identities, at times pointedly appropriating Spratling's experiences within circulations of homosexuality.[16] Joel Williamson, drawing upon Spratling's "Chronicle of a Friendship," offers this account of the men's first night in Genoa on their European sojourn: "They went immediately to a bar with some of the ship's officers. Spratling, drinking lustily, got into a difficulty with a group of prostitutes and their pimps. The police came and he spent the night in jail. Faulkner met him as he emerged from his incarceration the next day. 'You no longer look so vulgarly healthy,' he declared. Spratling accused him of sounding irritated. 'What the hell,' Faulkner replied. 'Why shouldn't I be? Missing an experience like that.'"[17] (Drawing upon Italian newspaper accounts from 1925, Massimo Bacigalupo confirms the basics of the story: "Bill Spratling was arrested at the Caffè Belloni in downtown Genoa on the evening of 2 August 1925, to be released the next afternoon, none the worse for this bad luck."[18]) Williamson continues: "Apparently, Spratling told Faulkner that while he was in jail, he participated in a homosexual act. Later, when Bill told Ben Wasson about the incident, he said that it was he who got into difficulty and was thrown into jail. Presumably, however, Bill did not tell Ben about a sexual encounter."[19] And yet Faulkner, knowing the link between the incarceration and same-sex acts, even if it remained unacknowledged to Wasson, *did* share the anecdote, alter the identities of the participants, and hint at a desire to be similarly transgressive for the "experience" it would provide, even if—or especially if—homosexual sex punctuated the episode. He does the same in the aborted novel "Elmer," composed largely in Paris that same year, and in that novel's reworking as the short story "A Portrait of Elmer" by having the autobiographical eponymous figure engage in a variation on Spratling's activities in Genoa.

Faulkner's literary production of this era further documents that he was preoccupied with his relationship with Spratling, who seems, directly or indirectly, to inform characters in no less than a dozen of these early works, many of which are homoerotically inflected. In two of the 1925 sketches for the New Orleans *Times-Picayune* ("Out of Nazareth" and "Episode") and in the uncollected "Peter," an artist named Spratling appears as the companion of the narrator, a surrogate for Faulkner himself. In "Divorce in Naples," with its notably nonchalant depiction of a long-term male couple, George both recalls Spratling physically and engages in behavior directly rehearsing Spratling's on the 1925 European trip, while in *Mosquitoes* and its prefiguring "Don Giovanni," Gordon and Morrison respectively cite Spratling with both their physicality and their living arrangements, especially if one accepts Talliaferro and Herb as Faulkner's mocking self-representations. Faulkner also, according to Spratling, "depicted some of my own traits in one of his characters" in *Soldiers' Pay*.[20] Finally, in four other early stories ("The Big Shot,"

"Mistral," "Snow," and "Evangeline"), a character named Don, often an artist of some sort ("an architect by vocation and an amateur painter by avocation" in "Evangeline"; a newspaperman in "The Big Shot"), consistently engages with another unnamed narrator in an elaborate process to master through narration a perplexing set of events.[21] These last four figures are clearly less directly representational than those designated as "Spratling," but even Faulkner's recurring use of the name *Don* conjures Spratling, who, after his research summers in Mexico between 1926 and 1928, assumed as a nickname the natives' appellation of "Don Guillermo" as he grew to identify with Mexican culture.

Unsurprisingly yoked with the recurrence of this male figure is the saturation of these early pieces with male homosociality, as the New Orleans sketches repeatedly depict men and their relationships to one another, usually at the exclusion of women. "New Orleans," which appeared in the January-February 1925 issue of *The Double Dealer*, is emblematic of the larger set of stories. Of its eleven sketches, only "Magdalen" focuses centrally on female identity, that of a prostitute. The rest celebrates or meditates on the Quarter's variegated male homosociality engaged in by wealthy Jews, priests, sailors, cobblers, African American longshoremen, cops, and male beggars. The piece's only other significant female presence is New Orleans itself, characterized in the final sketch, "The Tourist," and repeated in *Mosquitoes*, as a "courtesan, not old and yet no longer young, who shuns the sunlight that the illusion of her former glory be preserved."[22] Although Faulkner here associates the city with valorized sexual experience—"And all who leave her, seeking the virgin's unbrown, ungold hair and her blanched and icy breast where no lover has died, return to her when she smiles across her languid fan" (14)—and, assuming a male tourist, deploys a heterosexual metaphor, the depiction is simply that, a metaphor, in which there is a female presence but not that of an actual woman.

When Faulkner offers a literal heterosexual pairing, as in the sketch "Frankie and Johnny," the relationship still emerges through a focus on the man's actions and expressions. Faulkner allows the female Frankie only a single line, one virtually devoid of meaningful content—"Oh, Johnny!" (6)—amid his lengthy characterization of their relationship. But his narrative not only silences Frankie and sexistly infantilizes her to "baby," it also constructs her value to Johnny as determined only relative to other men. It is not until a "drunk bum stopped you and said what he said to you and I walked up and slammed him" (6) that she gains Johnny's notice. Even then, as he attempts to express his thrill when she kisses him, he opts for similes that draw on his relationships with other men: "and when you kissed me it was like one morning a gang of us was beating our way back to town on a rattler and the bulls jumped us and trun [sic] us off and we walked in and I seen day breaking acrost the water" (6).[23] What may at first seem a valorization of heterosexual chivalry and courtship thus remains male-focused.

The broader set of New Orleans sketches reveals the persistence of male homosociality while also featuring distinct homoerotic inflections. The sardonically entitled "Damon and Pythias Unlimited," for example, published in the *Times-Picayune* on 15 February 1925, is a sly comic depiction of a conman's attempt to fleece the narrator. However, the initial pickup on Jackson Square, a standard early- and mid-twentieth-century locale for men to cruise other men for public sex, recalls a male hustler securing a client. Certainly those witnessing the pairing of the narrator and the "round, very dirty" Morowitz, with his "soft, melting brown eyes—like a spaniel's"—that so affix the narrator's attention, are disconcerted by what the duo may represent.[24] When Morowitz, despite his bedraggled attire, imperiously demands to the cabdriver, "Drive over here; my friend and I wanta go to our hotel," the driver "weighed the two of us in his mind, and then he addressed me. 'Are you with him?'" (21), leaving unclear if he is potentially offended by Morowitz's class or sexuality. Moreover, the man does not live at the St. Charles Hotel, as he initially claims, but rather stays at a local bathhouse: "My friend works in the Alhambra Baths right next door to the St. Charles, so what's the good of me staying at a hotel when my friend insists I stay with him, huh?" (22). Even more than Jackson Square, during the 1920s the Alhambra Baths would have been associated with male same-sex activity, and Faulkner thus encodes a sexual availability—a "cruisiness" in current gay slang—to the initial interactions between these two men.

Even if one divests Morowitz of associations with environs of male homosexual activity, the story stays firmly rooted in expressions of male desire—if not necessarily sexual ones—especially once the pair arrives at the race track. There Morowitz and his "cousin," the jockey McNamara, compete for the narrator's attention, his money, and eventually his physical body. When the narrator wins his bet on one of the horses, the two hustlers "both offered to deliver it, the boy with insistent politeness; while the other, still vocal, demanded, insisted, cajoled; pawing and rubbing my arms, trying to take the bill from my hand" (25). The contest grows so violently heated that eventually the "other leaped upon him, shrieking. They struggled. Locked in close embrace they swayed about the floor" (27). Faulkner continues: "The other surged between us, breathing heavily. 'Say, fellow, move off and let me speak to my friend in private, will you?' The lad shook my hand, gave me a meaning look, and drew back. The other pawed me affectionately, trying to put his arms around my neck. I won, and he was forced to hiss his message from at least a foot's distance" (27). The constant throughout the second half of the story is triangulated desire but not that of two men and a woman, as famously theorized by Eve Sedgwick, but rather that of three men; indeed, the story mentions no women at all.

As intimated, within these early pieces there is near-constant anxiety about heterosexuality, anxiety that scholars have amply documented and contextualized within the vexed currents of Faulkner's relationships with, among others, Maud Faulkner, Estelle Oldham, and Helen Baird, whom he first met through Spratling. Consider the blatant "Jealousy," the sketch that appeared in the 1 March 1925 *Times-Picayune* in which a fanatically jealous restaurant owner, convinced of his wife's romantic involvement with an attractive waiter, seeks revenge by shooting the younger man. The ironic result is self-inflicted suffering and punishment when the antique pistol bursts in the husband's hand. Faulkner compounds the irony by establishing that, unlike in the scenario of triangulated desire that evinces a pronounced homoerotic connection between the two men, the young waiter desires neither the wife nor the husband, the presumed desire being simply the husband's projection, and he thus debases and abuses himself for nothing. If anything, the waiter seems stereotypically gay. Consistently flashing a "white satirical smile," he flatly denies the husband's accusations with bitchily overprecise diction—"You are already mad. Had you not been I should have killed you ere this. Listen, tub of entrails, there is nothing between us: for her sake whom you persecute, I swear it. I have said no word to her that you have not seen, nor she to me. If she be attracted to someone, it is not I"—and the confrontation culminates when he prissily slaps the husband.[25] Finally, when the waiter wishes to present "the signora" with a parting gift, he chooses glass beads purchased in "a curio shop where such things were sold—an orderless jumble of pictures, vases, bric-a-brac, jewelry, firearms and brass" (40), the stock gay milieu that Truman Capote famously rehearses in *Other Voices, Other Rooms*. The only homoerotic desire seems that which colors the descriptions of the waiter as offered by the narrative focalized through the husband. A "tall young Roman god in a soiled apron" (34), the waiter and his "supple grace" disconcert the husband and make him aware of "his own bulky figure" (36). In all of these images, the man marked by heterosexuality is preoccupied, anguished, and embarrassed, whereas the man *not* involved with heterosexuality remains "courteous and efficient," moving "deftly and swiftly about" (36), a model of productivity. Faulkner underscores this difference with the two men's contrasting economic scenarios: to "protect" his wife, the jealous husband sells the successful restaurant to the waiter, trading a fiscally secure future for one of uncertainty further destabilized by eventual incarceration. From almost every perspective, heterosexuality is unenviable.

This understanding continues in both "Episode" and "Peter," which depict horrific images of heterosexual interaction inside and outside marriage. In "Episode," Spratling's sketch reflects the shifting image of a beggar as her body reveals the evolution of her marriage. At first posed as "they had been photographed . . . on their wedding day. . . . She was a bride again, young and fair, with her trembling hand on young Joe's shoulder."[26] When repositioned, "[a]t once she became maternal. She was no longer a bride; she had been married long enough to know that Joe was not anything to be either loved or feared very passionately, but on the contrary he was something to be a little disparaging of; that after all he was only a large, blundering child. (You knew she had borne children by now—perhaps lost one.)" (106). This evolution's final phase is her current face, that of a "woman of sixty, toothless and merry as a gnome's" (107). If Faulkner thus suggests a dismal narrative for women within marriage, he offers in "Peter" an equally repulsive scenario outside it. As Spratling sketches the young mixed-race boy guarding his mother's room in a brothel, the callousness of the apparently heterosexual activity is inescapable:

> A voice— Baby!
> Another voice— Break dem springs, if you can.
> Peter— That's Euphrosy: she got more sense than any of these gals, mamma says.
> . . . .
> A voice— Baby, wrap me round!
> A voice— You goddam whore, I'll cut your th'oat.
> . . . .
> A voice— Come on, big boy, git done. I cant lay here all day.[27]

Here heterosexuality is little more than violent interaction divorced of pleasure and squarely within the grim realities of economic exchange.

Faulkner likewise mercilessly spoofs heterosexuality in the ironically titled "Don Giovanni" and *Mosquitoes*, especially through Talliaferro's ill-fated attempts at seduction, while the similarly themed and structured "Mistral" and "Snow" focus on how tales of heterosexuality, usually involving denigrated female behavior, impinge upon idealized male homosociality that has, per Parini, "homoerotic undertones."[28] As James Ferguson asserts, here "Don and the narrator descend from a pure, clean world of masculine companionship in the mountains into valleys, where they must be initiated into what is for them the corrupt, often morally destructive effects of female sexuality. . . . While the two young men are not directly involved and only learn about the horrors at second hand, it is clear that they are thoroughly shaken by their experiences, that they now know some profoundly unsettling things about the power of sex and the nature of evil."[29] Although "Evangeline" does not feature this romanticized homosociality, its inset tale, that prefiguring the sordid narrative of Thomas Sutpen's children in *Absalom, Absalom!* (albeit here devoid of Charles and Henry's homoeroticism), echoes "Mistral" and "Snow" in its disturbing depiction of heterosexuality. Finally and most overtly, "Divorce in Naples" features George's homosexist frustration at his partner Carl's botched foray into heterosexuality, a frustration expressed in part by gynophobic assessments of female genitalia and sexuality: "For a minute I thought he was crying, then I seen that he was just trying not to puke. So I knew what the trouble was, what had been worrying him. I remember the first time it come as a surprise to me. 'Oh,' I says, 'the smell. It don't mean nothing.'"[30] "[E]verything associated with the female," Edmond Volpe unequivocally states of the story, "is sordid, tainted with the putrefaction of evil."[31] Yet, for the repulsed Carl, heterosexuality is ultimately disposable, as symbolized in his change of clothes: "Then I watched him lift from the floor the undergarment which he had removed and thrust it through a porthole quickly, with something of the air of a recovered drunkard putting out of sight an empty bottle" (888).

If anxiety about heterosexuality is thus constant in these works, one element that varies is how Faulkner represents the Spratling figure relative to this anxiety. The usual case, however, is a careful divorcing of male artistry from male same-sex desire. In both "Peter" and "Episode," where Spratling's artistic capabilities are central, Faulkner establishes little about the artist's sexual desire. In "Peter," Spratling deliberately replaces heterosexual recreation with artistic creation. When the boy asks, "But you aint going up to mamma's room, are you?" Spratling tersely replies, "No, no. I'll draw the passage" (491), emphatically repeating, "I won't bother her. I'll just draw a picture of the stair case" (491). Similarly, in both "The Big Shot" and "Evangeline," although Don's presence is minimal, especially in the former story, where this presence is reduced to three- and five-sentence framing paragraphs for the inset tale, it is his professional productivity—his work on the *Sentinel* newspaper in "The Big Shot" and his "squatting behind an easel about the countryside, sketching colonial porticoes and houses and negro cabins" (583) in "Evangeline"—rather than his sexuality that defines him. Don is much more central in "Mistral," and, though Faulkner divorces the figure of associations with artistic production, he emphatically—even comically—heterosexualizes the character: "In the Tyrol last summer Don held us up three days while he was trying to make the girl who sold us beer at the inn."[32]

Faulkner dequeers the Spratling figure even further in *Mosquitoes*, casting Gordon, one of the novel's few talented, productive male artists as significantly heterosexual. Although Gwin does not assess this alteration in her discussion of the novel, focusing instead on Talliaferro's "mixed feelings about Gordon's muscular body" in the opening "scene drenched in male homoerotic suggestiveness," on Faulkner's overt depictions of lesbian sexual activity later in the novel, and on the editing of these images for publication, her final assessment remains appropriate: "Faulkner found the terrain, especially the male homoerotic terrain, of the queer abject treacherous footing for the successful male writer in the U.S."[33] In each of these instances, the dequeering of the Spratling figure suggests that Faulkner hesitated to depict fully what Spratling was in actuality: a man who was simultaneously overtly gay, artistically talented, and professionally successful. In fact, if one continues to consider *Mosquitoes*, the only male character exhibiting the same-sex desire identified by Gwin is Talliaferro, conspicuously one of the few *non*-artists aboard the *Nausikka*.

This particular treatment of Talliaferro has as its parallel Faulkner's handling of the Spratling figure in two other texts within this early production, texts in which implied or overt male same-sex desire manifests in this figure only when he is dissociated from artistic production. Although "Don Giovanni" clearly anticipates *Mosquitoes*, Morrison, a prefiguring of Gordon, has no identified profession, a fact that seems all the odder when he is juxtaposed against the unnamed writer who strongly recalls Anderson and furiously bangs away on his typewriter in the downstairs apartment. What Faulkner hints at with Morrison, however, is his conspicuous, if jesting, focus on phallic size and prowess when Herb reveals his new resolve in his preposterous schemes to seduce women: "'Certainly. That's the only way to win battles, you know. Napoleon taught us that.' 'Napoleon also said something about the heaviest artillery, too,' his friend remarked wickedly. He smiled with compliance. 'I am as I am,' he murmured. . . . 'Especially when it hasn't been used in some time,' his host continued."[34] This intimated homoerotic interest is overt in "Divorce in Naples," but there too the Spratling figure is distinctly uninvolved in artistic production. George, like Carl, instead consumes art, as encoded in his constant accompaniment by the "portable victrola" (879) and the cracked solitary record that provides the music to which the men dance "in pants and undershirts" (879).

For all this careful separation of male artistry and same-sex desire, the early Faulkner nevertheless reveals a recurring fusion of the elements in at least two ways. Critics have exhaustively analyzed the first of these: the eroticism of narrative game playing. Repeatedly in his fiction and perhaps reaching its finest articulation in Quentin and Shreve's contourings of Sutpen's narrative on *Absalom, Absalom!*, Faulkner foregrounds a youthful male duo who establishes itself as artistically creative not through solitary efforts within the visual arts or the written word but rather through same-sex interactions that construct a communal narrative. As Ferguson notes, both "Mistral" and "Snow" not only draw upon Faulkner's European sojourn with Spratling but also fit this model perfectly: "Both of these strikingly similar works are about two young Americans—'Don' and the unnamed narrator—who in the course of their travels in Europe encounter mysterious situations, the significance of which they puzzle over and finally piece together (although we can never be sure that their conclusions are correct)."[35] "Evangeline" too is structured in this fashion and, with its early negotiation of the Sutpen material, is even more closely tied intertextually to the male homoerotics of *Absalom*. In these three stories, however, Faulkner not only depicts male identities that unify artistic production with thinly encoded homoerotic desire but, through the unnamed first-person narrators, also fashions this identity for himself.

But the early Faulkner also offers more direct depictions of himself alongside Spratling as recognizable artists casually and comfortably immersed in a homosocial realm inflected by same-sex desire. If the early story "Peter" largely divorces Spratling from both hetero- and homosexual desire, Faulkner, both the author of the piece and the self-representational unnamed narrator, nevertheless tinges the Quarter's multicultural homosocial realm of men taxiing for entry into a brothel with a sexual energy eddying with homoeroticism. Until the final pages, when Peter's mother appears, the focus is incessantly on scrutinized, assessed, and appreciated male bodies, those of the "Chinaman, his face rife with sex" (490); the longshoreman Eagle Beak, whose name encapsulates his hypermasculinity and physical prowess; and Baptist, a "Hercules in dark bronze" (490). Peter is no exception, since his body, intrinsically sexualized by his name, is the object of the appreciative male gaze of first the writer, eventually the painter, and even the sexually excited Chinese man, who repeatedly designates Peter a "plitty boy" (489, 492). He seems, however, to have little anxiety at this quasi-pedophilic desire; rather, with "sad incongruity," as Volpe expresses it, the boy functions—and understands himself to function—within the matter-of-fact erotics, seductions, and rituals of the sex trade, not only regulating sexual access to his mother in a parody of St. Peter regulating entry into Heaven but also participating in the securing of clients through the advertisement of *his* body and its performance of supplication to these men.[36] After the set polite exchange with Baptist, the all-too-knowing Peter explains to Spratling, "He's all right. That's the way he always acks. You got to treat 'em like that, mamma says. And we do" (490). This *we* disconcertingly evinces that the boy sees himself as performing a vital role within the brothel, prostituting himself—a pretty little Peter—in the assistance of his mother in her profession.

Faulkner further links the boy, his mother, and prostituted bodies through their conspicuous creolization. "Peter's face," Faulkner offers, "is round as a cup of milk with a dash of coffee in it" (489), as yellow as the Chinaman's "flat Mongol face" (489), whereas his mother is "languorous as a handled magnolia petal. She is as light in color as Peter" (493). Differences of age and sex are thus tempered by the similarity of embodied race, which seems here to function as a racist—if historically grounded— marker of prostitution. Moreover, the form of the story makes parallel the overheard sexual interactions taking place within the whorehouse and the exchanges between Peter and Spratling as he sketches the boy. In both instances, Faulkner opts for direct discourse, offering simply the speaker's name and his or her words. Within this context, readers are invited—even forced—to see the exchange between Peter and Spratling as a version of prostitution, with the young boy's body appropriated for the older man's gratification, and Faulkner has their dialogue echo the violent sentiments of the quoted passage between the men and the female whores:

> Spratling— Lean against the wall, Peter. Stop wiggling so much! Stand as if God was looking at you.
> Peter— Like this? His dark sailor suit took an impossible shape against the azure restful wall. His young body was impossible and terrible.
> . . . .
> A voice— Oh, Christ, dont! I never meant it! Dont!
> Peter (weeping)— My arm hurts.
> Spratling— All right, move then.
> Peter— I cant! You wont draw me no more. (492–93)

Both inside and outside the brothel's bedrooms, bodies are painfully contorted for adult male pleasure, and Peter, no less than his mother, defers to these desires. With this depiction, Faulkner not only suggests a Freudian inextricability of artistic creation and sexual recreation but conspicuously aligns artistic creativity with homoerotically inflected interactions. Moreover, after a striking silence, Faulkner interjects himself in the final exchange between Spratling and Peter, reminding that the Faulkner figure too eschews the heterosexuality upstairs for the homosociality of the street and, deferred and brief though it may be, participates in the symbolic *ménage à trois* centered on Peter.

Even more overt in this conflation of artistry and male same-sex desire is "Out of Nazareth." Published on Easter Sunday, 12 April 1925, in the *Times-Picayune*, this story, as much as either "Elmer" or "Divorce in Naples," includes a striking homoeroticism, as Spratling and a yet-again-unnamed Faulknerian narrator meander through Jackson Square and encounter a dazzlingly handsome seventeen-year-old drifter: "Spratling saw him first. 'My God,' he said, clutching me, 'look at that face'" (47). The narrator, however, immediately articulates his own appreciation through a telling allusion to the Old Testament's identification of the desire "surpassing the love of women": "And one could imagine young David looking like that. One could imagine Jonathan getting that look from David, and, serving that highest function of which sorry man is capable, being the two of them beautiful in similar peace and simplicity—beautiful as gods, as no woman can ever be. And to think of speaking to him, of entering that dream, was like a desecration" (47).[37]

The story's other mythological allusions work to shore up these homoerotic currents. The Easter publication, for instance, reminds of the constellation of homoerotic images surrounding Christ's death and resurrection: the disciples' homosociality; Judas's same-sex kiss of betrayal; Christian iconography's fetish of the eroticized pierced and naked male body; and so on. But Faulkner also draws on Greek mythology. The rather unrealistic and instead symbolic flora of Jackson Square is exclusively "narcissi and hyacinths like poised dancers" (46). Both flowers allude to homoerotic images of male beauty—Hyacinth, the beloved of Apollo, and Narcissus, the beloved of himself—but the latter myth has been particularly associated with male same-sex desire, whether negatively in Freudian theories of male homosexuality and more positively in works by André Gide and Oscar Wilde.

Within the story, this desire significantly circulates among three men, all of whom are artists. Spratling is a painter who muses on Cezanne's skill and begs the boy to pose as a model; the narrator, like Faulkner, "a writing man" (50), confesses that "words are my meat and bread and drink" (53); and even the boy offers a "blundering and childish and 'arty'" (53) but nonetheless powerful Whitmanic narrative to the duo. Strikingly absent here is any anxiety about this conflation of male artistry and homoeroticism; indeed, it all seems divinely sanctioned when, in the closing lines, the boy's "young face stared into an ineffable sky, and the sun was like a benediction on him" (54).

This particular image thus suggests the fitness of John Duvall's and Minrose Gwin's characterizations of same-sex desire in Faulkner's early work. Like the sum of his career, it indeed "does not disavow male homosexuality," as Duvall carefully phrases it, and instead puts "into play moments of homoerotic figuration and possibility."[38] However, what Gwin identifies in her assessment of the textual history of *Mosquitoes* as his potential self-censoring of depictions of male homoeroticism is equally revealed in his broader literary production of the 1920s that takes Spratling as a significant source of inspiration. Initially untroubled, it seems, at conflations of male artistry, homoeroticism, and homosexuality in pieces like "Peter" and "Out of Nazareth," Faulkner appears to have grown increasingly anxious about this link and worked studiously to wrench apart these elements in subsequent Spratling figures, even as his relationships with gay men remained significant, especially within the "artful and crafty" subcultures of the French Quarter.

NOTES

1. John N. Duvall, "Faulkner's Crying Game: Male Homosexual Panic," in *Faulkner and Gender*, ed. Donald M. Kartiganer and Ann J. Abadie (Jackson: University Press of Mississippi, 1997), 50; Minrose C. Gwin, "Did Ernest Like Gordon?: Faulkner's *Mosquitoes* and the Bite of 'Gender Trouble,'" in *Faulkner and Gender*, 124.

2. Jay Parini, *One Matchless Time: A Life of William Faulkner* (New York: Harper Perennial, 2005), 76–77.

3. Tennessee Williams, *Suddenly Last Summer*, in *Four Plays* (New York: Signet, 1976), 81.

4. W. Kenneth Holditch, "William Spratling, William Faulkner, and Other Famous Creoles," *Mississippi Quarterly* 51, no. 3 (Summer 1998): 427.

5. Parini, *One Matchless Time*, 129.

6. William Spratling, *File on Spratling: An Autobiography* (Boston: Little, Brown and Company, 1967), 17, 16.

7. James G. Watson, ed., *Thinking of Home: William Faulkner's Letters to His Mother and Father, 1918–1925* (New York: Norton, 1992), 165.

8. William Spratling, "Chronicle of a Friendship: William Faulkner in New Orleans," in *Sherwood Anderson and Other Famous Creoles* (1926; reprint, Austin: University of Texas Press, 1966), 12.

9. Spratling, *File on Spratling*, 28.

10. Parini, *One Matchless Time*, 93.

11. Spratling, *File on Spratling*, 99, 100. See also Holditch, "William Spratling, William Faulkner, and Other Famous Creoles," 427–28.

12. Taylor D. Littleton, *The Color of Silver: William Spratling: His Life and Art* (Baton Rouge: Louisiana State University Press, 2000), 231, 234. This characterization stands in marked contrast to Parini's unequivocal one of "the rowdy young (and openly homosexual) painter William Spratling." See Parini, *One Matchless Time*, 74.

13. Littleton, *The Color of Silver*, 33.

14. William Faulkner, "Out of Nazareth," in *New Orleans Sketches*, ed. Carvel Collins (1958; reprint, Jackson: University Press of Mississippi, 2002), 46, hereafter cited in the text by page number.

15. Spratling, "Chronicle of a Friendship," 13.

16. For other accounts of Faulkner's artistic appropriations of scenes relayed by Spratling from his biography, see Littleton, *The Color of Silver*, 80.

17. Joel Williamson, *William Faulkner and Southern History* (New York: Oxford University Press, 1993), 202.

18. Massimo Bacigalupo, "New Information on William Faulkner's First Trip to Italy," *Journal of Modern Literature* 24, no. 2 (Winter 2002–2001): 325.

19. Williamson, *William Faulkner and Southern History*, 202.

20. Spratling, "Chronicle of a Friendship," 13.

21. William Faulkner, "Evangeline," in *Uncollected Stories of William Faulkner*, ed. Joseph Blotner (1979; reprint, New York: Vintage, 1997), 583, hereafter cited in the text by page number.

22. William Faulkner, "New Orleans" in *New Orleans Sketches*, 13, hereafter cited in the text by page number. See also William Faulkner, *Mosquitoes* (1927; reprint, Liveright, 1997), 10.

23. This sketch within "New Orleans" should not be confused with the later uncollected story with the same title. See William Faulkner, "Frankie and Johnny," in *Uncollected Stories*, 338–47.

24. William Faulkner, "Damon and Pythias Unlimited," in *New Orleans Sketches*, 20, hereafter cited in the text by page number.

25. William Faulkner, "Jealousy," in *New Orleans Sketches*, 34, 37–38, hereafter cited in the text by page number.

26. William Faulkner, "Episode," in *New Orleans Sketches*, 105, hereafter cited in the text by page number.

27. William Faulkner, "Peter," in *Uncollected Stories*, 491–92, hereafter cited in the text by page number.

28. Parini, *One Matchless Time*, 96.

29. James Ferguson, *Faulkner's Short Fiction* (Knoxville, University of Tennessee Press, 1991), 65–66.

30. William Faulkner, "Divorce in Naples," in *Collected Stories* (1950; reprint, New York: Vintage, 1995), 892, hereafter cited in the text by page number.

31. Edmond L. Volpe, *A Reader's Guide to William Faulkner: The Short Stories* (Syracuse: Syracuse University Press, 2004), 66.

32. William Faulkner, "Mistral," in *Collected Stories*, 874.

33. Gwin, "Did Ernest Like Gordon?," 126, 130, 139.

34. William Faulkner, "Don Giovanni," in *Uncollected Stories*, 483–84.

35. Ferguson, *Faulkner's Short Fiction*, 30.

36. Volpe, *A Reader's Guide to William Faulkner: The Short Stories*, 27.

37. Edwin T. Arnold reminds that, in the story "A Meeting South," Sherwood Anderson names his textual surrogate for Faulkner "David." "A Meeting South" and "Out of Nazareth" thus engage in an intertexual dialogue that consistently foregrounds Faulkner within intergenerational mentorships of male artists and their sexualized—and potentially homoeroticized—bodies.

38. Duvall, "Faulkner's Crying Game," 53.

"And You Too, Sister, Sister?":
Lesbian Sexuality, *Absalom, Absalom!*,
and the Reconstruction of the Southern Family

JAIME HARKER

In *Confessions of a Failed Southern Lady*, Florence King recounts her sexual adventures and misadventures in the late 1950s, under her grandmother's iron curtain of Southern ladyhood. After various transgressions—including fooling around with frat boys and an affair with a married man—Florence arrives in Oxford, Mississippi, and embarks on a torrid lesbian affair with the languid Cajun Bres. Florence ruminates on the appeal of Bres's earthy Southern sexuality:

> I was still not used to the Deep South's exquisite balance between hatred and hospitality. Making love in a ground-floor bedroom in Mississippi reminded me of *The Lady—Or the Tiger?* It would have been no more surprising to look up from Bres's twat and see a shotgun coming through the window than to see a smiling face saying, "Hey, how y'all doin'?"
>
> Because I expected death, that Thanksgiving night shines in my memory as a festival of lubricity. The old adage about danger enhancing sexuality is all too true, and the reason why Southerners are so horny. Much has changed now; liquor is in and racism, at least the blood-and-thunder kind, is out, but old-time religion is still flourishing and those black velvet nights are still ominous. I have a feeling that Mississippi is still the best place to be a consenting adult, and might even be our national G-spot. Just press Jackson and every woman in America will come.[1]

Why, you may ask, am I beginning an academic presentation on William Faulkner with a decadent celebration of Southern, and lesbian, sexuality? King's portrait of "transgressive" sexuality in the South is surprising not only for its candor but for its absolute absence of angst. As this conference attests, the study of sexuality has become increasingly important in Faulkner studies over the last fifteen years, resulting in a remarkable array of scholarship. The tone of much of this scholarship, however, is somber, an investigation of tortured racial and sexual politics. Corncobs and castration have haunted the scholarly psyche.

Scholars have been further burdened by biases about homosexuality and women's sexuality. Homoerotic desire must end tragically, especially in the South; women are victims, ghosts, sneaky ladies, but not desiring subjects—and certainly not with each other.

This is true of perhaps the most overanalyzed novel in the Faulkner pantheon: *Absalom, Absalom!* Given its extensive critical history, one might reasonably wonder if there is anything new to say about this novel. But the critical blind spots regarding this novel astonish me, quite frankly. So I want to propose a polymorphously perverse reading of *Absalom, Absalom!*—one that places it as a foremother, of sorts, to Florence King and places the novel in an intertextual conversation with contemporary Southern lesbian literature.

Absalom, Absalom! has been read, consistently, as the map of Thomas Sutpen's, and the old South's, tragic decline. The male narrators construct an Oedipal struggle between father and sons, one that repudiates the sons' homoerotic desires. Rosa refuses Judith's or Clytie's agency by calling them prisoners of a "sentient" house.[2] But then, as Olivia Carr Edenfield writes, Rosa "spends her life searching for a way into the patriarchy,"[3] from her odes to dead Confederate soldiers to her final punishment of Henry's racial and sexual border crossings.

This reading of *Absalom, Absalom!* as the embodiment of the doomed, noble South is consistent with what Michael Kreyling argues is Faulkner's legacy in Southern Studies.[4] We have required Faulkner to embody "The South," a unified entity that is equal parts nostalgia and heritage, a burden imprisoning Faulkner criticism. The South is usually imagined as "grounded," a "fixed" space immune to the changes, materialism, and moral relativism of modernity. "Sense of place" brings with it any number of clichéd ideologies: family, stability, morality, tradition. We have imposed a simple, two-dimensional map onto the multilayered excavations of Faulkner's fiction—a map of *the* Southern experience, with an ideology, and an ending, we already know.

Geographers, of course, have been rewriting such two-dimensional topographies for years, undoing common conceptions of place as fixed and permanent. Doreen Massey, for example, argues in *Space, Place, and Gender*:

> That recognition of the duration in external things and thus the interpenetration, though not the equivalence, of space and time is an important aspect of the argument in this book. It is what I am calling space as the dimension of multiple trajectories, a simultaneity of stories-so-far. Space as the dimension of a multiplicity of durations. The problem has been that the old chain of meaning-space-representation-stasis continues to wield its power. The legacy lingers on.[5]

Massey articulates a notion of space that contrasts sharply with fixed stereotypes of a patriarchal, homophobic, doomed South. Inspired by this geographical reimagination, Hortense Spillers has written a detailed spatial critique of *Absalom, Absalom!*, claiming that "the subjective component of space turns it into an infinite series of authorships."[6] Work like Spillers's reimagines the South not as a fixed pole of a simple binary (city/country, North/South, out/closeted), but as a crossroads, a fluid, intersecting, unfinished trajectory of narratives. Global South scholarship, recently explored in an *American Literature* special issue, edited by Kathryn McKee and Annette Trefzer, highlights the South as a complex contact zone, enmeshed in competing notions of empire, and situated at a racial, linguistic, and national crossroads.[7] It is, in other words, a geography of multiple, competing, sometimes invisible desires.

Faulkner has always provided a palimpsest of multiple Souths. During the Cold War, Faulkner's complex narratives inspired equally complex literary readings that nonetheless often yearn for closure—one clear map of the South. Subsequent analyses, notably Minrose Gwin's gynocritical reading, feel less need to construct an ultimate closure in Faulkner's complex narrative structures.[8] I want to suggest that thinking of Faulkner geographically, rather than simply formally, may help critics to avoid univocal conclusions about his Southern narratives.

Like Faulkner, contemporary Southern lesbian writers have always understood the complexity of the Southern terrain, and they explore these different notions of space in both essays and fiction. Minnie Bruce Pratt's essay "Identity: Skin, Blood, Heart" maps out her complicated relationship to the South through a memory that morphs into a metaphor.

> When I try to think of this, I think of my father. When I was about eight years old, he took me up the front marble steps of the courthouse in my town. He took me inside, up the worn wooden steps, stooped under the feet of folks who had gone up and down to be judged, or to gawk at others being judged, up past the courtroom where my grandfather had leaned back in his chair and judged for over forty years, up to the attic, to some narrow steps that went to the roof, to the clock tower with a walled ledge. . . . I never got to the top. When he told me to go up the steps in front of him, I tried to, crawling on hands and knees, but I was terribly afraid. I couldn't, or wouldn't, do it. He let me crawl down; he was disgusted with me, I thought. I think now that he wanted to show me a place he had climbed to as a boy, a view that had been his father's and his, and would be mine. But I was not him: I had not learned to take that height, that being set apart as my own, a white girl, not a boy. . . .
>
> So this is one gain for me as I change: I learn a way of looking at the world that is more accurate, complex, multilayered, multidimensioned, more truthful.

To see a world of overlapping circles, like movement on the mill pond after a fish has jumped, instead of the courthouse square with me at the middle, even if I am on the ground.[9]

Pratt's model of "overlapping circles" highlights Southern space as a place of multiple layers—simultaneous stories that can be rewritten. She eschews the "bird's-eye view" of clear hierarchy for complex overlapping circles, with only the ripple effect visible.

Pratt's perspective is informed by her experience as a Southern lesbian, one whose "overlapping circles" include both the powerful and the marginalized. Southern lesbian novels, particularly in the last thirty years, suggest a complex rewriting of the geography of "home" in Southern lesbian literary imaginations—a home that is a crossroads of marginal "stories so far," notably but not exclusively lesbian. Mab Segrest, for example, argues for a lesbian literary tradition as a legitimately Southern space, one without the nostalgia of the lost, and noble, cause.[10]

This linkage of contemporary Southern lesbian writers with Faulkner may seem counterintuitive. Frann Michel first suggested this provocative thesis in her 1989 essay, "William Faulkner as a Lesbian Author."[11] Michel notes Faulkner's attribution of his own poetry to a lesbian character in *The Mosquitoes* and argues that as a male Southern writer, Faulkner identified with the marginality of lesbians.

Yet Faulkner constructed a place for himself in Oxford society that was both queer and central, a space, if you will, simultaneously within and without. Southern lesbians, as I will argue, have constructed a similarly complex but authentically Southern space. So rather than claim a lesbian identity for Faulkner, I want to suggest an affinity.[12]

What I notice in *Absalom, Absalom!* is Faulkner's complex and precise rendering of Southern lesbian space, a rendering consistent with a later Southern lesbian literary tradition. I am interested in excavating a Southern literary tradition that is "shockingly pink," and I have discovered in Faulkner an unexpected ally.[13] Sutpen's Hundred becomes Judith's Hundred, a queer contact zone, one both within and outside of Southern patriarchal structures.

Absalom, Absalom!, as Joseph Allen Boone notes, undoes the unified narrative of The South. The novel is filled with mulattas and poor whites and spinsters and queers; "these subversive elements," Boone claims, "*do* escape the father's fascistic plotting, and in the form of the return of the textually repressed, threaten to wreck his transcendent designs and call into question the invisible, hypostatized authority upon which his identity as the superior sex and superior race rests" (298).[14] I would go further; the subversive elements do not just threaten to "wreck his transcendent designs"; they actually *do* wreck them. And yet we persist in seeing the novel as a tragedy, ending in homosexual homicide (Bon) or suicide (Quentin), tropes John Howard identifies as the most common narratives of gay life.[15]

Howard's *Men Like That* constructs other narratives of gay life, but these counternarratives also coexist in *Absalom, Absalom!* Though critics, notably Norman W. Jones, have explicated the gay homoerotics of the novel in brilliant fashion, hardly anyone has noticed the lesbian shadowing of the larger plot. Indeed, Jones's brief mention of their relationship, an aside in a larger explication of Bon and Henry, is about the only critical attention.[16] Bon and Henry, it seems, use Judith as a conduit for their own relationship, but why isn't it just as plausible that Judith uses Bon as a replacement for Henry? And since both Bon, the feminine, kimono-wearing seductress, and Henry, the sissy to Judith's tomboy, are feminized, could not that initial triangle, for Judith, express her lesbian desire, in concert with Bon and Henry's homoerotics? That this possibility has not occurred to critics suggests that they have been overly influenced by the narrators of the novel, who cannot attribute agency to any woman. But there is Judith, strong, independent, defiant, who achieves the ultimate hat trick, a widow without ever having been a wife, living unmolested until her death.

She does not, however, live alone. *Absalom, Absalom!* provides a nontragic alternative to the homosexual panic that invades the Bon/Henry, Quentin/Shreve dyads.[17] Henry killed Bon rather than admit his homoerotic desire for his own brother, but another sibling duo live out their lives with no negative consequences. Clytie, remember, is also a half-sibling, and Clytie and Judith live together from their childhood, when they watched their father's naked wrestling matches, until Judith's death. And Clytie continues to live in the house, caring for Henry, who looked so like Judith that one narrative regards them as twins. Why don't we read this as a triumph of love? A celebration of a decades-long marriage, that continues beyond the death of one partner?

Critics have not paid much attention to their relationship. But Rosa did. The famous touch between Rosa and Clytie in the entry hall (to which I will return in a moment) sparks Rosa's inarticulate memory of lesbian panic:

> We just stood there—I motionless in the attitude and action of running, she rigid in the furious immobility, the two of us joined by that hand and arm which held us, like a fierce rigid umbilical cord, twin sistered to the fell darkness which had produced her. As a child I had more than once watched her and Judith and even Henry scuffling in the rough games which they (possibly all

children; I do not know) play, and (so I have heard) she and Judith even slept together, in the same room but with Judith in the bed and she on a pallet on the floor ostensibly. But I have heard how on more than one occasion Ellen has found them both on the pallet, and once in the bed together. But not I. Even as a child, I would not even play with the same objects which she and Judith played with, as though that warped and Spartan solitude which before I could comprehend and to understand before I even heard, had also taught me not only to *instinctively fear her and what she was*, but to shun the very objects which she had touched. (112, italics added)

The touch, forbidden, familiar, between the two women makes them "twin-sistered," and leads Rosa to muse upon the unspeakable intimacy between Clytie and Judith—an intimacy she recognizes without being able to name. She would not touch the objects they touched, for fear it was "catching." Yet Rosa kept coming back, and back, until that final, fateful invasion. Fear and desire animate all her storytelling.

Rosa "instinctively fear[s] her and what she was." It is unclear which "she" Rosa avoids, but in some sense the unnamed "she," "twin-sistered," was both Judith and Clytie. "What she was" is easier to define: the prototypic Southern lesbian, hiding in plain sight. Yet, Rosa must, at all costs, not name this unspeakable truth:

I cried—perhaps not aloud, not with words (and not to Judith, mind: perhaps I knew already, on the instant I entered the house and saw that face which was at once both more and less than Sutpen, perhaps I knew even then what I *could not, would not, must not believe*)—I cried 'And you too? And you too, sister, sister?' (112–13, italics added)

Again, the thing she "could not, would not, must not believe" cannot be Clytie's familial relationship; everyone knows. It is something so terrifying to Rosa that even when she tells all, she cannot tell that. But she desperately wants to be part of the Southern sisterhood, as her haunting refrain, half-reproachful, half-longing, indicates. "Sister, sister," echoes the title, "Absalom, Absalom," King David's lament for the death of his treasonous but well-loved son. Like David, Rosa gladly would have died for Judith, but her place was usurped, and thwarted by love, she could only cry out against the two "sisters" whose relationship excluded her.

In later Southern lesbian novels, lesbian desire is similarly figured in familial terms, sisters or mother/daughter. In *The Color Purple*, Shug and Celie both act like mothers and children, for example.[18] Rosa's attraction to the "sisters" runs underneath her ode to the "summer of wisteria," as does her jealousy at being left out. After this encounter, she insinuates herself into their room, their bed, after imagining and constructing the closest place possible to Judith, her wedding undergarments. What did she expect when she arrived at Sutpen's Hundred? Did she expect Judith to fall into her arms? She clearly resented Clytie's claim of equality, her assertion of a primary relationship. Rosa remained so obsessed with Judith that she memorialized her tombstone like one of her lost confederate soldiers. Was it really her obsession with Judith, not Thomas Sutpen, that keeps her focused on the house? Indeed, was marrying Sutpen the only way to get close to Judith, who only, through that engagement, finally focuses on Rosa's body, sewing a wedding dress that envelops Rosa? And that unwelcome reminder of her role as "breeder" in the Sutpen household, the intimate relation with Thomas, not Judith, represents the traumatic break, her inability to possess Judith?

Let us go back, then, to that oft-quoted passage, when Clytie touches Rosa:

> Then she touched me, and then I did stop dead. Possibly even then my body did not stop, since I seemed to be aware of it thrusting blindly still against that solid yet imponderable weight (she not owner: instrument; I still say that) of that will to bar me from the stairs; possibly the sound of the other voice, the single word spoken from the stair-head above us, had already broken and parted us before it (my body) had even paused. I do not know. I know only that my entire being seemed to run at blind full tilt into something monstrous and immobile, with a shocking impact too soon and too quick to be mere amazement and outrage at that black arresting and untimorous hand on my white woman's flesh. Because there is something in the touch of flesh with flesh which abrogates, cuts sharp and straight across the devious intricate channels of decorous ordering, which enemies as well as lovers know because it makes them both:—touch and touch of that which is the citadel of the central I-Am's private own; not spirit, soul; the liquorish and ungirdled mind is anyone's to take in any darkened hallway of this earthly tenement. But let flesh touch with flesh, and watch the fall of all the eggshell shibboleth of caste and color too. Yes, I stopped dead. (111–12)

Critics have tended to read this in universalized terms—a paean to racial harmony. We forget that its impetus is two women touching, touching like lovers. It may be no more than verbal wordplay to suggest the verbal similarities of "Clytemnestra" and "clitoris."[19] When she is touched by Clytie, or "clittie," Rosa "thrusts blindly" against it; the effect is "liquorish" and "ungirdled," naked and liquid; and Rosa tells us twice, this touch makes her "stop dead"—perhaps the "little death" of orgasm the French have so carefully inscribed. Clytie's touch sends Rosa into the "citadel of the central I-Am's private own"—or in more colloquial terms,

Clytie makes Rosa see God. We know that after this touch by Clytie, Rosa moves in, lies literally between Judith and Clytie, her ungirdled mind anyone's to take. (Sadly, no one did.)

Jay Watson suggests "that when Clytie presses Rosa's arm, the whole novel 'comes.'"[20] Rosa, in other words, is the novelistic G-spot of *Absalom, Absalom!* Certainly, the novel moves toward explicit explorations of queer desire in the aftershocks of Rosa's ecstasy. Lesbian desire remains the unspoken drive behind the narrative; Clytie's touch is both transformative and inscrutable.

Clytie and Rosa were, in Rosa's words, "open, ay honorable, enemies," Clytie always barring her unspeakable desire for Judith. Yet Clytie's touch remains her sole link to Judith, one that continues to arouse her. When, forty years later, she returns to Sutpen's Hundred to see what is hidden in the house, she is trembling with breathless anticipation. Quentin feels "something fierce and implacable and dynamic driving down the thin rigid arms and into his palms and up his own arms; lying in the Massachusetts bed he remembered how he thought, knew, said suddenly to himself, 'Why, she's not afraid at all. It's something. But she's not afraid'" (293). It's something, all right—something that Rosa, both times, must destroy with violence, with the epithet "nigger" (used, like Bon used it, to break the intimate homoerotic bond) and, in the end, with her fists. But what Rosa and Quentin feel and then disavow is the revolutionary potential of queer desire. In so much of Faulkner, sexuality is simply another weapon to enforce hierarchy. Rape, abandonment, exploitation, commodification—all pervert sexual expression. Here, queer desire provides an escape from such hierarchies, a liberatory impulse that breaks down the "eggshell shibboleth of color and caste."

Queer desire and queer space circle Judith like a constellation. Judith is the shadowy protagonist behind the explicit tale of Thomas Sutpen as originary father, the unacknowledged originary lesbian mother. The novel's narrators compress her into patronizing stereotypes of spinsters, ghostly ladies, but she cannot be imprisoned there, by any of them. Despite the narrators' repeated attempts to define Judith as a spinster, the term never seems to fit a woman as self-possessed, as independent, as intimidating as Judith. Indeed, in Diane Roberts's excellent discussion of spinsters, she discusses Rosa in depth, but never mentions Judith.[21]

Rather than discuss the bachelor/spinster dyad, a more useful excavation of Faulkner's lesbian characters would build on Gary Richards's sissy/tomboy binary. The tomboy, I want to argue, is a recurring trope for the Southern lesbian. Judith fits this perfectly; watching fights (with Clytie), racing hell-bent for leather to church, plowing and working like a man, supporting herself instead of living in oblivious dependence like Rosa, facing tragedy and heartbreak without flinching—which, according to Henry James's Basil Roscomb, is the epitome of the "masculine spirit." Indeed, despite the narrators' attempts to dismiss her with the other hysterical women, Judith always exceeds and triumphs over their patronizing labels. The male narrators treat Judith like a tragic virgin but then must acknowledge that she is "unbereaved."

Unlike Cousin Druscilla in *The Unvanquished*, Judith is never brought to heel by the larger community. Judith, as Rosa instinctively knows, is twice the man her father was, the true and legitimate heir, who seizes her inheritance and, unlike Ike McCaslin, actually gives the unacknowledged inheritors of the land their birthright.

Clytie is another tomboy, perfectly matched with Judith, decimating stereotypes about "mammies" and "house slaves," just as Judith destroys myths of the "plantation belle." Quentin's encounter with her as a boy unnerves his sense of gender, racial, and geographical hierarchy:

> *You didn't even know she was there until all of you started and whirled as one and found her watching you from a chair tilted back against the cabin wall—a little dried-up woman not much bigger than a monkey and who might have been any age up to ten thousand years, in faded voluminous skirts and an immaculate headrag, her bare coffee-colored feet wrapped around the chair rung like monkeys do, smoking a clay pipe and watching you with eyes like two shoe buttons buried in the myriad wrinkles of her coffee-colored face, who just looked at you and said without even removing the pipe and in a voice almost like a white woman's: 'What do you want?' and after a moment one of you said 'nothing' and then you were all running without knowing which of you began to run first nor why since you were not scared, back across the fallow and rain-gutted and brier-choked old fields until you came to the old rotting snake fence and crossed it, hurled yourselves over it, and then the earth, the land, the sky and trees and woods, looked different again, all right again.* (173–74)

Clytie is beyond any known categories—no age, no discernible gender, with a voice like a "white woman's," who demands and claims her space. She so unnerves the boys that the very ground beneath their feet feels unfamiliar, and they must run away to reclaim their familiar superimposed geography. This is the queer space, as I will discuss, that animates Southern lesbian literature.

This trope of the tomboy continues in later Southern lesbian literary traditions. In *Bastard Out of Carolina*, Bone's nascent sexual difference is defined by gender; her cousin tells her, "You got a man-type part of you. Rock-hard and nasty and immune to harm. But hell, Boatwright women come out that way sometimes."[22] The identification of lesbians as "man-type" varies in these novels. Raylene is grouped with her infamous Boatwright brothers: "Glen was right, Mama told me, she didn't want me to grow up as wild and mean as Earle or Beau or even Raylene" (111). In *Getting Mother's Body*, Dill actually passes as a man, hanging out with the men at the barber shop, accepting what male privilege he has as a black man in a small Texas town.[23] The men in town notice that Dill never seems to need a shave, but in typical Southern fashion, they never mention it, and neither does Dill. In *Fried Green Tomatoes at the Whistle Stop Cafe*, Idgie is accepted as a man in Whistle Stop—hunting, carousing, drinking, taking care of Ruth, going to the whorehouse, being a father to Stump.[24] In *The Color Purple*, Shug is an object of desire for men, of course, but she also acts like a man in her approach to sex and relationships. When she and Albert were young, they would cross-dress, Shug taking the "masculine" role and Albert the "feminine," their own inverted butch-femme roles.

White lesbians sometimes define their difference in terms of race. Bone's lesbian aunt Raylene, in *Bastard Out of Carolina*, "was always telling people that we had a little of the tarbrush on us, but the way she grinned when she said it could have meant she was lying to make somebody mad, or maybe she just talked that way because she was crazy angry to start out" (53). The conflation here of racial and sexual deviance is common in Southern literature, and Bone initially articulates one in terms of the other—as Raylene does herself, mischievously. Bone is similarly different, "all black-headed and strange," as her cousin asserts. Molly Bolt, in *Rubyfruit Jungle*, adopted and different, often wonders if she is part black, a marker of her sexual differences.[25] Florence's lover Bres in *Confessions of a Failed Southern Lady* is hounded by the local white citizens' council, because her lesbianism marks her as a "nigger-loving Jew communist." Of course, Clytie is mixed race, and Judith dies of yellow fever—an implied miscegenation to the "high yellow" of her mulatto siblings and nephew.[26]

These tomboys, racially and sexually indeterminate by Southern hierarchies, consistently remake the landscape, creating autonomous havens within and among the more dominant Southern narratives. Sutpen's Hundred was never a stable space. It started as Indian land, then became an egalitarian, cross-racial men's haven before it was reinvented as a legitimate plantation. Even the French architect undoes some of Sutpen's tacky grandeur. These multiple stories, if you will, overlap; once Sutpen's Hundred becomes the site of paterfamilias, he still has boxing matches with his Haitian slaves. The transformation continues long after the demise of the Sutpens: Major De Spain's hunting camp becomes a homosocial haven for Ike McCaslin and other men, a haven undone by capitalism.

During the Civil War, of course, Judith constructs an autonomous queer space on her father's plantation. Her father's return is dramatic, disruptive, and mercifully brief; he manages to send one potential wife screaming into the night and then provoke his most loyal subject to murder. With the exception of this interlude, Judith continues her queer contact zone until her death. She is one of the few, if not the only, Faulkner characters who not only escapes the burdens of Southern history but triumphs over them, creating a radically different social order.

Judith's escape, her liberation, comes through an embrace of work. Rosa describes this, while insisting on seeing it as a tragedy:

> We led the busy eventless lives of three nuns in a barren and poverty-stricken convent: the walls we had were safe, impervious enough, even if it did not matter to the walls whether we ate or not. And amicably, not as two white women and a negress, not as three negroes or three whites, not even as three women, but merely as three creatures. . . . We grew and tended and harvested with our own hands the food we ate, made and worked that garden just as we cooked and ate the food which came out of it: with no distinction among the three of us of age or color but just as to who could build this fire or stir this pot or weed this bed or carry this apron full of corn to the mill for meal with least cost to the general good in time or expense of other duties. It was as though we were one being, interchangeable and indiscriminate, which kept that garden growing, spun thread and wove the cloth we wore, hunted and found and rendered the meager ditch-side herbs to protect and guarantee what spartan compromise we dared or had the time to make with illness. (125)

Judith constructs a space in which everyone does her share to survive— no one passes the burden onto others. In other words, Judith establishes a household in which the exploitive racial and gender hierarchies of the plantation South, which Rosa saw as her birthright, are completely undone. They are not black, or white, or women—they are creatures, equal and unprivileged. Remember that Judith left her feather bed to join Clytie on the pallet, with one exception; her disavowal of exploitive privilege destroys the hierarchical corruption of the plantation system, at least at Judith's Hundred.

Judith's poverty never turns into Rosa's Protestant "penury"; she maintains a generosity of spirit that Rosa can only attribute to profligacy and fear. Judith "(abetted by Clytie) would cook twice what we could eat and three times what we could afford and give it to anyone, any stranger in a land already beginning to fill with straggling soldiers who stopped and asked for it" (26). Rosa eventually runs from this world, preferring the hypocritical helplessness that never makes her recognize where her food comes from, but Judith stays in this queer space until the end of her life.

Judith's generosity extends both to strangers and to family, broadly defined. After her father's death, Judith remakes the Southern family by appropriating its most hallowed institutions. She buys tombstones to commemorate Charles Bon and his son in the family plot. Mr. Compson, after revealing this fact, editorializes:

> Yes. They lead beautiful lives—women. Lives not only divorced from, but irrevocably excommunicated from, all reality. That's why, although their deaths, the instant of dissolution, are of no importance to them since they have a courage and fortitude in the face of pain and annihilation which would make the most spartan man resemble a puling boy, yet to them their funerals and graves, the little puny affirmation of spurious immortality set above their slumber, are of incalculable importance. (156)

Consider the context in which Mr. Compson makes this remark. He has just told the story of Thomas Sutpen traveling in the middle of war with ornate, expensive tombstones for himself and his wife, a gesture made even though he knew that the war was lost, and yet Mr. Compson does not talk about how Southern men's lives are irrevocably excommunicated from all reality. Nor was Sutpen's gesture isolated; Miles Orvell, speaking at this conference several years ago, traced the larger cultural trend toward Confederate War memorials in the reconstruction period, one that divorced Southerners further from the reality of the Civil War into a romanticized myth of the lost and noble cause.[27] Those memorials, still standing, were anything but empty gestures; they were a material remaking of the Southern landscape, a superimposed story that sought to become the only story of Southern identity.

In this context, Judith's commemoration was not quixotic but subversive, even revolutionary. She combated the larger, romanticized commemoration of the Civil War, so common in the reconstruction South, with her own institutionalization of illegitimate, mixed-race siblings. This behavior continued throughout her life. She invited Charles Bon's octoroon "widow" to visit his grave, violating another Southern cultural taboo by recognizing her as family. And after the war, she adopted Charles Bon's son, setting him up as the heir apparent, even inviting him to call her "aunt Judith." She attempted to create a space in which black and white were irrelevant, keeping him from "niggers" and "planters." Valery St. Bon, like Rosa, was uncomfortable with the freedom from Southern patriarchal values that Judith's queer contact zone provided. The judge's outraged question to Valery, *"What are you? Who and where did you come from?"* (165) would have been directed more fruitfully to Judith, but it is never asked in the refuge Judith provides, nor is it asked of Jim Bond, the miscegenated future of the South and the nation, and one that Judith's queer contact zone made possible.

Judith's construction of a liberatory lesbian space is echoed in contemporary Southern lesbian novels. One example is Raylene's house in *Bastard Out of Carolina*. Raylene lives in a rented house, but unlike her siblings, she stays in the same place. Her home is "easy to get to on the Eustis Highway but set off by itself on a little rise of land" (178). It is strategically situated at the bend of a river, with "all the trees had been cut back and the scuppernong vines torn out" (17). "'I don't like surprises,' she always said. 'I like to see who's coming up on me'" (179). She acknowledges and defies danger. (It is significant, I think, that Bone's rape takes place, not as the movie version suggests, at Raylene's, but at another aunt's house, one that had already been the site of another horrifying scene of domestic violence.)

Raylene's home serves as a different kind of haven, not just for Bone from the abuse of her stepfather, but for her male nephews, who come to the river because she encourages absolute freedom. She provides a model of self-sufficiency, living on her garden and whatever trash she can salvage from the river and sell. In fact, her insistence on inhabiting the margins, turning the discarded refuse of the society into an independent life, gives Bone her only refuge from the cycle of abuse she witnesses and experiences. Raylene's is a Southern prototype of the lesbian commune, a commune anchored by lesbians but not exclusive to them.

Other lesbian spaces are less independent and more integrated into the larger community. Rita Mae Brown's *Bingo* maps out a town dissected by the Mason-Dixon line, and other divisions in town—including gay and straight identity—are equally bifurcated and violated.[28] (Nickel Smith, the town lesbian, has an affair with her best friend's husband, and then marries the town queer to provide a quasi-heteronormative "family"—thus earning Rita Mae Brown the ire of gay and lesbian critics everywhere). In *Fried Green Tomatoes at the Whistle Stop Cafe*, Ruth and Idgie's café is the meeting place for everyone in town, black and white (though with separated entrances), klan members and lesbians. Ruth and Idgie's centrality to the workings of the town becomes evident in the local newspaper, included in the narrative—they are integrated seamlessly into the town's events. In *The Color Purple*, there are multiple and changing sites: Sofia and Harpo's house, which becomes a juke joint, an alternative to the local church; Celie's house, first the site of her abuse, and then a home in which her lover, her ex-husband, her ex-husband's son and wife and son's ex-lover, and finally her children can find refuge;

Shug's Memphis mansion, Celie's refuge and then the site of her business and independence. Most of these novels feature towns, and houses, which allow for contact between disparate classes, groups, races, and cliques in the South.

In lesbian novels by African American women, such contact zones are less likely to be cross-racial. White people are generally constructed as outside threats to the community, a means of uniting black people who differ, not just in sexual orientation, but in beliefs and perspective. In *The Color Purple*, Sofia's imprisonment comes from a hostile white community, and the group that considers how to free her includes ex-lovers, her jilted husband, and her husband's lover—whose attempt to free Sophie leads to her own abuse.

In novels by white lesbians, by contrast, the cross-racial character of these intersecting spaces is essential. White lesbians also become key connectors in their Southern communities between black and white. *Fried Green Tomatoes* becomes the prototype for this—Ruth's and Idgie's insistence on serving black patrons, their relief for the poor by stealing from the trains, their acceptance of Big George as part of the family, Idgie's attempted protection of George by going on trial. Minnie Bruce Pratt and Mab Segrest are deeply invested in civil rights activism, as is Rita Mae Brown (she was actually kicked out of college for her activism, though Molly Bolt is kicked out for lesbianism).

"Family" is much more fluid in these novels as well, including extended families and family-like relationships. I've already mentioned the complex "solution" in *Bingo*, which involves a gay man and a lesbian setting up house together, supported by a larger web of relationships in the novel, including the wife of Nickel's baby's father, her best friend. Dill serves as surrogate parent to her ex-lover's daughter, however unwillingly.

In *Bastard Out of Carolina*, Raylene is clearly a part of the complex web of family relationships and accepted there. Allison shows her role in a larger ethics of care. When Bone's mother loses the baby, for example, "Aunt Raylene showed up in her overalls and low boots to clean the house from one end to the other. . . . carried her out to sit on the couch in the fresh air. . . . I cried until Aunt Raylene took me out in her truck and rocked me to sleep with a damp washcloth on my eyes" (49). The "families" in these novels include ex-lovers, aunts, nephews, employees, and friends, an inclusive family of affinity, not of blood.

By acknowledging these lesbian contact zones, I don't mean to construct them as utopian. In *Absalom, Absalom!*, as in later Southern lesbian novels, the liberatory space is always at risk, violated and often defended by violence. Raylene kept the bushes cut back for a reason; she, like Clytie, remained ever vigilant about intruders. Frank's attempted kidnapping of his son from the Whistle Stop Café is prevented only by the violence and deception of a multiracial community.

Clytie, defender of the lesbian contact zone, destroys it rather than let it be violated by the patriarchal forces of the Jim Crow South, and she, like Judith, dies protecting her liberatory queer space.

> Then for a moment maybe Clytie appeared in that window from which she must have been watching the gates constantly day and night for three months— the tragic gnome's face beneath the clean headrag, against a red background of fire, seen for a moment between two swirls of smoke, looking down at them, perhaps not even now with triumph and no more of despair than it had ever worn, possibly even serene above the melting clapboards before the smoke swirled across it again. (300)

Fragile and transitory, these lesbian contact zones construct refuges from *the* South's hegemonic metanarrative. These contemporary redneck lesbian communes extend from their tomboy lesbian foremother, Judith. The male narrators of *Absalom, Absalom!* see this dynamic queer refuge as a symbol of the South's decay, an apocalypse in which "the Jim Bonds are going to conquer the western hemisphere" (302). For Judith, though, who gave her life to save Charles Bon's descendents, Jim Bond's eventual triumph would simply extend the logic of the queer contact zone across the Southern landscape. She considered her dead fiancé's mixed race grandson as not only family but legitimate heir, the proper representative of the mulattas, queers, spinsters, and maroons of her family tree. Judith's Hundred, and the other lesbian contact zones of Southern literary traditions, are integrated into the larger Southern community, providing a refuge from heteronormative restrictions for gay and straight alike.

NOTES

1. Florence King, *Confessions of a Failed Southern Lady* (New York: St. Martins Press, 1985), 232.

2. David L. Coss, "Sutpen's Sentient House," *Journal of the Fantastic in the Arts* 15.2 (2005): 101–18, 101.

3. Olivia Carr Edenfield, "'Endure, and then Endure': Rosa Coldfield's Search for a Role in William Faulkner's *Absalom, Absalom!*," *Southern Literary Journal* 32.1 (Fall 1999): 57–68, 58

4. Michael Kreyling, *Inventing Southern Literature* (Jackson: University Press of Mississippi, 1998).

5. Doreen Massey, *Space, Place, and Gender* (Minneapolis: University of Minnesota Press, 1994), 24.

6. Hortense Spillers, "Topographical Topics: Faulknerian Space," *Mississippi Quarterly: The Journal of Southern Cultures* 57.4 (Fall 2004): 535–68, 535.

7. Kathryn McKee and Annette Trefzer, eds., "Global Contexts, Local Literatures: The New Southern Studies," *American Literature* 78.4 (December 2006).

8. Minrose Gwin, *The Feminine and Faulkner: Reading (Beyond) Sexual Difference* (Knoxville: University of Tennessee Press, 1990).

9. Minnie Bruce Pratt, "Identity: Skin, Blood, Heart," in *Rebellion: Essays, 1980–1991* (Ithaca, N.Y.: Firebrand Books, 1991) 27–82, 32–33.

10. Mab Segrest, *My Mother's Dead Squirrel: Lesbian Essays on Southern Culture* (Ithaca, N.Y.: Firebrand Books, 1985).

11. Michel Frann, "William Faulkner as a Lesbian Author," *Faulkner Journal* 4.1–2 (Fall 1988–Spring 1989): 5–20.

12. That affinity was not simply conceptual; Jay Parini and Gary Richards have highlighted Faulkner's comfortable relationships with gay people. Jay Parini, *One Matchless Time: A Life of William Faulkner* (New York: Harper Collins, 2004); Gary Richards, "The Artful and Crafty Ones of the French Quarter: Male Homosexuality and Faulkner's Early Prose Writing," in *Faulkner's Sexualities: Faulkner and Yoknapatawpha, 2007*, ed. Annette Trefzer and Ann J. Abadie (Jackson: University Press of Mississippi, 2010).

13. Gary N. Richards articulates a Southern tradition tinged with lavender, not shockingly pink, in his *Lovers and Beloveds: Sexual Otherness in Southern Fiction, 1936–1961* (Baton Rouge: Louisiana State University Press, 2005).

14. Joseph Allen Boone, *Libidinal Currents: Sexuality and the Shaping of Modernism* (Chicago: University of Chicago Press, 1998).

15. John Howard, *Men Like That: A Queer Southern History* (Chicago: University of Chicago Press, 1999).

16. Norman W. Jones, "Coming Out through History's Hidden Love Letters in *Absalom, Absalom!,*" *American Literature* 76.2 (June 2004): 339–66, 354–55.

17. William Faulkner, *Absalom, Absalom!* (New York: Vintage, 1991).

18. Alice Walker, *The Color Purple* (New York: Pocket, 1990).

19. Many thanks to my colleague Doug Robinson for this playful suggestion.

20. E-mail to the author, 18 July 2007. Many thanks to Jay Watson for this brilliant insight.

21. Diane Roberts, *Faulkner and Southern Womanhood* (Athens: University of Georgia Press, 1994).

22. Dorothy Allison, *Bastard Out of Carolina* (New York: Plume, 2005), 54.

23. Suzan-Lori Parks, *Getting Mother's Body* (New York: Random House, 2003).

24. Fannie Flagg, *Fried Green Tomatoes at the Whistle Stop Cafe: A Novel* (New York: McGraw-Hill, 1988).

25. Rita Mae Brown, *Rubyfruit Jungle* (New York: Bantam, 1980).

26. Jay Watson, e-mail to the author, 18 July 2007.

27. Miles Orvell, "Faulkner, Photography, and a Regional Ethics of Form," in *Faulkner and Material Culture: Faulkner and Yoknapatawpha, 2004*, Joseph Urgo and Ann J. Abadie, eds. (Jackson: University Press of Mississippi, 2007).

28. Rita Mae Brown, *Bingo* (New York: Bantam Books, 1988).

Faulkner, Marcuse, and Erotic Power

MICHAEL ZEITLIN

*I have noticed in my psychoanalytical work that the whole frame of mind
of a man who is reflecting is totally different from that of a man who is
observing his own psychical processes . . . the man who is reflecting . . .
and this is shown amongst other things by the tense looks and wrinkled
forehead . . . is also exercising his critical faculty; this leads him to reject
some of the ideas that occur to him after perceiving them, to cut short
others without allowing the trains of thought which they would open
up to him, and to behave in such a way towards still others that they
never become conscious at all and are accordingly suppressed before
being perceived. The self-observer on the other hand [note his "restful
expression"] need only take the trouble to suppress his critical faculty. If
he succeeds in doing that, innumerable ideas come into his consciousness
of which he could otherwise never had got hold.*
—Freud, The Interpretation of Dreams

Following the publication of *The Portable Faulkner* in 1946, and until his
death in 1962, William Faulkner produced a series of essays, speeches,
and public letters in which he addressed himself to a wide range of social
and political topics. How Faulkner defined the major concerns of this
period may cast a light upon the entire body of his fictional work, especially as it involves the exploration of an astonishing range of resolutely
flesh-and-blood human beings, each struggling with the "problems of the
human heart in conflict with itself" while standing in various attitudes of
opposition to the power structures of a highly organized society.

Given their polemical quality, Faulkner's public discourses of the Cold
War period might be read alongside the largely contemporaneous "critical theory" of the Frankfurt School, whose members included Walter
Benjamin (who died in France by his own hand soon after the Nazi invasion in June 1940) and his fellow refugees from Hitler's Europe, Theodor
Adorno, Max Horkheimer, and Herbert Marcuse. These three colleagues
landed in New York in 1933, becoming naturalized American citizens in
1940, after which they enjoyed highly visible careers. Like these Frankfurt School thinkers, Faulkner felt that American society after World War
II was undergoing a nightmarish transformation, becoming, essentially,

a paranoid state virtually hypnotized by the prevailing Cold War map of the globe. As Faulkner put it in the Nobel speech, with dismay: "There is only the question: When will I be blown up?" To be sure, the prospect of nuclear apocalypse was something of a real concern, but the dominant picture of two immense power blocks "objectively" intent on atomic collision was also one, as Adorno put it at the time, that "delude[d] [the people] with false conflicts which they [were] to exchange for their own."[1] In an "Address to the Graduating Class University High School" (31 May 1951), Faulkner explained the matter in this way:

> What threatens us today is fear. Not the atom bomb, nor even fear of it, because if the bomb fell on Oxford tonight, all it could do would be to kill us, which is nothing, since in doing that, it will have robbed itself of its only power over us: which is fear of it, the being afraid of it. Our danger is not that. Our danger is the forces in the world today which are trying to use man's fear to rob him of his individuality, his soul, trying to reduce him to an unthinking mass by fear and bribery . . . the economies or ideologies or political systems, communist or socialist or democratic, whatever they wish to call themselves, the tyrants and the politicians, American or European or Asiatic, whatever they call themselves, who would reduce man to one obedient mass for their own aggrandisement and power. . . . So, never be afraid. Never be afraid to raise your voice for honesty and truth and compassion, against injustice and lying and greed. If you, not just you in this room tonight, but in all the thousands of other rooms like this one about the world today and tomorrow and next week, will do this, not as a class or classes, but as individuals, men and women, you will change the earth. In one generation all the Napoleans and Hitlers and Caesars and Mussolinis and Stalins and all the other tyrants who want power and aggrandisement, and the simple politicians and time-servers who themselves are merely baffled or ignorant or afraid, who have used, or are using, or hope to use, man's fear and greed for man's enslavement, will have vanished from the face of it. (122–24)[2]

Part 1
Privacy, Fear, and State Power

In Faulkner's view, the broadest problem of his time was that the distinction between the individual and the general society was collapsing altogether, the individual losing his or her power to resist the invasive agencies and coercive seductions of the latter. As "the individual" as a term came to signify the "atomization" of the collective people (who become what Don DeLillo has called "the TV audience. . . . The crowd broken down into millions of small rooms"),[3] the "conviction of individual significance," as Faulkner put it in a review of a novel by Erich Maria Remarque in 1931 (*ESPL* 187), became (dialectically) more intense, more polemically urgent. André Malraux, in his 1931 preface to *Sanctuary*, was perhaps the first to remark upon the "powerful, and savagely personal" dimension of Faulkner's fiction—what Faulkner himself, in *Absalom, Absalom!*, would call "the I, myself, that deep existence which we lead," and "the citadel of the central I-Am's private own."[4] Because, in the words of Adorno, "the sphere of private existence" had become that of "mere consumption, dragged along as an appendage of the process of material production, without autonomy or substance of its own,"[5] the very concept of the precious and embattled private self was "an ideological reflex and echo" (in Marx's formulation)[6] of the extent to which that self was becoming an "integer" (Faulkner's word here) (*ESPL* 61, 73, and elsewhere) within the socioeconomic system.

In his preface to *Eros and Civilization: A Philosophical Inquiry into Freud* (1955), Marcuse declared that "psychological categories . . . have become political categories": "The traditional borderlines between psychology on the one side and political and social philosophy on the other have been made obsolete by the condition of man in the present era: formerly autonomous and identifiable psychical processes are being absorbed by the function of the individual in the state—by his public existence. Psychological problems therefore turn into political problems: private disorder reflects more directly than before the disorder of the whole, and the cure of personal disorder depends more directly than before on the cure of the general disorder. The era tends to be totalitarian even where it has not [in the West, so far] produced totalitarian states."[7] Psychology, designating the realm of private and personal interiority, had become a political category, that is, precisely because the private and personal domain was under siege by the penetrative and imperializing forces of corporate capitalism, governmental control, and the media—what the Frankfurt School often referred to as "the culture industry," an alliance of powers Faulkner described in the following way in his "Address upon Receiving the National Book Award for Fiction" in 1955, for *A Fable*: "the giants of industry and commerce, and the manipulators for profit or power of the mass emotions called government, who carry the tremendous load of geopolitical solvency, the two of which conjoined are America" (*ESPL* 144). In Faulkner's formidable essay, "On Privacy (The American Dream: What Happened to It?)" (published originally in *Harper's*, July 1955), America (so conceived) was intent on transforming the individual into "one more identityless integer in that identityless anonymous unprivacied mass which seems to be our goal" (*ESPL* 71). Faulkner goes on to sketch out a brief history of "the

American individual" as a figure in opposition to powerful sources of authority emanating from beyond the self. In seventeenth-century New England this individual believed that he "could be free not only of the old established closed-corporation hierarchies of arbitrary power which had oppressed him as a mass, but free of that mass into which the hierarchies of church and state had compressed and held him individually thralled and individually impotent" (*ESPL* 62). Now this unique version of American freedom was disappearing. "It is gone now. We dozed, slept, and it abandoned us" (*ESPL* 65). In one sense the outlines of the crisis could still be defined with a degree of clarity: the private individual was, again, now, pitted against "powerful federations and organizations and amalgamations like publishing corporations and religious sects and political parties and legislative committees" (*ESPL* 73). Yet this vast conglomeration of powerful institutions (like "the amplifyer" [sic] in Faulkner's novel of 1935, *Pylon*) was "sourceless, inhuman, ubiquitous,"[8] and hence mappable only in terms of an almost hallucinatory inflation of figures. We must imagine the "puny" and isolated human form trembling (and possibly "still talking" to itself) in the foreground of "that furious blast, that force, that power rearing like a thunder-clap into the American zenith, multiple-faced yet mutually conjunctived, bellowing the words and phrases which we have long since emasculated of any significance or meaning other than as tools, implements, for the further harassment of the private individual human spirit, by their furious and immunised high priests: 'Security.' 'Subversion.' 'Anti-Communism.' 'Christianity.' 'Prosperity.' 'The American Way.' 'The Flag'" (*ESPL* 73). (See also "An Innocent at Rinkside," *Sports Illustrated*, 1955 [*ESPL* 48–51], where Faulkner wonders "just what a professional hockey-match, whose purpose is to make a decent and reasonable profit for its owners, had to do with our National Anthem") (*ESPL* 51). Faulkner is referring here of course to the prevailing atmosphere of "suspiciousness and repressiveness" in the general American culture, that McCarthyism "represented by requiring oaths of loyalty, by putting people under surveillance, by inquiring into the ideas and attitudes and pasts and associations of men and women holding civic positions."[9]

By the 1950s, the contest between the individual and what Karl Zender has designated, in a vivid condensation, as "the power of sound" had become a master theme linking liberals and radicals alike (in Nazi Germany, the Frankfurt School had learned, liberals surrounded by fascists were radicals by definition).[10] In Lionel Trilling's *Freud and the Crisis of Our Culture* (a short book based on his Freud Anniversary Lecture of 1955 at the New York Psychoanalytic Institute and Society to mark the day of Freud's birth, 6 May 1856), for example, the author's rhetorical composure belies a barely restrained sense of panic: "One does not need to have a very profound quarrel with American culture to feel uneasy because our defenses against it, our modes of escape from it, are becoming less and less adequate. One may even have a very lively admiration for American culture, as I do, and yet feel that this defenselessness of the self against its culture is cause for alarm. . . . We must, I think, recognize how open and available to the general culture the individual has become, how little protected he is by countervailing cultural forces, how unified and demanding our free culture has become" (49–50, 53–54).

For Marcuse, the subversion of the autonomy of the individual subject produces his atomization and isolation. This isolated condition of the "integers," in turn, prepares the ground for their re-formation into masses held together by group psychologies based on an *immediate* identification with the images of authority. This "democratic introjection of the masters into their subjects" (Marcuse, *Eros* xv) describes how Faulkner understood the matter in the 1950s. Joseph Urgo in *Faulkner's Apocrypha* cites Faulkner's letter of 4 March 1959 to Muna Lee of the State Department: "All evil and grief in this world stems from the fact that man talks. I mean, in the sense of one man talking to a captive audience."[11] Faulkner continues: "Except for that, and its concomitants of communication—radio, newspapers, such organs—there would have been no Hitler and Mussolini. I believe that in the case of the speaker and his captive audience, whatever the reason for the captivity of the audience, the worst of both is inevitably brought out—the worst of the individual, compounded by the affinity for evil inherent in people compelled or persuaded to be a mass, an audience, which in my opinion is another mob."[12] The problem now, as it was in the Fascist 1930s and 1940s, concerned the impoverishment of the resistant individual ego from which something like genuine privacy, creative resistance, and a real collective strategy of refusal might flow.[13] As Marcuse elaborates, "The shrinking of the ego, its reduced resistance to others appears in the ways in which the ego holds itself constantly open to the messages imposed from outside. The antenna on every house, the transistor on every beach, the jukebox in every bar or restaurant are as many cries of desperation—not to be left alone, by himself, not to be separated from the Big Ones, not to be condemned to the emptiness or the hatred or the dreams of oneself."[14]

This general description provides the background against which I should now like to place my main subject, that is, the manner in which Faulkner and these Frankfurt School thinkers conceived the possibilities of imaginative freedom, of opposition to or even liberation from "the totality" or "the system" (as Marcuse tended to call it, in a way that would influence the language of the 1960s social revolutions in America), or what, more recently, DeLillo again has called "the whole apparatus of assimilation."[15] This "apparatus" is understood by Marcuse as one vast interlocking structure of "machines": "the political machine, the corporate machine, the cultural and educational machine which has welded blessing and curse into one rational whole" (*Eros* xvii).

Their answer to the question of opposition or liberation involved, I suggest, a radical conception of human interiority centered in the very biological substance, the flesh and blood, of the individual human being who, on the basis of being so grounded, could join together with others in a genuine collective strategy for social change: Thus "Eros begins its cultural work of combining life into ever larger units" (Marcuse, *Eros* 79). As one goes deep into the interior of the human subject, one encounters a resistant soul closely interwoven with a critical mass of sexuality and eros serving, potentially, latently, as a dynamic source of rebellious and creative expression. Any liberation of the human subject in this context takes for granted Freud's radical conception of the polymorphous "pleasure principle" as defined in his revolutionary *Three Essays on the Theory of Sexuality* (1905). At the danger of reduction, one might put the matter in the form of an equation thus: Our biology generates polymorphous forms of eroticism, these in turn generate powerful phantasies, and phantasies keep alive the possibilities of liberation from a repressive apparatus (or what Marcuse called a "performance principle" dominated by "surplus repression"), an apparatus that has become too severe in its restriction of a dynamic form of human potential and emancipatory energy. As Marcuse puts it, "The psychoanalytic liberation of memory explodes the rationality of the repressed individual. As cognition gives way to re-cognition, the forbidden images and impulses of childhood begin to tell the truth that reason denies. Regression assumes a progressive function" (*Eros* 19). Hence the key question for Marcuse in *Eros and Civilization* is "Can we speak of a juncture between the erotic and political dimension?" (xxi).

One of the major ironies here is that the general culture I am describing is one very much to be understood as post–Kinsey Report America. I am referring of course to that great survey of *Sexual Behavior in the Human Male* (1948) to which the origins of the 1960s sexual revolution have been traced.[16] As Lionel Trilling in *The Liberal Imagination* wryly notes in his fascinating review of the Kinsey Report, all this massive, 800–page document really seems to be saying is "that there is an almost universal involvement in the sexual life and therefore much variety of conduct. This was taken for granted in any comedy that Aristophanes put on the stage." Trilling continues: "[I]t is one of the great points of the Report how much of every kind of desire there is, how early it begins, how late it lasts." The report is thus to be understood both "as symptom and as therapy. The therapy lies in the large permissive effect the Report is likely to have, the long way it goes toward establishing the *community* of sexuality. The symptomatic significance lies in the fact that the Report was felt to be needed at all. . . . Nothing shows more clearly the extent to which modern society has atomized itself than the isolation in sexual ignorance which exists among us."[17] Marcuse, writing in the aftermath of the report, notes, "Today compared with the Puritan and Victorian periods, sexual freedom has unquestionably increased (although a reaction against the 1920's is clearly noticeable)." At the same time, however, and this is the key point, "the sexual relations themselves have become much more closely assimilated [into the general social apparatus] . . . sexual liberty is harmonized with profitable conformity" (*Eros* 94). (Think of how cigarette companies in this period aggressively associated their product with images of glamorous lifestyles and the "healthy" sexuality of young men and women—an especially pernicious example of what Marcuse would call "repressive desublimation.")[18] Along such lines, Laura Mulvey, in a classic essay, suggests that our fascination with the proliferation of sexuality in contemporary film (not to mention, say, the multibillion dollar internet pornography industry) "is reinforced by pre-existing patterns of fascination already at work within the individual subject and the social formations that have moulded him." Mulvey's analysis considers "the way film reflects, reveals and even plays on the straight, socially established interpretation of sexual difference which controls images, erotic ways of looking and spectacle."[19]

If, as Marcuse noted, "[t]he technique of mass manipulation [has] developed an entertainment industry which directly controls leisure time" (*Eros* 48), it seeks also, directly, to organize, that is, even the sexuality of the masses. "The individual is not to be left alone. . . . With his consciousness co-ordinated, his privacy abolished, his emotions integrated into conformity, the individual has no longer enough 'mental space' for developing himself . . . for living with a conscience [and an erotic sexuality] of his own" (*Eros* 99). The problematic of what Marcuse called this "immediate, external socialization of the ego, and the control and management of free time—the massification of privacy" ("Obsolescence" 238) might be seen as continuous with our own "postmodern condition." For the recently deceased French cultural theorist, Jean Baudrillard, our contemporary has become something of a general "pornographic" nightmare: "No more hysteria, no more projective paranoia, properly speaking, but [the] state of terror proper to the schizophrenic: too great a proximity of everything, the absolute proximity, the total instantaneity of things, the feeling of no defense, no retreat. It is the end of interiority and intimacy, the overexposure and transparence of the world which traverses him without obstacle. He can no longer produce the limits of his own being. . . . He is now only a pure screen, a switching center for all the networks of influence."[20]

One encounters a more prosaic but no less harrowing vision of this Pavlovian state of affairs in the work of Faulkner's brilliant 1930s contemporary, Nathanael West: "Men have always fought their misery with dreams. Although dreams were once powerful, they have been made puerile by the movies, radio and newspapers. Among many betrayals, this one is the worst" (*Miss Lonelyhearts*).[21] In *The Day of the Locust*, West continues:

> [The people] don't know what to do with their time. They haven't the mental equipment for leisure, the money nor the physical equipment for pleasure. . . . Their boredom becomes more and more terrible. They realize that they've been tricked and burn with resentment. Every day of their lives they read the newspapers and went to the movies. Both fed them on lynchings, murder, sex crimes, explosions, wrecks, love nests, fires, miracles, revolutions, wars. The daily diet made sophisticates of them. The sun is a joke. Oranges can't titillate their jaded palates. Nothing can ever be violent enough to make taut their slack minds and bodies. They have been cheated and betrayed. They have slaved and saved for nothing. (178)

Given the situation in which the modern state extends its "executive arm into the soul of the masses" (Marcuse, *Eros* xxiii), one must somehow "get beneath" that level of being and consciousness that has proven all-too-susceptible to co-option by the endless (though highly organized, methodical, and strategic) images flowing from the culture industry's myriad illuminated surfaces. "The very depth at which the sexual instinct operates protects it from such a systematic and methodical organization," Marcuse suggests (*Eros* 51). The depth metaphor here implies a resolutely Freudian, and Darwinian, conception of what Ilse Gubrich-Simitis has called "the pleasure-creating, mortal biological-organic substrate," which is "the final anchoring of all human behavior."[22] It is only by moving in this direction, "down" toward the "pleasure principle," which "precedes" the "reality principle," that one might recover the image of the resistant and creative core of human being itself. In a complex reading of Freud's *Beyond the Pleasure Principle*, Marcuse argues that the death drive, which lies *beyond* (i.e., even further back in time in the direction of the archaic and elemental) the pleasure principle, is engaged with Eros in ensuring that the human being follows his or her own *natural* "detour toward death": the key issue for Marcuse is the extent to which "the death drive" has been commandeered by the state and its "purveyors of Death" (*Eros* xi) who produce the massive numbers of those who die violently before their natural-biological time.[23]

This Freudian biological conception is in so many ways at odds with our prevailing discursive categories of thought, but, thinking historically, or trying to, we might allow Trilling, once again, to isolate the critical power such a conception seemed to have in its own time—the conception of the subject as "the living substance of history" (Marcuse, *Eros* 106), as a "biological fact," as "a *given*, a *donnée*–a gift" (Trilling, *Freud* 47). Trilling suggests that "Freud may be right or he may be wrong in the place he gives to biology in human fate, but I think we must stop to consider whether this emphasis on biology, whether correct or incorrect, is not so far from being a reactionary idea that it is actually a liberating idea. It proposes to us that culture is not all-powerful. It suggests that there is a residue of human quality beyond the reach of cultural control, and that this residue of human quality, elemental as it may be, serves to bring culture itself under criticism and keeps it from being absolute" (Trilling, *Freud* 48).

Part 2
Faulkner at West Point

On 19 April 1962, Faulkner visited the United States Military Academy at West Point, New York, and in the book commemorating this last major public appearance (he would die less than three months later), a photograph on page 110 shows the writer sitting at a large table in a room crowded with cadets. The cadets are in uniform; they have brush cuts; they hang on every word Faulkner speaks into the microphone; some are taking notes. This is Captain James R. Kintz's class on "The Evolution of American Ideals as Reflected in American Literature," and appearing reasonably comfortable though fatigued, Faulkner fields question after question. At one point someone asks:

> Q. Sir, have you ever desired to be anything besides a writer?
> A. Why sure, I'd like to be a brave, courageous soldier; I have thought of all sorts of things I'd like to be. I'd like to be a beautiful woman. I'd like to be a millionaire.[24]

No one pursues this intimate theme any further, the next questioner asking Faulkner's opinion of Mr. Khrushchev, but Faulkner's statement is perhaps worth pondering for what it suggests about the origins and implications of his imaginary desire, a desire that, in its sheer libidinal range and multiplicity, generates that astonishing "plurality of lives" that we encounter throughout the fiction.[25]

Perhaps it should not be surprising that, in his waning (though still dignified) power as a man, Faulkner should contemplate such revitalizing sources: virile courage, feminine beauty, opulent wealth, the primary fantasies of the artist as a young man. We are told (by French psychoanalyst Jacques Lacan) that such fantasies, whose "internal thrust is precipitated from insufficiency to anticipation," help "situate the agency of the ego, before its social determination, in a fictional direction."[26] One thinks of the first spectacular version of this imaginary dialectic, Faulkner's attempt to mirror and so give birth to himself as a novelist, and hence of Donald Mahon (brave soldier) and Margaret Powers (beautiful woman) of *Soldiers' Pay* (1926), with which Faulkner first sought to establish his fame and fortune as a great American modernist, if not the greatest novelist who ever wrote. The dream of wealth and abundance always contains the fantasy of fame, which was never unconnected in Faulkner's mind with "the ultimate intention of impressing some woman," as Dawson Fairchild puts it in *Mosquitoes*.[27] The simultaneously real and imaginary person may be mother, "sister," Estelle, Helen, or other women "for whom the creator of the phantasy performs all his heroic deeds and at whose feet all his triumphs are laid."[28] As it turned out, Faulkner did achieve more worldly fame than he ever wanted or needed, but perhaps what continued to drive him was that kind of fame whose essential locus is fantasy, the domain of "the subject's 'impossible' relation to the object-cause of its desire."[29]

Equally one might say that "I'd like to be a brave, courageous soldier" also harbors its own dimension of "impossibility." Recalling the Faulkner on whom they stopped the war before he could fly—the Faulkner of the postwar limp and the steel skull plate—such a wish, now articulated before real soldiers soon to be shipped off to Vietnam, must also be understood as a kind of (belated) confession that he was never really one of them at all, except in his fiction.[30] But if we see in this confession a touch of admiration for these real soldiers before him, there is an additional dynamic element in Faulkner's fantasy of bravery that we might contemplate. Consider, for example, how Faulkner earlier in the same session describes the moral action of the dive-bombing pilot in his short story "Turnabout": "'I think that when he dove his bomber down on the roofs of that chateau, it was a gesture of revolt against all the brassbound stupidity of the generals and admirals that sit safe in the dugouts and tell the young men to go there and do that. That that was something that probably every soldier in war has felt. They have cursed the whole lot of them—that my brother is the man I am trying to kill. But you people safe at home—curse all of them. I am sure every soldier has felt that'" (*Faulkner at West Point* 102). This is a powerful condemnation of the way in which warfare routinely sacrifices the "grunts" to the strategic purposes, or ineptitude, of the military command and their civilian overlords; it is also a remarkable thing to say when you are the personal guest of Major General William C. Westmoreland, whose "brassbound stupidity" (he was not alone) in Vietnam would soon become notorious.[31] For Faulkner in this statement, courage implies disobedience, transgression, the demystification of military authority (as it had—and does—in *A Fable*, as Joseph Urgo above all has argued in *Faulkner's Apocrypha*). We might therefore imagine that, had he lived, he would have been on the crest of that tidal antiauthoritarian, antiwar wave of the mid to late 1960s. I believe he would have been. As for the audience of cadets, we can only speculate that Faulkner's seditious declaration must have generated at the very least some mild levels of nervous perplexity and discomfort. (See the expression on the face of Major Joseph Fant in the photo on page 89.)

Perhaps even more radical, potentially, of course, was the statement, "I'd like to be a beautiful woman," especially given its setting and audience. One can only speculate that the wish to be a beautiful woman was not often expressed (publically) in the halls of America's foremost military academy. It is absolutely impossible, for example, to imagine General Westmoreland admitting such a thing in front of a microphone. And yet here was America's most famous writer, a Nobel laureate, spokesman of "the eternal verities of the human heart," saying, with an air less of scandalous confession than casual truthfulness, that being a beautiful woman was among the things he would have wanted to experience. One wonders whether this is Faulkner in something like his sublime innocence not so much refusing to be intimidated as showing himself radically incapable of *being* intimidated by the public's—or even the military's—attitude toward his personal, artistic imagination. On the other hand, in a West Point class devoted to "The Evolution of American Ideals," surely Faulkner would have known, at some level, that anything other than the suggestion of an absolute, male-identified, heteronormative sexuality would be deemed at least mildly subversive if not suspiciously "un-American."

I use this latter term advisedly, not only because the tableau of Faulkner giving "testimony" into a microphone might suggest the contemporaneous hearings of the House Un-American Activities Committee, which was still operative in 1962, when J. Edgar Hoover, the FBI's ultimate "master of deceit"—"a man whose own sequestered heart [held] every festering secret in the Western world"[32]—was spying by wiretap on Martin Luther King Jr., ostensibly to protect the nation against racial and "communistic" insurgency, but also, one may speculate, in order to satisfy his own, more private fascination with moral, sexual, and political "perversion." As Stephen J. Whitfield writes, "In an era that fixed so rigidly the distinction between Communist tyranny and the Free World, and which prescribed that men were men and women were housewives, perhaps only one peril seemed, if anything, worse than Communism. 'The overriding fear of every American parent,' a visiting English anthropologist noticed in 1950, was that a son would become a 'sissie.'"[33] One suspects that only Faulkner could have gotten away with incarnating at the United States Military Academy, West Point, an exquisite paradox (to anybody who chose to contemplate it): a great man (surely no sissie), a great American, a beautiful woman in his imagination.

Of course, as this scene, "Faulkner at West Point," puts into graphic perspective, Faulkner, from even before his first novel, *Soldiers' Pay*, and throughout his work thereafter, assiduously imagined himself not only into the consciousness and psychology of women (Margaret Powers, Eva Wiseman, Narcissa Benbow, Temple Drake, Dewey Dell, Addie Bundren, Rosa Coldfield, Charlotte Rittenmeyer, Eula Varner) but also into their bodies and sexualities. Indeed, the notion of a man's desire for a special intimacy or identification with women announced itself as a comic metatheme in his earliest fiction. We might recall that one of Faulkner's first fictional incarnations was as a wholesale buyer of women's undergarments in the short story "Don Giovanni," whose protagonist, Herbie, "knew women's clothes and, interested in women, it was his belief that his knowledge of the things they liked gave him a grasp which no other man had on the psychology of women."[34]

But the motif of the man who identifies with women, as incarnated in Herbie's contemporaries and successors, Elmer Hodge, Ernest Talliaferro, Byron Snopes, Horace Benbow, Quentin Compson, and Harry Wilbourne (who, as a writer of pulp fiction, begins one of his narratives, "I had the body and desires of a woman yet in knowledge and experience of the world I was but a child")[35] was also a theme capable of the highest possible seriousness. With respect to conventional definitions of masculinity and femininity, these Faulknerian subjects are invariably misaligned and uncertain. And it is this uncertainty, in turn, that helps to maintain an oscillatory identification with both genders, as in Elmer Hodge's fantasy as he fondles the tubes of paint sent to him by his sister Jo-Addie: "thick-bodied and female and at the same time phallic: hermaphroditic."[36] Preventing any clear demarcation (at the level of phantasy) between the two sexes that might lead to certainty of sexual identity, this region of hermaphroditic ambiguity seems (especially as the earliest work suggests) the very ground of Faulkner's revolutionary narrative explorations of mental process and unconscious phantasy.

The early Faulknerian protagonist is "polymorphous," that is, in the historically specific sense of Freud's *Three Essays on the Theory of Sexuality* and Joyce's *Ulysses*: possessing multiple "erotogenic zones" linked with a rich and shifting array of psychological identifications and physical and mental "objects."[37] These objects are invariably "cathected" (invested with erotic value and force) in relation to that complex of unconscious drives, emotions, phantasies, and proscriptions ever flowing from (the dynamic mnemonic presence of) childhood experience. That is, the polymorphous Faulknerian subject of desire is always entangled—at the level of phantasy life and so in symbolic repetition through changing social contexts—in the conflicts and calamities of the original family drama. "The past is never dead. It's not even past."

We can further say of this "polymorphously perverse disposition" (*Three Essays* 320) (to use Freud's phrase while recalling Dawson Fairchild's in *Mosquitoes*: "a perversion that builds Chartres and invents Lear is a pretty good thing") (*Mosquitoes* 191) that, by definition, it centrifugally resists coming to a focus in the location of an exclusively genital sexuality or upon the image of an ideally adapted, wholly masculine or feminine personhood. If, as some have argued, the Freudian therapeutic and adaptive teleology leads in the direction of an ideal coherence and integration organized around the stability of a "central ego," which is itself necessary to the anchoring of the subject in heterosexual, monogamous, genital (i.e., "bourgeois") sexuality, it does so precisely because it recognizes the formidable force and quintessential humanity of all that threatens, interrupts, and exceeds "normalization."[38] Horace Benbow, as the nodal point of a rich intertextual series of figures, is perhaps the clearest Faulknerian example of the sexual subject who persistently fails in this sense to "adapt": we can read the signatures of this resistance to normalization in his incestuous focus on his sister Narcissa, in his complex of fetishistic substitutions for her—glass blowing for instance—in his masochistic identification with Temple, and in his disastrous marriage to Belle Mitchell. With Horace, that is, Faulkner gives us an imaginary blueprint of the region in which the subject's "normal" range of affects and sensations is compulsively exceeded. And, with Horace, and before him Elmer Hodge, he gives us the points of origin from which every subsequent kind of sexual expression whether of man or woman in Faulkner's fiction might be traced.[39]

In "The Sexual Life of Human Beings," one of the *Introductory Lectures on Psycho-Analysis*, Freud gives a kind of gothic inventory of perverse types whose attempts to exercise a progressive control over their own erotic drives have failed spectacularly, and whose sexual characters have therefore become warped and distorted, in sometimes comical, sometimes hideous ways during the conflict of desire itself with a repressive reality. These suffering souls are "individually thralled and individually impotent" (*ESPL* 63) with respect to their own sexual compulsions, yet it is the very violence of their erotic contortions, the fury of their rebellion, the intensity of their commitment to a *"jouissance* beyond the pleasure principle"[40] that mark the biological refusal of Eros to forego expression. The perversion of Eros postulates, at least for Marcuse, its own dynamic negation, a utopian image of what a humane liberation of erotic potential might look like: "This image of man was the determinate negation of Nietzsche's superman: man intelligent enough and healthy enough to dispense with all heroes and heroic virtues, man without the impulse to live dangerously, to meet the challenge; man with the good conscience to make life an end-in-itself, to live in joy a life without fear. 'Polymorphous sexuality' was the term which I used to indicate that the new direction of progress would depend completely on the opportunity to activate repressed or arrested *organic*, biological needs: to make the human body an instrument of pleasure rather than labor" (*Eros* xiv–xv).

As we listen in on Freud's inventory of perverted human types it will be as difficult to sustain Marcuse's vision, perhaps, as it will be *not* to think of their Faulknerian analogues: "[W]e now come to a long series of abnormal people whose sexual activity diverges more and more widely from what seems desirable to a sensible person. In their multiplicity and strangeness they can only be compared to the grotesque monsters painted by Breughel for the temptation of St. Anthony or to the long procession of vanished gods and believers which Flaubert leads past, before the eyes of his pious penitent. Such a medley calls for some kind of arrangement if it is not to confuse our senses."[41]

Freud begins to sort them out in the following terms. There are those, for example,

who have abandoned the genital as an object altogether, and have taken some other part of the body as the object they desire—a woman's breast, a foot or a plait of hair. After them come others for whom parts of the body are of no importance but whose every wish is satisfied by a piece of clothing, a shoe, a piece of underclothing—the fetishists. Later in the procession come people who require the whole object indeed, but make quite definite demands of it—strange or horrible—even that it must have become a defenceless corpse, and who, using criminal violence, make it into one so that they may enjoy it. But enough of this kind of horror![42]

. . . Next come the sadists, puzzling people whose tender endeavours have no other aim than to cause pain and torment to their object, ranging from humiliation to sever physical injuries; and, as though to counterbalance them, their counterparts, the masochists, whose only pleasure it is to suffer humiliations and torments of every kind from their loved object either symbolically or in reality. There are still others in whom several of these abnormal preconditions are united and intertwined; and lastly, we must learn that each of those groups is to be found in two forms: alongside of those who seek their sexual satisfaction in reality are those who are content merely to *imagine* that satisfaction, who need no real object at all, but can replace it by their phantasies.

Now there cannot be the slightest doubt that all these crazy, eccentric and horrible things really constitute the sexual activity of these people. . . .

Well, Ladies and Gentlemen, what attitude are we to adopt to these unusual kinds of sexual satisfaction? ("The Sexual Life of Human Beings" 306).

Freud's answer is that of the medical scientist: "Unless we can understand these pathological forms of sexuality and can co-ordinate them with normal sexual life, we cannot understand normal sexuality either. In short, it remains an unavoidable task to give a complete theoretical account of how it is that these perversions can occur and of their connection with what is described as normal sexuality" (307).

Perhaps these passages from Freud make you think of such Faulkner characters as Januarius Jones, Ernest Talliaferro, Bryon Snopes, Benjy Compson, Quentin Compson, or the petty fascist officer of *Pylon* who is literally maddened by the vision of Laverne Shumann in parachute harness: "Then he began to struggle and scream again, cursing now, screaming at Laverne, calling her whore and bitch and pervert in a tone wild with despair until the engine blotted it" (*Pylon* 912). Or that strange little man dressed in a tight black suit, his "face wrung above his absent chin, his bluish lips protruding as though he were blowing upon hot soup, making a high whinnying sound like a horse,"[43] a sound described by my esteemed coeditor at the *Faulkner Journal*, Edwin (Chip) Arnold, as "the love song of J. Alfred Popeye." As T. H. Adamowski has observed of him, "[Popeye] does not give up on Eros because of the tyranny of a useless genital."[44]

What this all suggests is Faulkner's tolerance, his sympathy for the full range, his ability to identify with and to embody the human multitudes in all their variety and contradiction. I am interested therefore in the mysterious connection between, on the one hand, this persistent series of polymorphous Faulknerian subjects and, on the other, some notion of the "myriadminded" artist (Coleridge's word for Shakespeare, repeated by Joyce in the "Scylla and Charybdis" chapter of *Ulysses*, where Stephen Dedalus elaborates his theory of Shakespeare's *Hamlet*). Myriadminded Faulkner—who as a writer continues to be reborn at the hypothetical point at which the self is shattered beyond singular identity into multiplicity and excess. Somehow Faulkner's staging of the scene of turbulent nonadaptation and rebellious failure—of the "alibi" of a subject always perpetually "elsewhere" (with respect to the norm of what society deems healthy, conventional sexuality) —is linked dialectically with the scene of his accumulating power as an artist, and thus with his greatness as a human being. What drives the entire dynamic is Faulkner's unmistakably transgressive and polymorphous desire. As he had written to Joan Williams on 12 August 1952, "[As a writer] You have got to break your wall. You have got to be capable of anything, everything, accepting them I mean, not as experiments, clinical, to see what it does to the mind, like drugs or dead outside things, but because the heart and the body are big enough to accept all the world, all human agony and passion."[45]

Faulkner's ability to stage and embody a multitude of fictional incarnations can be traced to the site of one of his many beginnings, the *New Orleans Sketches* of 1924–25, where one encounters a series of first-person incarnations: Wealthy Jew, Priest, Sailor, Cobbler, Longshoreman, Cop, Beggar, Prostitute, Tourist, and, of course, Artist, whose essential being and consciousness are rendered thus: "A dream and a fire which I cannot control, driving me without those comfortable smooth paths of solidity and sleep which nature has decreed for man. A fire which I inherited willy-nilly, and which I must needs feed with talk and youth and the very vessel which bears the fire. . . . I, too, am but a shapeless lump of moist earth risen from pain, to laugh and strive and weep, knowing no peace until the moisture has gone out of it, and it is once more of the original and eternal dust."[46] A dream and a fire which I cannot control: this formulation takes us into the heart of the paradox which I sought to invoke with my epigraph from Freud's *The Interpretation of Dreams*: the place of artistic and visionary power is the region of the dream's freedom which ranges beyond the ego's horizon of control. And as the unmistakably feminine-gendered figures of "the vessel" and the "shapeless lump of moist earth" suggest, the desire inherent in the dream and the fire drives beyond "those comfortable smooth paths of solidity" (and, we might add, "identity"), toward the wellsprings of the preoedipal, hermaphroditic unconscious, a "deep" and yet decentered realm, archaic and "prior to" the interpellation of the masculine self into the symbolic order of patriarchal civilization—or the U.S. Military Academy at West Point.

NOTES

1. Theodor Adorno, "The Culture Industry Reconsidered," in Stephen Eric Bronner and Douglas MacKay Kellner, eds., *Critical Theory and Society: A Reader* (New York: Routledge, 1989), 133.

2. "Address to the Graduating Class University High School," in James B. Meriwether, ed., *William Faulkner: Essays, Speeches, and Public Letters*, updated version (New York: Modern Library, 2004), 123–24. Abbreviated hereafter as *ESPL*.

3. Don DeLillo, "The Art of Fiction No. 135," Interview with Adam Begley, *Paris Review* 128 (Fall 1993), 296.

4. André Malraux, "A Preface for Faulkner's *Sanctuary*," in Robert Penn Warren, ed., *Faulkner: A Collection of Critical Essays* (Englewood Cliffs, N.J.: Prentice-Hall, 1966), 273. William Faulkner, *Absalom, Absalom!* (New York: Vintage International, 1990), 109, 112.

5. Theodor Adorno, *Minima Moralia: Reflections from Damaged Life*, trans. E. F. N. Jephcott (1951; London: Verso, 1978), 15.

6. Karl Marx, "Existence and Consciousness," in T. B. Bottomore and Maximilien Rubel, eds., *Karl Marx: Selected Writings in Sociology and Social Philosophy*, trans. T. B. Bottomore (New York: McGraw-Hill, 1956), 75.

7. Herbert Marcuse, *Eros and Civilization: A Philosophical Inquiry into Freud* (1955; Boston: Beacon Press, 1966), xvii.

8. William Faulkner, *Pylon*, in *William Faulkner: Novels 1930–1935* (New York: Library of America, 1985), 801.

9. Lionel Trilling, *Freud and the Crisis of Our Culture* (Boston: Beacon Press, 1955), 42–43.

10. Karl Zender, *The Crossing of the Ways: William Faulkner, the South, and the Modern World* (New Brunswick: Rutgers University Press, 1989). See chapter 1, "The Power of Sound," 3–42.

11. Quoted in Joseph R. Urgo, *Faulkner's Apocrypha: "A Fable," Snopes, and the Spirit of Human Rebellion* (Jackson: University Press of Mississippi, 1989), 36.

12. Joseph Blotner, ed., *Selected Letters of William Faulkner* (New York: Vintage, 1978), 424–25.

13. *A Fable* seems to represent a post–Gandhian ethos of "noncooperation" and hence the characteristic gesture of the civil rights movement: "that all we ever needed to do was just to say, Enough of this"; "just enough of us, all of us in the mud here saying together, Enough of this, let's have done with this." William Faulkner, *A Fable* (1954; New York: Vintage, 1978), 58, 66. For a discussion of Faulkner's complex responses to the early civil rights movement, see Theresa M. Towner, *Faulkner on the Color Line: The Later Novels* (Jackson: University Press of Mississippi, 2000), especially chapter 5, "Race and the Nobel Prize Winner."

14. Herbert Marcuse, "The Obsolescence of the Freudian Concept of Man," in Bronner and Kellner, eds., *Critical Theory and Society: A Reader*, 237.

15. "This is why we need the writer in opposition, the novelist who writes against power, who writes against the corporation or the state or the whole apparatus of assimilation. We're all one beat away from becoming elevator music" (Don DeLillo, "The Art of Fiction No. 135," 290).

16. Alfred C. Kinsey, Wardell B. Pomeroy, and Clyde E. Martin, *Sexual Behavior in the Human Male* (Philadelphia: W. B. Saunders Company, 1948).

17. Lionel Trilling, "The Kinsey Report," in *The Liberal Imagination: Essays on Literature and Society* (New York: Charles Scribner's Sons, 1950), 223–24, 229, 223.

18. See Helen Epstein, "Getting Away with Murder," a review of *The Cigarette Century: The Rise, Fall, and Deadly Persistence of the Product that Defined America*, by Allan M. Brandt (Basic Books, 2007), in the *New York Review of Books* 54:12 (19 July 2007), 38–40.

19. Laura Mulvey, "Visual Pleasure and Narrative Cinema," in Gerald Mast and Marshall Cohen, eds., *Film Theory and Criticism: Introductory Readings*, 3rd ed. (New York: Oxford University Press, 1985), 803.

20. Jean Baudrillard, "The Ecstasy of Communication," trans. John Johnston, in Hal Foster, ed., *The Anti-Aesthetic: Essays on Postmodern Culture* (Port Townsend, Wash.: Bay Press, 1983), 132–33.

21. Nathanael West, *Miss Lonelyhearts & The Day of the Locust* (New York: New Directions, 1933), 39.

22. Ilse Gubrich-Simitis, "Metapsychology and Metabiology: On Sigmund Freud's Draft Overview of the Transference Neuroses," in Ilse Gubrich-Simitis, ed., *A Phylogenetic Fantasy: Overview of the Transference Neuroses*, by Sigmund Freud, trans. Axel Hoffer and Peter T. Hoffer (Cambridge: Belknap Press of Harvard University Press, 1987), 106.

23. See especially Marcuse's "Political Preface 1966" to *Eros and Civilization*: "The inferno is still concentrated in certain far away places: Vietnam, the Congo, South Africa, and in the ghettos of the 'affluent society': in Mississippi and Alabama, in Harlem. These infernal places illuminate the whole" (xiii).

24. Joseph L. Fant III and Robert Ashley, eds., *Faulkner at West Point* (New York: Random House, 1964), 112.

25. "In the realm of fiction we find the plurality of lives which we need." Sigmund Freud, "Thoughts for the Times on War and Death," in James Strachey, ed. and trans., *The Standard Edition of the Complete Psychological Works of Sigmund Freud* (London: Hogarth Press and the Institute of Psycho-Analysis, 1966), 14:291.

26. Jacques Lacan, "The Mirror stage as formative of the function of the I as revealed in psychoanalytic experience," in *Écrits: A Selection*, trans. Alan Sheridan (New York: Norton, 1977), 4, 2.

27. William Faulkner, *Mosquitoes* (1927; New York: Liveright, 1955), 250.

28. Sigmund Freud, "Creative Writers and Day-Dreaming," in *The Standard Edition*, 9:147.

29. Slavoj Žižek, *Looking Awry: An Introduction to Jacques Lacan through Popular Culture* (Cambridge: MIT, 1991), 6.

30. See Malcolm Cowley, *The Faulkner-Cowley File: Letters and Memories, 1944–1962* (New York: Penguin, 1966), 71–91.

31. See Neil Sheehan's damning portrait in *A Bright Shining Lie: John Paul Vann and America in Vietnam* (New York: Random House, 1989): "I asked the general if he was worried about the large number of civilian casualties from the air strikes and the shelling. He looked at me carefully. 'Yes, Neil, it is a problem,' he said, 'but it does deprive the enemy of the population, doesn't it?'" (621).

32. Don DeLillo, *Underworld* (New York: Scribner, 1997), 51. See also J. Edgar Hoover, *Masters of Deceit: The Story of Communism in America and How to Fight It* (New York: Holt, 1958).

33. Stephen J. Whitfield, *The Culture of the Cold War* (Baltimore: Johns Hopkins University Press, 1991), 43. See also Whitfield's discussion of the 1950 Senate report, "Employment of Homosexuals and Other Sex Perverts in Government" (44).

34. William Faulkner, "Don Giovanni," in Joseph Blotner, ed., *Uncollected Stories of William Faulkner* (New York: Random House, 1981), 480. Herbie's prototype is Joyce's Leopold Bloom in *Ulysses*. A considerable mass of Faulkner criticism has stressed the complex, troubled nature of Faulkner's early representations of and fictional identifications with women. A brief representative selection might include Fran Michel, "Faulkner as Lesbian Author," *Faulkner Journal* 4 (Fall 1988/Spring 1989): 5–20; Lisa Rado, "'A Perversion that Builds Chartres and Invents Lear Is a Pretty Good Thing': *Mosquitoes* and Faulkner's Androgynous Imagination," *Faulkner Journal* 9 (Fall 1993/Spring 1994): 13–30; Minrose

Gwin, *"Mosquitoes'* Missing Bite: The Four Deletions," *Faulkner Journal* 9 (1993 Fall–1994 Spring): 31–41; John N. Duvall, *Faulkner's Marginal Couple: Invisible, Outlaw, and Unspeakable Communities* (Austin: University of Texas Press, 1990); Robert Dale Parker, "Sex and Gender, Feminine and Masculine: Faulkner and the Polymorphous Exchange of Cultural Binaries," in Donald M. Kartiganer and Ann J. Abadie, eds., *Faulkner and Gender: Faulkner and Yoknapatawpha, 1994* (Jackson: University Press of Mississippi, 1996), 73–96. In much of this work, Gordon's sculpture of the female torso is deemed a particularly expressive trope of masculine "gender trouble" and misogyny. Naturally, as Faulkner imagined himself into the souls and bodies of women—Margaret Powers, Temple Drake, Addie Bundren, and Rosa Coldfield—he also discovered how they suffered, and resisted, their oppression.

35. William Faulkner, *The Wild Palms*, in *William Faulkner: Novels* 1936–1940 (New York: Library of America, 1990), 577. For a discussion of this moment and related matters, see Candace Waid, "The Signifying Eye: Faulkner's Artists and the Engendering of Art," in Donald M. Kartiganer and Ann J. Abadie, eds., *Faulkner and the Artist: Faulkner and Yoknapatawpha, 1993* (Jackson: University Press of Mississippi, 1996), 208–49.

36. William Faulkner, *Elmer*, ed. Dianne L. Cox, *Mississippi Quarterly* 36 (Summer 1983), 345.

37. "As we all know, it is not until puberty that the sharp distinction is established between the masculine and feminine characters. From that time on, this contrast has a more decisive influence than any other upon the shaping of human life." Sigmund Freud, *Three Essays on the Theory of Sexuality*, *Standard Edition*, 7:141, 219. See also Robert C. Bak's classic essay, "The Phallic Woman: The Ubiquitous Fantasy in Perversions," *The Psychoanalytic Study of the Child* 23 (1968): 15.

38. See Leo Bersani, *The Freudian Body: Psychoanalysis and Art* (New York: Columbia University Press, 1986). Or Harry Wilbourne, who only learns too late "that love no more exists just at one spot and in one moment and in one body out of all the earth and all time and all the teeming breathed than sunlight does." William Faulkner, *The Wild Palms*, 523.

39. See Noel Polk's discussion of Horace Benbow in *Children of the Dark House: Text and Context in Faulkner* (Jackson: University Press of Mississippi, 1996), 36–73.

40. Slavoj Žižek, *Welcome to the Desert of the Real!: Five Essays on September 11 and Related Dates* (London: Verso, 2002).

41. Sigmund Freud, "The Sexual Life of Human Beings," *Introductory Lectures on Psycho-Analysis*, in *The Standard Edition*, 16: 305.

42. If this is not proof that Freud had read "A Rose for Emily" at least it is proof that "life—and Freud—imitate Faulkner."

43. William Faulkner, *Sanctuary: The Corrected Text* (1931; New York: Vintage, 1993), 159.

44. T. H. Adamowski, "Faulkner's Popeye: The 'Other' as Self," *Canadian Review of American Studies* 8 (1977): 40.

45. Joseph Blotner, ed., *Selected Letters of William Faulkner*, 338.

46. William Faulkner, "The Artist," in Carvel Collins, ed., *William Faulkner: New Orleans Sketches* (New York: Random House, 1958), 12.

Faulkner's Sexualized City: Modernism, Commerce, and the (Textual) Body

PETER LURIE

"Oh, my Lolita, I have only words to play with!"
—*Humbert Humbert,* Lolita[1]

In a deleted passage from the middle of Faulkner's second novel, *Mosquitoes*, a young girl named Jenny is corrected in her kissing style by another girl. Jenny's partner in a barely illicit scene of what the other characters in the book call "petting," an eighteen-year-old on her way to Yale, breaks off the kiss with distaste when she tells Jenny that her way of kissing is not "refined." After some brief discussion, Jenny agrees to be tutored in a supposedly more elegant approach to the arts of love. The lesson apparently works. For, returning to her boyfriend later in the scene, a working-class tough named Pete, Jenny instructs him in turn. Initially resisting the more stylish smooching, Pete eventually defers, declaring "I guess I can stand being refined for a day or two."[2]

I open with this admittedly obscure detail for several reasons. Briefly, I will mention that the kissing scene was deleted from *Mosquitoes* initially not through Faulkner's decision, but one made by his publisher, a slightly more cautious Horace Liveright with whom, at a still early stage in his career, Faulkner felt compelled to comply.[3]

Despite appearances, in *Mosquitoes* and elsewhere, refinement counts for a good bit in Faulkner. Some of his most memorable characters or narrators speak in a heightened or "refined" idiom, often one that appears out of step with the more rustic world they inhabit or beyond their expected verbal capacity. (I have in mind Darl Bundren, the narrator of *The Hamlet*, or even Benjy Compson, whose native poeticism is part of his narration's beauty.) What is interesting for our purposes are the ways in which in *Mosquitoes* and, at a quite early point of his career, Faulkner linked such stylistic refinement—often a category for aesthetic considerations—to the erotic. We might note in passing that a diminutive form of the French word for language, *langue*, is the same as their word for tongue.[4] It might be interesting to speculate in this light about the manner of kissing practiced in *Mosquitoes* by the sculptor Gordon. Whereas we are asked to appreciate his natural (and therefore, unrefined) sexual appeal (Tallifierro speculates about what appeals more to women: his own tailored sleeve or Gordon's ripped T-shirt),[5] Gordon produces an artwork that suggests its own refined formalism: a headless, limbless statue of a female nude that appears neoclassical in its simplicity and directness.

Such classicism is the aesthetic opposite of what Faulkner demonstrates at moments in *Mosquitoes* and that would go on to become his famously *baroque* style. In the discussion that follows, I will be asking a number of questions about that development, among them the following: What is the role in Faulkner of a baroque, highly refined language, especially when Faulkner uses it to convey sexuality? And what connections (or disconnections) might that style have to Faulkner's use of the setting of the city, as in *Mosquitoes*, or elsewhere of the rural countryside? As we will see, changes in these locations occurred during the period of Faulkner's modernity that caused their differences to become obscured. As a consequence he fashions a third, textual space or "location" for his more fully realized version of sexuality.

In an earlier and very different approach to Faulkner's verbal flourishes, another critic once wrote, "Faulkner's style loves to perform."[6] Readers familiar with Faulkner will recognize the aptness of such a statement, particularly when we consider some of the sections of novels I will take up here, including some of Faulkner's most celebrated passages. Nowhere else is such flourish evident as it is in Rosa Coldfield's narrated chapter of *Absalom, Absalom!* and, in a departure from his approach to narrating *The Hamlet* generally, in Faulkner's rapturous descriptions of Ike Snopes and Jack Houston's cow. The critic cited above, John T. Matthews, seeks to answer what lies behind that language's "performance"— in Faulkner's modernism generally as well as in these two novels. What motivates it, or, as Matthews suggests in a number of ways, for what does it compensate or seek to make up? His answer is that such stylistic "play" points up a recurring theme in both Faulkner's stories and in the French poststructuralist theory on which Matthews draws: a narrative in both cases of lack, longing, and desire. Faulkner makes this connection explicit when, in his "Introduction" to *The Sound and the Fury*, he relates the act of writing, or "marring" the unmarked page, with sexual despoilment.[7] Yet it is significant that the kind of writing Faulkner produced in *The Sound and the Fury* is what we have come to associate with Faulkner's signature methods and his discovery of them in this, his first major novel. Throughout his mature work, but including early novels like *Mosquitoes*, as we will see, Faulkner's writing was always "refined," if by refined we mean something beyond a straightforward or transparent narrative technique or style. And as the earlier passage from *Mosquitoes* suggests, such refinement was already associated for Faulkner with sexuality.

Yet other ideas about modernism and writing like Faulkner's may allow us to see his refined style differently. At certain moments and in relation to particular contexts, that style owes something, not to the lack inherent in writing (or in desire, as Matthews and others point out), but to what we may recognize as writing's fullness—even its own "body." Understood as a response to what Faulkner saw as the deadening effects on sexuality of the city and the role in the modern metropolis of an abstract, impersonal market economy, Faulkner's use of an increasingly heightened prose style moves his fiction closer to an expression of physicality and eroticism.

In order to illustrate this, I trace a move forward from one of Faulkner's earliest novels, set mainly in New Orleans and its outskirts, through other city stories and scenes in *Sanctuary* and the anomalous *Pylon*, to Faulkner's later, mature works such as *Absalom, Absalom!* and *The Hamlet* that appear to offer an alternative to his earlier depictions of urban anomie. Closer consideration of these last works, however, will suggest that during the modern period of Faulkner's life and writing, the (Southern) countryside too acquired a quality of displacement, such that natural feelings of attraction and desire find few "natural" outlets or means of expression.

That is the bad news. The good news is that these very works furnish what we might call a saving grace for Faulknerian sexuality. And they do so by way of a "geography" that is neither urban nor rural. Rosa Coldfield's chapter in *Absalom*, like *The Hamlet*'s infamous episodes involving Ike Snopes and the cow, show Faulkner pursuing a strategy of fulfillment, not through characters who seek contact with an absent paramour (for example, Rosa with Charles Bon) or even through a genuine human relationship (in the case of Ike), but through his own highly figurative, erotic use of language. In light of ongoing critical debates about the role in literary studies of form as well as beauty, we might say that these examples make a claim on being erotic *because* they are figurative. This is so especially when we view them as examples of Faulknerian writing at its most ingenuous. Sexuality may be purely imaginative (in Rosa's case) or whimsically perverse (in Ike's). But, Faulkner presents it in a style that is itself deeply, provocatively pleasurable—because of its baroqueness and attendant difficulties, not in spite of them—and in so doing he accomplishes one of his truest expressions of the erotic.

Sex and the City

Marjorie Levinson has written recently about the return to formalist literary approaches, considerations of the inherent pleasures of reading, and of the role in such considerations of *affect*.[8] Levinson offers her remarks in response to a preponderance of historical and political approaches to literature that, until recently, have dominated critical discussion such as Cultural Studies and the New Historicism, both of which sought to downplay emphases on literature's beauty or form. In *The Ideology of the Aesthetic*, Terry Eagleton labels such emphases as a sign of an ideology that equated aesthetic appreciation with capitalist systems. Eagleton makes hard claims against the aesthetic, specifically what he sees as its role securing a privileged space, mentally and economically, in which a particular class subjectivity finds occasion to identify itself. Yet at the same time, he acknowledges its more progressive potential.[9] Where I agree most specifically with Eagleton and others like Christopher Beach is in their account of the aesthetic as a "politics of the body."[10] The view here is that genuine aesthetic experience, of the sort that revels in verbal or visual or tactile sensuousness, can bring the subject back to contact with his or her material reality—in all its social or political configurations. Beach draws on the Frankfurt School critic Theodor Adorno and the Russian theorist Mikhail Bakhtin to connect a certain kind of aesthetic encounter to bodily and, hence, to political awareness and identity. For such critics, the key to such (aesthetic) experiences was their connection to noninstrumental or irrational modes of thought that avoided coopting by economic or ideological systems. Adorno is particularly useful here for what he offers about the potential resistance of modernist language to such coopting by modern economic structures, including and above all the culture industry.[11]

Characters in *Mosquitoes* are concerned with the aesthetic; they talk about it, pronounce their sensitivity to it, and claim to be devoted to it. Yet where they fail in their several artistic pursuits, the novel itself offers a uniquely Faulknerian example of formalist (aesthetic) writing, a quality that is in part at least owed to its setting. For, in addition to introducing Faulkner to certain issues about eroticism and language, *Mosquitoes* plays a specific role in his career in terms of his depictions in it of the city. The novel offers two examples of Faulkner's vision of New Orleans, each of which illustrates one of the two poles of my analysis: the modernist-aesthetic, and the commercial.

At the start of *Mosquitoes* appear several telling descriptions of setting. These include the self-consciously aesthetic, almost surreal depictions of the New Orleans cityscape, images that, as Cleanth Brooks has suggested, show the young writer "who was already conscious of his own real mastery of [words]."[12] Leaving Gordon's building, Talliaferro confronts a scene as ravishing and genuinely beautiful as anything the artist has produced in his studio:

> The violet dusk held in soft suspension lights slow as bellstrokes, Jackson square was now a green and quiet lake in which abode lights round as jellyfish, feathering with silver mimosa and pomegranate and hibiscus beneath which lantana and cannas bled and bled. Pontalba and cathedral were cut from black paper and pasted flat on a green sky; above them taller palms were fixed in black and soundless explosions. (14)

The passage is striking, immediately, for its visual evocativeness and aural pleasure: the alliterations and assonance; the aqueous green light that seems a faint extension of New Orleans's very real connections (like those of Venice) to its maritime culture and location; the hints at the overripe, decadent atmosphere that links Faulkner's imaginary city to a fin-de-siècle European scene. Yet, unlike other passages in *Mosquitoes* that, as Brooks indicates, show Faulkner's style as more derivative—such as the novel's very first description of place, to which Brooks traces several high-literary "borrowings" by a Faulkner who is looking back rather than forward—the paragraph quoted above hints at several stylistic flourishes that Faulkner continues to use in his later fiction. The synesthesia of lights that appear, or sound, "slow as bellstrokes," the imagery of pasting and collage, the oxymoron of the palm trees' "soundless explosions"—all of these techniques appear in later Faulkner and, as here, operate to dazzlingly original effect. This is an example of what Faulkner could "do" with language; it shows already in his second novel the kind of aesthetic, if not also erotic, pleasures, as I will claim.[13]

Elsewhere in *Mosquitoes*, the city appears in a rather different light and toward rather different ends. The night before the boating trip, Gordon pauses during his meaningless wandering and lingers around the dock. Above him, we're told,

> The warehouse . . . was a formal rectangle without perspective. Flat as cardboard, and projecting at faint motionless angles above it, against a lighter spaciousness and a sky not quite so imminent and weary, masts of a freighter lying against the dock. . . . Beneath it, within the somber gloom of the warehouse where men had sweated and labored, across the empty floor lately thunderous with trucks, amid the rich overripe odors of the ends of the earth—coffee and resin and tow and fruit—he walked, surrounded by ghosts, passing on. (47)

Earlier we are told of other "ghosts" that linger around Gordon and his studio: the "shades" of slaves who had once resided there (11). Through these references to (slave) labor and to New Orleans's once-rich history of trade, Faulkner makes clear the economic base on which the city's vitality depended and that also supported its rise as a center of creative life. Particularly as mediated by the artist figure, Gordon, and the rest of the boat's retinue, *Mosquitoes* highlights the connection between New Orleans as a locus for aesthetic life and as a center of commerce.[14]

Although no one in *Mosquitoes* owns slaves, and few members of the boating outing seem to actually work, the novel nevertheless implies that the activity of retailing extends to realms outside of commerce—including both the community's artistic circle and their failed sexual adventures. Dawson Fairchild, we are told several times, is a successful novelist, but his most creative work seems to be opining. More importantly, his views are part of an ongoing intellectual exchange that passes for profundity and that holds the ship's male company in thrall. The book's putative protagonist, Talliaferro, especially, seems convinced that the true end of being an artist means being able to seduce women (for him, another form of exchange). Yet Talliaferro's own ambitions in either arena are pathetically unrealized. Related to this is the fact that nothing very much happens in *Mosquitoes*, least of all the aims of seduction that on one level the trip is meant to facilitate. Mosquitoes buzz about and bother everyone. The opportunities for sexual liaison and for other productive, purely pleasurable acts of artistic creation are thus everywhere thwarted by both the insects themselves and the vehicle for which they act as a metaphorical tenor: the thickened, clouded atmosphere of the city, even beyond the confines of New Orleans. This idea of the city as the site of a failed or, at best, sublimated sexuality is evident from the novel's opening sentence. "The sex instinct," Talliaferro declares (and repeats, the narrator tells us), "is quite strong in me" (9). Clearly harkening back to Eliot's Prufrock, and despite his tentative overtures to Jenny later on the boat, Talliaferro shows that he is far too timid to possess an active sex drive—let alone act on it. Like everyone else in the book, he is too interested in talking—in what passes for urbane sophistication—than in any full-blooded action, sexual or otherwise.

Despite its story's various misfirings, *Mosquitoes* is largely comic in tone; its depiction of urban sexuality mostly seemed to give Faulkner a chance to poke fun at certain contemporaries in his own extended social circle and to play with words. A slightly later novel also set in an urban environment, *Pylon* has both a different tone and wordplay from *Mosquitoes*. The importance of *Pylon* is two-fold: it is set in the city and, related to that setting, it depicts a barren, seemingly loveless coupling. The pilot Roger Shumann and Laverne may very well love each other; more than any other pairing in the book they seem to possess a genuine, if unspoken affection. Yet their exchanges are also marked throughout by a terse friction over their winnings and troubled cash flow.[15] And in a true rarity for Faulkner, a memory of their affair provides a fairly graphic love scene.

I use the term "love scene" deliberately here, and with an eye toward its familiar cinematic version. For, like the airplane race itself, the scene of Roger and Laverne's in-air lovemaking is both offered and consumed as an entertainment spectacle. The extended air meet is attended by an anonymous and, it turns out, bloodthirsty crowd. For, while the onlookers' interest in the event is based in part on their curiosity about the planes and the pilots' skill in maneuvering them, the novel's story and, in a crucial scene, the newspaper editor Hagood make clear that they are also interested in the very real danger the air race poses. Rather than encourage the kind of human-interest approach *Pylon's* nameless reporter wants to write, Hagood is utterly clear about what kind of story he thinks will interest his papers' readers and, by clear implication, the racing meet's paying viewers:

> "You listen to me a minute. If one of [those pilots] takes his airplane or his parachute and murders [Laverne] and the child in front of the grandstand, then it will be news. But until they do, what I'm paying you to bring back here is not what you think about somebody out there nor what you heard . . . nor even what you saw: I expect you to come in here tomorrow night with an accurate account of everything that occurs out there tomorrow that creates any reaction excitement or irritation on any human retina."[16]

Hagood's emphasis on vision—the irritation "on any human retina"—is key. For it points up the way in which, in the context of *Pylon*, what determines human interest and what makes for news stories as well as popular entertainments that will sell is sensationalistic spectacle. This imperative runs through the novel, evident in the bold-faced headlines in the newspaper about the air show and its fatalities, which Faulkner reproduces typographically in his text.[17]

This visual scheme extends, crucially, to the erotic scene late in the novel when the narrator describes an event from Roger and Laverne's earlier life together. The flashback relates the episode when, in the midst of performing a mid-air stunt of Laverne "wing walking," she and Shumann end up having sex in his cockpit. But however tender their lovemaking may be, it turns out to be part of the air show "performance." Flying above a small Kansas town and far from New Valois, the site of the novel's events and the spectacle of the racing meet, Roger and Laverne's coupling is "viewed" not only by the reader, but by a crowd of what turns out to be overappreciative men. Following Laverne's postcoital parachute from the plane, she lands in a field naked from the waist down and is greeted by a group of eager spectators, one of whom, in particular, seeks to turn what he takes to be the pornographic display into a more partici-patory venture. And in another Faulkner rarity, he uses a profanity (and a notably unrefined language) in offering to pay for his pleasure. "'I'll pay you,' the man screamed [to Shumann]. 'I'll pay her! I'll pay either of you! Name it! Let me fuck her once and you can cut me if you want!'" (912).

I offer this summary not for its prurience. What is of note about this section of *Pylon* is the way that it extends qualities of the urban, New Orleans scene to the depiction of events far beyond it. That is to say: the uses to which sexuality end up being put in the book (here, Roger and Laverne's lovemaking during the air show) ultimately serve the same imperative as the novel's other example of a mass cultural "entertain-ment," the newspaper. As with Hagood's exhortation that the reporter supply copy that can perform visually or act "on any human retina," so the novel's graphic depiction of sexuality shows that it too can be readily coopted for a sensationalist, voyeuristic pleasure. My suggestion here is that Roger and Laverne are unwittingly complicit in a commercial system that exploits human sexuality. Though they are not performing their love-making for the crowd, it grows out of and is an extension of an activity that is offered specifically for spectators (the air show). Compelled by circumstances to perform the in-air stunt of walking across the airplane wing, Laverne's act of climbing into the cockpit with Shumann seems both a desperate attempt to assert some fleeting autonomy from the eco-nomic pressures she and Shumann face, as well as evidence of the erotic frisson that arises from them. In either case, and as events after their lovemaking reveal, the pleasure they find together seems connected to the more impersonal workings of commercialism. Like the urban crowd that demands risk and that the newspaper means to serve, Laverne and Roger's audience demonstrates a type of pleasure—or the longing for it—that seeks to satisfy itself violently (with Laverne's rape by the agitated, insane onlooker). Sexuality in *Pylon*, like in *Mosquitoes*, is thus marked by the influence of the city, as well as by urban, mass-cultural organs like the newspaper. Moreover, and as part of the purely pecuniary motives of the paper, that pleasure becomes coopted by forces that control and channel such examples of human sexual appetite as we see, managing and controlling them for profit, like other consumer pleasures.

In *Pylon*, as well as in the earlier *Sanctuary*, Faulkner shows that sex-ual debasements follow from the economic and abstract ways in which he understood human relations were experienced in the city. Such abstrac-tions were further facilitated by Faulkner's awareness of the role played in urban experience by vision—again, and as in *Pylon*, the voyeuristic and objectifying habits of primarily male characters that act as substitutions for genuine erotic life. Such objectifying serves well the workings of a modern, abstract money economy. At the start of the twentieth century, the German cultural critic Georg Simmel describes this process in a seminal essay from 1903, "The Metropolis and Mental Life."[18] Simmel refers to the shifting visual patterns in the city such as the constant flow of traffic and trolley cars, the appearance and disappearance of faces and bodies in one's view, and the ubiquitous presence of advertising. Simmel also claims that the constant encounters with strangers on city streets and in urban transit, combined with the increasing estrangement of a market economy, causes urban dwellers to become more introverted and remote from one another—a phenomenon that would have obvious consequences for sexuality.

Alan Trachtenberg examines this development in American cities in a series of observations that resonate with Faulkner's impersonal, commercial, and thus nonsexualized city. In *The Incorporation of America*, Trachtenberg refers to the metropolis's increasing dependence on the market as well as how it came to organize visual stimulus and spectacle: "As the domestic making of goods receded [in the late nineteenth century], city dwellers became more and more enmeshed in the market, more and more dependent on buying and selling, selling their labor in order to buy their sustenance; the network of personal relations, of family, friends, neighbors, comes to count for less in the maintenance of life than the impersonal transactions and abstract structures of the marketplace."[19] Elsewhere Trachtenberg claims that urban experience—of the sort we find in *Mosquitoes*, *Pylon*, and, as we will see, in *Sanctuary*—as well as new media technologies and forms of mass entertainment "began to erode direct physical experience of the world" (122)—and hence, of other people and their bodies. "Viewing and looking at representations, words, and images, city people found themselves addressed more often as passive spectators than as active participants, consumers of images and sensations produced by others" (122). This includes the viewing, not only of the city itself, but of massive urban spectacles such as spectator sports, amusement parks, and, of course, the cinema.[20]

This perspective offers a useful frame for the connections *Sanctuary* shows between an abstracting, depersonalizing market and an increasing cultural emphasis on vision. There is no mass-cultural, city-based entertainment in *Sanctuary*, such as *Pylon*'s homologous air show and newspaper. There are, however, any number of examples in the book of characters' acts of viewing. Several moments leap to mind, such as Tommy spying on Temple through the peephole while she undresses; Popeye watching her in bed with Red at Miss Reba's—and Clarence

Snopes watching him watching through the keyhole; Horace's low-level sexual contemplation of his stepdaughter's image in her photograph. The most persistent of these examples, of course, is Popeye, a character notable for his (urban) scopic drive and attendant remoteness. For despite all his menace and quite real violence, Popeye is also an oddly passive figure. He rapes Temple with a prosthetic, and, as we learn, he does so in part because of his sexual impotence. As we also learn about Popeye early in the book, he is a thoroughly mechanical man. He appears to Horace as though he is "stamped [from] tin" and has "rubber" eyes and "doll-like hands."[21] He is notably out of his element and fearful in the forest pathways near Lee Goodwin's, and when Popeye hears a bird singing, Horace is right when he points out that the only names of birds Popeye knows are those he would buy in a restaurant meal. Popeye is, in other words, a consumer. As a result, and like many other examples of modern, urban consumers, Popeye is decidedly alien—cut off from not only other people but from any capacity for potency or genuine human desire. Defined by his affinity with the visual, Popeye suggests a modern and urban malaise.

What is also clear in *Sanctuary*—and related to this role of looking—is the way the city operates as a marketplace for human flesh. Of particular interest to us is a brief episode in the book that exposes not only the facts of prostitution or the effects on Temple of Popeye's rape and abduction, but the singular power of abstraction around sexuality that obtains in Memphis. I have in mind the only chapter in which the characters Virgil Snopes and Fonzo Winbush appear. Two young men in the city for the first time, they find themselves staying as guests at Miss Reba's because they can't afford a regular hotel. One evening after having been led by an acquaintance to another brothel, the boys encounter their cousin, Clarence Snopes, back at Miss Reba's. When they complain about the prices of the prostitutes where they've been, Clarence leads them to another section of the city—a "negro" district, where they look into another building with "red shades in the lighted windows" (316). "Through an open door," the narrator tells us, the boys and Clarence "saw a room filled with coffee-colored women in bright dresses, with ornate hair and golden smiles."

> "Them's niggers," Virgil said.
> "Course they're niggers," Clarence said. "But see this?' he waved a banknote in his cousin's face. "This stuff is color-blind." (316)

In the context of an essay about the dulling of affect in the city, Clarence's comment makes a certain kind of historical sense. In the modern

American city (as in the European modernity that Simmel describes) individuals become indifferent to qualitative differences; they judge and consider products only on the basis of cost. This scene is central in *Sanctuary*, for in it we find a supremely shorthand version of the enormously abstracting power of money. In a market economy, where everything, including and perhaps especially human relations, is mediated through an impersonal cash nexus, qualitative distinctions melt away into a color-blind exchange of capital for goods. The fact that these "commodities" are also human beings is entirely to the point. We find a similar case of African American prostitutes in *Absalom, Absalom!*, when Charles Bon reveals to Henry "a row of faces like a bazaar of flowers—the supreme apotheosis of chattelry."[22] There, however, the courtesans are part of a nineteenth-century New Orleans economy, draped in the rhetoric of Charles Bon's ideas about nobleness and honor. Here in *Sanctuary*, their condition reveals much more about the circumstances of the modern city—and not only for the women who sell their sexual labor. As Popeye's mechanical, voyeuristic relations with Temple make clear, *Sanctuary*'s color-blind world operates according to an imperative in which sexuality becomes reduced to a cash value. Urban sexuality in *Sanctuary*'s Memphis—as it had been in *Pylon*'s New Valois or in the New Orleans environs in *Mosquitoes*—is part of a market system. Faulkner's city novels all reveal how in modernity, individual sensibility became hollowly indifferent to qualitative, substantive variations, judging and considering "products" only on the basis of quantitative measures like cost.

"Rural" Sexuality

It would seem that there would be many occasions in Faulkner to find events and human relations with emotional, economic, or interpersonal bases that are both rural and real. Indeed, two of Faulkner's most well-known and canonical works, *Absalom, Absalom!* and the first Snopes novel, *The Hamlet*, seem a deliberate return on his part to the Yoknapatawpha countryside. Following the excursions into urban sexuality respectively, first in *Pylon* (1935) and then in the "Wild Palms" section of *If I Forget Thee, Jerusalem* (1939), and written after the city novels I have been discussing, both *Absalom, Absalom!* and *The Hamlet* go back to earlier periods in the county's history, when its inhabitants might have been less affected by urban commercialism, market forces, or a compromised, abstract-impersonal sexuality. Although urban sexuality in Faulkner can be bleak, there is hope for erotic life in his fiction outside of the metropolis. Such eroticism, though, in fact obtains in a quite different "geography," having contact with neither the city nor with what, we learn, is an increasingly urbanized countryside.

It is tempting to see Faulkner's portrayal of Frenchman's Bend in *The Hamlet* as an admittedly nostalgic return (well after novels like *Pylon*, *Sanctuary*, or *If I Forget Thee, Jerusalem*) to a way of life that relied on exchanges of goods, not cash; to a community defined by close social and family connections; and to a world in which human relations and indeed physical as well as emotional experiences were genuine. Yet as the novel shows in several ways, such is not the case. Or it is the case—but the terms of these connections and physical identity have been meaningfully qualified. As events from *The Hamlet* make clear and in the period its events depict, the urban and mercantile world has already begun to infiltrate supposedly remote regions like Frenchman's Bend. Flem Snopes's ascension to a position of prominence, above all, reveals the extent to which the countryside is not immune from modern, abstract forms of economic domination and exchange.

Several critics have referred to this split, including Richard Moreland, who perhaps as much as any critic has shown the ways in which the economy and culture of Frenchman's Bend had already become urbanized before the novel opens.[23] One clear example of this development appears early in the chapter "The Long Summer" when the narrator describes Mink's reversed days and nights after he's hidden Houston's body. Watching the coming of night, Mink "would sit there for perhaps ten or fifteen minutes longer, as the holder of the annual commuter's ticket sits on his accustomed bench and continues to read his paper after the train has already whistled for the stop."[24] There is no train near Mink's hideout—commuter rail or otherwise. Yet as Faulkner's simile reveals, the urban (or suburban) life of commuters and white-collar labor exists, if only as a trace,[25] in Yoknapatawpha.

Another example from *The Hamlet* brings us back to the city and visual pleasure, as well as to the associations between such pleasure, sexuality, and commodification. Oddly, this story about a small Southern village includes a scenario involving Ike Snopes at Mrs. Littlejohn's stall that resembles the kind of urban, mass-cultural spectacle that is suggested in Faulkner's city novels. I will turn to Ike's encounters with Houston's cow in the river bottom shortly. For they will provide a welcome—indeed, necessary—rejoinder to Faulkner's emphasis on the isolating lack of eroticism and intimacy in the city. For now, I would like to examine how the "hamlet" of Frenchman's Bend includes a space that operates quite like an urban cinema. The scene at Mrs. Littlejohn's stall includes paying viewers, "customers" whom Lump charges a price of admission for their acts of viewing Ike there with the cow. As Ratliff asks when he finds the men looking through the pried-off plank in the stable wall, "'Does he [Lump] . . . make you pay again each time, or is it a general club ticket good for every performance?'" (913). Although the immediate context of the story here is provincial and rural, but like the visual spectacle(s) in *Pylon* or the voyeurism in *Sanctuary*, the economic structure and management of viewing at the stall resembles the urban phenomenon of passive spectating at a peepshow.

With these hints of a connection between the city and rural space or of a burgeoning market economy, *The Hamlet* includes a commensurate threat to human intimacy. Flem Snopes is obviously a cold, indifferent man; his (urban) abstractness, like Popeye's in *Sanctuary*, also connects to his sexual impotence, which we learn about in the later Snopes novel *The Town*. Faulkner underscores this fact with irony when he has Flem marry Will Varner's daughter Eula, a character whose overwhelming sexual vitality appears irresistible to nearly every man she encounters. As readers have long recognized, Flem and Snopesism suggest Southern history's inexorable move to an impersonal business model for human agency and human relations. We will remember Flem's calculating mind, his machine-made shirts, and his abstract fixation on the bottom line. In the realm of a debased, commercialized sexuality and a reminder of events in Memphis in *Sanctuary*, we should also recall the young African American girl lying on the floor behind the counter asking Flem what he asks for a can of sardines (882).

Faulkner's Textualized Erotic

If we find in *The Hamlet* a rapidly changing rural scene and a decline in human relations typified by the metropolis, Faulkner's modernism nevertheless offers the possibility of genuine and physical love. Yet, it does so indirectly and apart from a particular location or geography: in his language. At the risk of asking too much interpretive sway from perhaps too little text, I move in the last section of my discussion to two highly suggestive examples of what I mean by Faulkner's eroticized style, what I call his poetics of Eros.

To trace this elusive erotic life, we need to turn to *Absalom, Absalom!* and to its infamous spinster, Rosa Coldfield. It may seem unlikely to consider Rosa sexually. By "consider," however, I mean to recognize the ways in which her language, as much as or more than any prose Faulkner wrote, conveys a quality of embodied fullness, a nearly physical presence that is the foil to the more fully racinated, abstract, and disembodied (and thus, asexual) perspective of so many Faulkner characters—particularly

male characters. This includes overly cerebral types such as Horace Benbow, Quentin Compson, Gail Hightower, or the reporter in *Pylon*. Paradoxically, sexuality in Rosa's chapter has something to do with her lonely
story, her memory of what she calls her *"barren youth"* (119). Despite
denying her claim to "leaf" or bloom and thus to a commensurate eroticism, what Rosa refers to as the *"warped bitter pale and crimped half-
fledging intimidate of any claim to green which might have drawn to it
the tender mayfly childhood sweetheart games or given pause to the male
predacious wasps and bees of later lust"* (119), Rosa is, indeed, a sexual
being—as the imagery in this passage suggests. And that imagery corre-
sponds with the way that Rosa's section operates generally. What emerges
in Rosa's chapter is not merely her memory of a libidinally charged teenage summer. What is noteworthy, in this argument, is the dense, bodily,
rhapsodic prose that Faulkner fashions in depicting that memory verbally.
As Rosa tells us, *"There is no such thing as memory, the brain recalls just
what the muscles grope for"* (118). True to that assertion, Faulkner shows
us a language with Rosa that is itself "groping."[26]

Readers too have to "grope" with Rosa's *langue*, her language or her
tongue. We have, that is, to try to hold it firm, to engage with its materiality, its body or its "thingness." The abstruse, dense prose of Rosa's
chapter, far from being too abstract or conceptual for many readers, I
suggest, is on the contrary too *physical*. Consider Rosa's characterization of herself as *"all polymath love's androgynous advocate"* (121) or
her assertion (again describing herself), *"who shall say what gnarled
forgotten root might not bloom yet with some globed concentrate more
globed and concentrate and heady-perfect because the neglected root was
planted warped and lay not dead but merely slept forgot?"* (119). Surely
the length of the clause here, the fact that Faulkner stretches syntax
to such a degree, makes demands on the reader's attention, our mental
impressions of the sentence's metonymic, forward-moving motion. Such
passages demand that we encounter them physically, as objects, before or
perhaps even apart from their semantic meanings. Such a verbal physicality is helped by the fact that Rosa is so mightily engaged in her own
bodily sensory memory of her *"summer of wistaria,"* a *"pervading everywhere of wistara"* that blended with and was animated by the *"summer
of a virgin's itching discontent"* (119–20). Such longing climaxes for Rosa
(again, paradoxically) when she was fourteen, *"four years younger than
Judith, [and] four years later than Judith's moment which only virgins
know: when the entire delicate spirit's bent is one anonymous climax-
less epicine and unravished nuptial"* (120). What other nonravishment
has ever been described so ravishingly? Even passages in Rosa's chapter
that are not "about" the body rhetorically or semantically, such as this,

are *of* the body, in the manner that metered verse acts on the reader bodily. Referring to an overheard conversation between Bon and Judith in the Sutpen garden during one of his visits, Rosa asks in a prose that mimics Elizabethan rhythms, and one we might even scan thus, *"'What suspiration of the twinning souls[/] have the murmurous myriad ears [/] of this secluded vine or shrub listened to?[/] what vow, what promise, this heavy rose's[/] dissolution, crowned[. . .]?'"* (122). Rendered by Faulkner as prose, such phrases nevertheless have the cadence of verse, the accented-syllabic patterns of a scheme like pentameter, as well as aural properties such as consonance that allow Rosa's voice to register for readers as something felt or experienced bodily.[27]

These examples from Rosa are striking. But the most unequivocally lush language about love that Faulkner wrote appears in a later novel and in a different register. That the love in *The Hamlet* is that of an "idiot" for a cow is both to the point and completely immaterial. It does not matter—in a "normative" sense—that Ike's love is outside the realm of ordinary sexual behavior. The fact that such language attends the relationship between a human being and an animal is important, however, to the Utopic dimension of Faulkner's treatment of sexuality—namely, that the occasions in which we find the highest state of erotic life in his corpus are those that operate in the realm of the potential.

Returning to *The Hamlet*, we may note that as Faulkner narrates the beginning of Ike's sensual encounter, he sets it off from the scene we have noted of the men watching Ike in Mrs. Littlejohn's stall. And as he does at other points in his work, Faulkner offsets two related but quite different perspectives on one event: the fact of Ike and the cow's encounter. Significantly, he does so through the use of decidedly different prose. The urban-seeming scenario of Lump charging "admission" to the stall spectacle is written in the matter-of-fact voice with which the narrator opens *The Hamlet* and relates its events generally. The language describing the scenes of Ike anticipating his object of desire in the creek in the spring morning could not be more stylized and hence, more different.

Then he would hear her, coming down the creekside in the mist. It would not be after one hour, two hours, three; the dawn would be empty, the moment and she would not be, then he would hear her and he would lie drenched in the wet grass, serene and one and invisible in joy, listening to her approach. He would smell her; the whole mist reeked with her; the same malleate hands of mist which drew along his prone drenched flanks palped her pearled barrel too and shaped them both somewhere in immediate time, already married. He would not move. He would lie amid the waking instant of earth's teeming life, the motionless fronds of water-heavy grasses stopping into the mist before his face in black, fixed curves, along each parabola of which the marching drops held in minute magnification the dawn's rosy miniatures, smelling and even tasting the rich, slow, warm barren-reek milk-reek, the flowing immemorial female, hearing the slow planting and the plopping suck of each deliberate cloven mud-spreading hoof, invisible still in the mist loud with its hymenal choristers. (883)

This is striking language—what in various contexts others have called "baroque" or "an exalted lyrical strain"[28] and which, I submit, is among the most rhapsodic prose Faulkner ever wrote.[29] Interestingly, this passage also emphasizes an engagement on Ike's part with his environment that privileges sensory experiences other than vision—that part of the sensorium that in modernity is so fully associated with the city.[30] I suggest that Faulkner indulges his writing so completely in this section of *The Hamlet* because, however earnestly he does so, Faulkner describes a relationship that is not exactly "real." As we have seen through several examples, human connections in Faulkner's world are hard. Whether this was due to some of Faulkner's own personal frustrations in life, his sense of the impossibility of actually possessing (or describing) the perfect woman, or, as I have been suggesting, the difficulties of human contact in an increasingly urban and abstract world, Faulkner finds his truest and most lovingly described love affair in his fiction between not a man and a woman (nor between two men or two women, as other examples in his life and fiction allow), or even between two human beings.[31] It is the fact of "displacement," then, away from the object of affection or even a fully attainable human love, but also from the increasingly urbanized spaces of twentieth-century America, that language affords—especially such refined language as Faulkner here fashions.

I say that what Ike pursues is not a real (human) relationship. And we would do well to remember that, for all its fulsome poeticizing, this section of *The Hamlet* never directly depicts Ike's coupling. It does, however, clearly intimate ecstasy. During this final encounter, Ike has a heady, almost out-of-body experience. Having left the barn and finding himself back at the spring, remembering again his time with the cow, Ike feels "the well of days, the still and insatiable aperture of earth. It holds in tranquil paradox of suspended precipitation dawn, noon, and sunset; yesterday, today, and tomorrow—star-spawn and hieroglyph, the fierce white dying rose, then gradual and invincible speeding up to and into slack-flood's coronal or nympholept noon" (903). Penetrating the hieroglyphics of Faulkner's prose, we go to the heart, or climax of this section of the novel: Ike's imaginative conflating of all time, past and present, in one rapturous moment.

Another way to put this would be that with Ike, as with Rosa Coldfield, Faulkner writes in ways that we cannot quite understand. The length of the sentences, the obscurity of the diction—these qualities make it difficult to clearly "see" the events that the narrator describes in *The Hamlet* or to follow the events of Rosa's chapter. Reading these passages, we are constantly aware of the material presence of the words in them as well as their semantic meanings. But such challenges to readers lead them somewhere productive: away from the scene(s) depicted and, by a circuitous route, back to both the textual and corporeal body. The obscurity of Rosa's chapter or sections of *The Hamlet*, their difficulty, in this view, are their force. They also fashion their own unique pleasure. Gesturing toward a Utopic, not-quite-realizable but nevertheless concrete encounter with the textual and the bodily real, these moments accomplish something crucial, offering a loving, even eroticized riposte to the flattened, affectless, "color blind" abstractions of Faulkner's earlier descriptions of sexuality. Life in Faulkner's city, particularly erotic life, was never as fully embodied as are Faulkner's later, somewhat idealized—but simultaneously, compellingly corporealized—descriptions of Ike's interlude and Rosa's longings.[32]

It is a material, formalist aspect of words that Faulkner shows both early and later in his career to such positive effects, as well as powerful affect. Faulkner finds in *The Hamlet* and *Absalom* a way of offering characters (and readers) something that does not seem available either in the city or, except in rare cases, the modernizing Southern countryside. After a series of questioning looks at several environments, Faulkner does find a space for eroticism. He finds it in characters who, although they appear in novels written after his early city fiction, live in a time period that antedates a full-blown urban modernity. Yet as we have seen, the novels in which they appear also show some connection to modern phenomena such as the metropolis and the market. In response Faulkner moves his search for a splendorous language of eros away from both the city and, to a degree, from the country. Eroticism and desire exist in Faulkner. Yet they do so in what, as a modernist, Faulkner may have felt was one of the only spaces free from the sway of commercial life available to him—the pure, "unretailed" space of his writing. More and more as he wrote, and the further he went from the city as a direct subject, Faulkner wrote in a manner that was "refined." That he most often did so to describe feelings of love is not simply fortuitous. Doing so allowed him to bring together his own love of language and its materiality as well as its aesthetic possibilities, its sensual beauty. Returning to the body and to sensuality in *Absalom* and *The Hamlet*, Faulkner also returns to the bodily quality of writing. As we have seen, the prose of *Absalom, Absalom!* and *The*

Hamlet is written in such a way that we have to grapple (or grope) with it. Yet that process allows readers to have an experience that is itself more than simply imaginative and that partakes of the bodily and the physical. In the context of a modernity that made greater and greater demands of abstraction, calculation, and reason, such a return to the body and the senses can make of reading a more powerful, even intimate occasion than many were able to find in their lives and in the period of Faulkner's career.

Faulkner's engagement with the erotic and with writing—and with the erotic *through* writing—follows a long line forward from *Mosquitoes*. This line traces the development of Yoknapatawpha and of Faulkner's (ostensible) move away from the city generally as well as from the baroque scene of New Orleans and the phony posturing of a group of sophisticated aesthetes. Such a group and such a scene, however, gave Faulkner ways to explore what it meant to be a writer and to approach certain experiences with words. And some of the lessons he learned with that group served him well as he returned to his "native postage stamp" and wrote about characters and environments with which he was more intimate and genuinely familiar. With Ike Snopes and Rosa Coldfield we are a long way, in one sense, from the scene of two girls kissing on a boat outside New Orleans. Yet in another regard, in the sense of how we kiss (or use our *langue*), our "playfulness," refinement, elegance, or style, as well as how we write or consider writing (in other words, how we read), we may not be so distant, after all.

NOTES

1. Vladimir Nabokov, *The Annotated Lolita*, ed. Alfred Appel Jr. (New York: Vintage, 1991), 32.

2. This passage and other deletions from *Mosquitoes* appear in Minrose C. Gwin's work of textual criticism, "*Mosquitoes*' Missing Bite: The Four Deletions," *Faulkner Journal* 9:1&2 (Fall 1993/Spring 1994), 31–41.

3. Gwin, 32.

4. Of course the same is true of English, in which "tongue" also connotes language or a way of speaking. Yet as the scene in question points up, the French apparently know something about tongues and kissing as well as about language, as a good deal of poststructuralist theory suggests (and to which my discussion attends).

5. William Faulkner, *Mosquitoes* (New York: Liveright, 1997), 9. Subsequent references are to this edition and appear parenthetically in the text.

6. John T. Matthews, *The Play of Faulkner's Language* (Ithaca, N.Y.: Cornell University Press, 1982), 15.

7. William Faulkner, "An Introduction for *The Sound and the Fury*," in *The Sound and the Fury*, ed. David Minter (New York: Norton Critical Edition, 2nd ed., 1994), 226, cited in Matthews 18.

8. Marjorie Levinson, "What Is New Formalism?," *PMLA* 122.2 (March 2007): 558–69.

9. Eagleton sees the aesthetic as a philosophical category that is "radically double-edged." On the one hand, it encourages "a mode of being which [especially after Kant] is entirely self-regulating and [which thus] . . . provides the middle class with just the ideological model of subjectivity it requires for its material operations," *The Ideology of the Aesthetic* (Oxford: Basil Blackwell, 1990), 9. On the other hand, Eagleton avers, the aesthetic offers "a vision of human energies as radical ends in themselves which is the implacable enemy of all dominative or instrumentalist thought. It signifies a creative turn to the sensuous body" (*The Ideology of the Aesthetic* 9). It is this second view that I see Faulkner enable with his own particularly aestheticized prose.

10. Christopher Beach, "Recuperating the Aesthetic: Contemporary Approaches and the Case of Adorno," in *Beauty and the Critic: Aesthetics in an Age of Cultural Studies*, ed. James Soderholm (Tuscaloosa: University of Alabama Press, 1997), 100.

11. See Adorno, *Aesthetic Theory*, trans. C. Lenhardt, ed. Gretel Adorno and Rolf Tiedemann (London: Routledge and Kegan Paul, 1984), 24, 6, and "The Culture Industry: Enlightenment as Mass Deception," in *Dialectic of Enlightenment*, trans. John Cumming (New York: Continuum, 1988), *passim*. I will return to the deleterious effects on sexuality of a managed, consumer culture shortly, as well as to Faulkner's efforts to critique and resist them.

12. Cleanth Brooks, *William Faulkner: Toward Yoknapatawpha and Beyond* (New Haven: Yale University Press, 1978), 132.

13. The passage appears on the novel's second page; its evocations of Eliot and British aestheticism are apparent: "Outside the window New Orleans, the vieux carré, brooded in a faintly tarnished languor like an ageing yet still beautiful courtesan in a smokefilled room, avid yet weary of ardent ways. Above the city summer was hushed warmly into the bowled weary passion of the sky. Spring and the cruellest [sic] months were gone, the cruel months" (10), cited in Brooks 132.

14. A similar connection exists between retail activity and artistic life in *If I Forget Thee, Jerusalem*. In *Mosquitoes* Tallifiero works in the women's section of a department store, a profession that supports him in his support (in turn) of the artistic community in New Orleans; in "The Wild Palms" Charlotte Rittenmeyer dresses department store windows in Chicago so as to be able to pursue her work sculpting erotically charged (if also perverse) figurines. See Taylor Hagood, *Faulkner's Imperialism: Space, Place, and the Materiality of Myth* (Louisiana State University Press, 2008) for an account of the particular economic history of New Orleans and its role in *Mosquitoes*.

15. John T. Matthews traces the elaborate and, indeed, desperate negotiations over income in the novel in "The Autograph of Violence in Faulkner's *Pylon*," in *Southern Literature and Literary Theory*, ed. Jefferson Humphries (Athens: University of Georgia Press, 1990). Interestingly, although Matthews pursues a Bahktinian reading of the book, emphasizing the importance of class antagonism, wage earning, and *Pylon*'s suggestions of revolutionary energy, he does not attend to the related (Bakhtinian) matter of bodies and sexuality that the novel also introduces.

16. William Faulkner, *Pylon*, in *Novels 1930–1935* (New York: Library of America, 1985), 808. Subsequent references are to this edition and appear parenthetically in the text.

17. Critics have suggested that the newspaper passages in *Pylon* show Faulkner emulating the direct visual as well as the semantic impact that the large-block lettering of the headlines make. See Karl Zender, *The Crossing of the Ways: William Faulkner, the South, and the Modern World* (New Brunswick: Rutgers University Press, 1989), 51.

18. Georg Simmel, "The Metropolis and Mental Life," in *The Sociology of Georg Simmel*, trans. and ed. Kurt Wolff (New York: Free Press 1964).

19. Alan Trachtenberg, *The Incorporation of America: Culture and Society in the Gilded Age* (New York: Hill and Wang, 1982), 121. Subsequent references are to this edition and appear parenthetically in the text.

20. This is a similar line of argument about the modern metropolis as we find in several European theorists of modernity, such as Guy Debord, Walter Benjamin, and Siegfried Kracauer, all of whom drew on Simmel. See Debord, *The Society of the Spectacle*, trans. Donald Nicholson-Smith (New York: Zone Books, 1994); Benjamin, "The Work of Art in the Age of Mechanical Reproduction," in *Illuminations*, trans. Harry Zohn, ed. Hannah Arendt (New York: Shocken Books, 1968) and *Charles Baudelaire: A Lyric Poet in the Era of High Capitalism*, trans. Harry Zohn (London: Verso, 1997); and Kracauer, "On Photography," in *The Mass Ornament: Weimar Essays*, trans. and ed. Thomas Y. Levin (Cambridge: Harvard University Press, 1947).

21. William Faulkner, *Sanctuary*, in *Novels 1930–1935* (New York: Library of America, 1985), 181, 182. Subsequent references are to this edition and appear parenthetically in the text.

22. William Faulkner, *Absalom, Absalom!*, in *Novels 1936–1940* (New York: Library of America, 1990), 92–93. Subsequent references are to this edition and appear parenthetically in the text.

23. Richard Moreland, *Faulkner and Modernism: Rereading and Rewriting* (Madison: University of Wisconsin Press, 1990).

24. William Faulkner, *The Hamlet*, in *Novels 1936–1940* (New York: Library of America, 1990), 944. Subsequent references are to this edition and appear parenthetically in the text.

25. "The trace is not only the disappearance of origin. . . . [W]ithin the discourse that we sustain . . . it means that the origin did not even disappear, that it was never constituted except reciprocally by a nonorigin, the trace" (Jacques Derrida, *Of Grammatology*, trans. Gayarti Chakravorty Spivak [Baltimore: Johns Hopkins University Press], 61).

26. We might recall the etymological root of "grope" from the Old English, now obsolete, which was to "grasp" or to "touch," or its connotations of sexual play (Oxford English Dictionary, online version). And while clinically speaking the tongue is an organ, it seems apt to consider it (in light of the implications of Rosa's statement here) as another of those muscles that grope (or reach or grasp) at memory or, as in Rosa's own example, at human connection.

27. See Elizabeth Harris Sagaser, "Flirting with Eternity: Teaching Form and Meter in a Renaissance Poetry Course," in *Renaissance Literature and Its Formal Engagements*, ed. Mark Rasmussen (New York: Palgrave, 2002), 185–206, for an account of the way that verse or rhythmic writing acts on readers corporally.

28. Richard Grey, *The Literature of Memory: Modern Writers of the American South* (Baltimore: Johns Hopkins University Press, 1977), 218. Andrea Diminio, "Why Did the Snopeses Name their Son 'Wallstreet Panic'? Depression Humor in Faulkner's *The Hamlet*," in *William Faulkner: Six Decades of Criticism*, ed. Linda Wagner-Martin (East Lansing: Michigan State University Press, 2002), 344.

29. Many critics have written about Faulkner's stylistic intensity, including Arnold Weinstein, who attributes this superlative to Rosa (*Vision and Response in Modern Fiction* [Ithaca: Cornell University Press, 1974], 140).

30. I have written elsewhere about the fact that, in his fiction after 1939, Faulkner moves away from an emphasis on vision and, as this scene with Ike illustrates, toward an effort to bring tactile, olfactory perceptions to the world of his characters and, by extension, his contemporary readers. See Peter Lurie, *Vision's Immanence: Faulkner, Film, and the Popular Imagination* (Baltimore: Johns Hopkins University Press, 2004), 174.

31. John Irwin has described how, over his career, Faulkner maintained a creative energy in response to a series of failed relationships. See "Not the Having but the Wanting: Faulkner's Lost Loves," in *Faulkner at 100, Retrospect and Prospect: Faulkner and Yoknapatawpha, 1997*, ed. Donald M. Kartiganer and Ann J. Abadie (Jackson: University Press of Mississippi, 2000), 154–64. For Faulkner's remarks about describing the "ideal woman," see *Lion in the Garden: Interviews with William Faulkner*, ed. James B. Merriwether and Michael Millgate (New York: Random House, 1968), 127.

32. In a very different interpretive context from mine, Tony Fabijancic points to moments in Faulkner in which his language restores his poor white farmers to a kind of perceptual life after their senses as well as their hope have been blunted ("Reification, Derification, Subjectivity: Towards a Marxist Reading of William Faulkner's Poor-White Topography" (*Faulkner Journal* 10:1 [Fall 1994]). Fabijancic offers examples such as Darl Bundren's lyrical utterances in *As I Lay Dying*, poetic flights that appear despite his family's difficulties both economically on their farm and more generally on their journey to bury Addie. In a gesture that relates to my discussion above, Fabijnancic refers to Fredric Jameson's account of writing like Faulkner's and examples from visual art, works whose effects Jameson says create a "semiautonomous space" and "an act of compensation which ends up producing a whole new Utopian realm of the senses" (Fredric Jameson, *Postmodernism, or, the Cultural Logic of Late Capitalism* [Durham: Duke University Press, 1991], 7, cited in Fabijancic 90).

"Must Have Been Love":
Sexualities' Attachments in Faulkner

Deborah E. McDowell

But there must have been love he thought. Some sort of love. Even what he would have called love: not just an afternoon's or a night's spittoon.[1]
—William Faulkner, Go Down, Moses

Years ago, George Kent made the passing observation that, while "there is considerable sexual activity in Faulkner"—as much, he said, as could be found in the Kinsey Report—there was "little sexuality, that is, if we define sexuality as that warm and unself-conscious endorsement of the role of the body in effecting transcendence of individual isolation."[2] That was 1974, and much has changed in the interim. I doubt that any contemporary student of sexuality as a topic of academic inquiry could endorse Kent's definition—indeed, many would likely find it quaint—for as is now axiomatic, sexuality is a social/discursive construction, a function of ideology. Its meanings and understandings are vexed, variable, and historically contingent. And as for Kent's assertion that there is little sexuality in Faulkner, the work of countless literary critics would contravene. The crudest Google Search for "Faulkner and Sexuality" yields 310,000 entries, including course descriptions, calls for papers, special issues of journals, and scholarly monographs. A random list of titles is instructive: "This Was the Answer to It: Sexuality and Maternity in *As I Lay Dying*," "Gender, Sexuality, and the Artist in Faulkner's Novels," "A Loving Gentleman and the Corncob Man: Faulkner, Gender, and Sexuality in *The Reivers*," "Trauma Studies and Faulkner's *Sanctuary*: Sex, Sexuality and Race," "Contextualizing *The Sound and the Fury*: Sex, Gender, and Community in Modern American Fiction." Taken together, as the repetition of the conjunction "and" suggests, these studies establish nothing more emphatically than that, as a concept, sexuality never stands alone. It is always coupled, always attached to some other conceptual matter: identity, difference, morality, reproduction, community, gender, power, kinship, market relations and, of course in Faulkner's corpus, race and region.

94

Any discussion of race, region, and sexuality in Faulkner must inevitably confront the sordid details and the brutal history of slavery and segregation at the heart of his entire Southern cycle—concubinage, incest, and tangled interracial genealogies—to say nothing of the abuses that segregation spawned: terrorism and lynching, dispossession and disenfranchisement, the day-to-day humiliations of Jim Crow. But in addition to this violent history, which Faulkner has chronicled unsparingly, we must also confront the reciprocal affective bonds, the emotional intimacies and attachments this history engendered simultaneously. Referring specifically to African Americans, James Baldwin argued decades ago that the "American Negro's situation" is "not simply the relationship of oppressed to oppressor, of master to slave, nor is it motivated merely by hatred; it is also, literally and morally, a blood relationship, perhaps the most profound reality of the American experience, and we cannot begin to unlock it until we accept how very much it contains of the force and anguish and terror of love."[3]

Scholars, even "Faulknerians" here and there, have begun to turn their attention to the complexities of these affective bonds or to what Peter Coviello terms, in another context, the "intimacy effects of sex."[4] I want to consider, though only in broad outline, one such "intimacy effect," one such "attachment" of interracial sex in Faulkner: love. At the risk of oversimplifying the matter, I would suggest, if only provisionally, that Faulkner's most significant work constitutes, fundamentally, his search for a language of love, for a means of capturing its elusiveness and expression in narrative. I agree with Judith Sensibar that, for Faulkner, "love was always 'opaque': symbolic of failure or anticipated failure."[5] Such opacity and failure were manifest most especially in Faulkner's representation of interracial love, a failure perhaps traceable to a relational and affective grammar of this emotion that he inherited and that, by the time he began to write, he had learned by heart.

By this I mean Faulkner drew repeatedly on preexisting discourses and Southern customs that sought to define and racialize emotion, as well as to dictate and codify what blacks and whites could/should/did feel for one another. Of course, Faulkner tried to unlearn this grammar that had historically structured the relation between race and emotion, but he was left, more often than not, to ponder whether or not, to borrow from George Kent, the "claims of love [could] ever supercede the Southern racial and aristocratic code"[6] that naturalized interracial sex but anathematized interracial love. Turning specifically to what he terms "the sexual commerce between black women and white men," Kent argues that such commerce "remained in an area tolerable to the white imagination as long as it did not include recognition of the black woman's personality

and interfere or threaten to interfere with white Anglo-Saxon domination" (Kent, 440). In other words, it was not *sex* between blacks and
whites that was so socially unsettling in the South; it was love. As Charles
Robinson explains, for example, "Until the Supreme Court struck down
the statutes in 1967, southern states prosecuted blacks and whites who
displayed genuine intimacy for one another. Interracial sex, however,
never became a casualty of the provision. In fact, anti-miscegenation
edicts actually encouraged those who dared to cross the sexual color line
to keep their relationships informal and strictly sexual. Benevolent acts
of kindness and affection subjected couples to legal penalties."[7]

"What Is This Thing Called Love?"

When Cole Porter titled his famous lyrics "What Is This Thing Called
Love?" he was simply posing for his time a question doggedly pursued for
centuries. My interest here is not in furthering that vain pursuit, nor in
reprising the philosophical distinctions among the kinds and categories of
love. My aim is much more modest: to examine how fervently Faulkner
chased the elusive question from the inchoate beginnings of his literary
career to its very end. From his very early cycle of poems in *Vision in
Spring*, to his early unpublished stories, including one titled "Love"—to
the major works on which his reputation rests, love or rather its absence,
as Judith Sensibar observes, is Faulkner's subject, particularly the nature
of sexual, of erotic love.[8]

I begin my exploration of Faulkner and the subject of love by turning
first to perhaps an unlikely source for such an examination, his 1950 Nobel
Prize Acceptance Speech. In this brief and rambling address, Faulkner
challenges future writers to leave "no room in [their] workshop for anything but the old verities and truths of the heart," the "old universal truths
lacking which any story is doomed."[9] Significantly, the first of the verities
Faulkner summons is "love." Here, as he would in other places, Faulkner
saw fit to distinguish love from lust, the heart from the glands. In the
course of this brief speech, he goes on to refer in various configurations
to the other "old verities": "honor and pity and pride and compassion and
sacrifice," followed by "courage and honor and hope." I have always been
struck by these proliferating abstractions, each linked or attached to each
through the repetition of that single conjunction, "and."

Alexander Welsh argues that these substantives are simply asserted
"to be 'truths,'" although Faulkner fails to form any "propositions about
them that could enable the audience to dispute the point."[10] We might
press Welsh's assertion still further. Perhaps Faulkner piled substantive

on substantive there in the Nobel Prize address, because he realized by this point in his career, his most significant work already behind him, that there *was* no proposition, certainly no single proposition to be formed about love or honor or courage or sacrifice, except at the meaningless level of abstraction, bloodless rhetorical ideal, or cultural piety. The abstractions that Faulkner treats as transparent, transcendent "givens" are, like sexuality, products of political, social, economic, and cultural processes and thus cannot be conceived apart from the means and modes of their inscription. In other words, Faulkner's universals are not universal; his eternal verities, not eternal; they are given meaning and substance only in time; they are by history and its discourses made.

I share with numerous theorists of emotion across the disciplinary spectrum the notion that emotions are not simply "personal" properties or feelings that one has inside, awaiting expression or enunciation, but are rather, much like sexuality, discursive and cultural constructs, as we have long been wont to say. It is difficult, then, to speak of love or any other emotion, without considering its construction or, shall we say, its "making." I am interested here, then, in "lovemaking" in the textual sense of the term, not so much in what love *is*, but rather in what it has been made to be and, further, how this making sweats, thwarts, ambiguates— and often censors—the matter of love across the color line.

I would argue that much of Faulkner's work is similarly invested less in defining love than in exploring its making but, more often, its unmaking. I am reminded here of Addie's much-quoted lines in *As I Lay Dying*: "Love, he called it . . . that word was like all the others: just a shape to fill a lack. . . . When the right time came, you wouldn't need a word for that anymore than for pride or fear." She goes on to say, "Sin and love and fear are just sounds that people who never sinned nor loved nor feared have for what they never had and cannot have until they forget the words."[11] But, as Hightower knows, there is no forgetting the words. As he remarks in *Light in August*, "Perhaps they were right in putting love into books. . . . Perhaps it could not live anywhere else."[12]

In light of the history that forms the foundation of Faulkner's fiction, it seems the better part of madness to propose that we talk not just about love but about interracial love; more specifically, about love between white men and black women. Let me meet immediately perhaps the most obvious objection, namely, how do we talk about love between the races within the context of intractable structures of violence, domination, and abuse? Within a legal context that historically prohibited its expression? Within a cultural and discursive context that has long appropriated the language of love for the purpose of sentimentalizing and rationalizing subjugation, particularly the subjugation of slavery?

In need of an ideology to justify slavery, slaveholders and apologists for slavery alike turned to the ideal of the sentimental family to represent the love that supposedly obtained between masters and slaves.[13] A passage from George Fitzhugh's *Cannibals All* provides but one example of what I mean: "Within the family circle, the law of love prevails, not that of selfishness. . . . Besides wife and children, brothers and sisters, dogs, horses, birds and flowers—slaves also belong to the family circle. . . . The interests of master and slave are bound up together and each in his appropriate sphere actually endeavors to promote the happiness of the other."[14] As many have observed, Fitzhugh's sentimental and paternalistic vision of the family as a "circle" where "the law of love prevails" supported the ideology of slavery as a benevolent institution and masked the inherent violence—especially the sexual violence—and domination of the system.[15] Countering such sentimentality and paternalism, they have documented the sexual abuses perpetrated against enslaved women. For example, Angela Davis argues that "there could hardly be a basis of 'delight, affection and love as long as white men, by virtue of their economic position, had unlimited access to Black women's bodies."[16] Countless scholars have extended Davis's argument, going so far as to insist that *all* sexual relationships between enslaved women and white men amounted to rape, largely because slavery denied these women property in their persons and, by extension, the rights of consent. For these reasons primarily, Jan Lewis rightly cautions us against "translat[ing] sex as love."[17]

Across the disciplines scholarship has so consistently denied that slavery and interracial love can be contemplated together that there seems little discursive space for even broaching the subject. While limited sources, to say nothing of the variable sociohistorical meanings of love, pose the most immediate and near insurmountable challenges to such a discussion, particularly within the context of slavery, ideology and the force of scholarly paradigms only compound the difficulty. In a compelling and nuanced article Adrienne Davis challenges this paradigm. Focusing on relationships between white male slaveholders and black enslaved women, she argues that the view we have inherited about these relations "leaves a monolithic and undeveloped rendering of both the relationships and the women." Moreover, it "fails to characterize and distinguish the multiplicity of forces, coercive devices, arrangements, and ideologies that the antebellum sexual economy made available to white men seeking interracial sex." She concludes that "analyses of miscegenation ought not devolve into flat attributions of total power and powerlessness to slaveholders and enslaved women, respectively."[18] Indeed, to deny outright and categorically that one of the effects of interracial intimacy could be love is to concede that three hundred years of history had no measurable effect on anything, which leads to an improbably static view of history. Though slavery must be and has been forcefully condemned, we should not underestimate the complexities that came of its duration, particularly in the realm of human relationships. We might heed Peter Parish's assertion that slavery must be understood in all its "contradictions and paradoxes," for it was a "growing, changing, mobile, flexible, and variable institution,"[19] which mobility and variation must surely have shaped and complicated the constellation of human affects and relations. The insistence that power asymmetries and forms of exploitation can only breed the "negative" emotions: hatred, anger, contempt, not compassion and love seems belied by even the fragmentary record of interracial relationships that have escaped the discurtive censors.

Going to Jefferson

Let me tip my hand and admit that my interest in how we might advance a conversation about love across the color line, especially as it pertains to black women and white men, stems from public responses to the 1998 revelations that, based on DNA testing, Thomas Jefferson very likely fathered at least one of Sally Hemings's six children. Not surprisingly, the revelation touched off a fierce debate—in both scholarly and popular arenas—and respondents were remarkably consistent in the question they raised: Did love have anything to do with the alleged relationship between Jefferson and Hemings? In "Sallygate," a *New York Times* Op-Ed piece, columnist William Safire put the question succinctly: "Was it lifelong love or heartless domination?"[20]

While the historian Fawn Brodie, the novelist Barbara Chase-Riboud, and generations of Hemings's descendants had long argued that Hemings and Jefferson enjoyed a love relationship, since the emergence of the DNA findings, this point of view has gained increasing force and credence, although diehard Jeffersonians persistently seek to discredit it. In her much-discussed and justly acclaimed book on the relationship between Jefferson and Hemings, Annette Gordon-Reed argues for a sustained love relationship.[21] Lucia Stanton and Diane Swann-Wright, codirectors of Monticello's African American Oral History Project, concur with Gordon-Reed that that there existed "a particularly strong oral tradition of a deep and abiding love between Jefferson and Hemings."[22]

Deep and abiding love? Drew Gilpin Faust answers "No," in thunder. Echoing a by-now familiar position, Faust counters: "In the context of American slavery," any "sexual liaisons between masters and slaves were almost certainly not romances, were in many cases rapes and were shaped by the woman's status as property."[23] Garry Wills classifies any relationship between Jefferson and Hemings as purely sexual and fully consistent with the practices of Jefferson's time. Men of Jefferson's era and station "use[d] prostitutes and use[d] women," he argues, but "there is no evidence he *cherished* her" (emphasis added).[24] In a more measured statement, historian Gordon Wood writes, "Even those historians willing to accept that Jefferson, like other Southern slaveholders, might have slept with his slaves have balked at the notion that Jefferson had a romantic and long-lasting love relationship with Hemings."[25] Perhaps Dan Jordan, director of the Thomas Jefferson Memorial Foundation, comes closest to a plausible conclusion about the Jefferson-Hemings affair: "whether it was love or just rape . . . no one knows and it's unlikely anyone will ever know."[26]

That we are unlikely to ever know what passed emotionally between Hemings and Jefferson, or whether theirs was a shared affection, does not prevent us from pondering the question. Moreover, it does not prevent us from asking just why, for many, particularly those fiercely invested in preserving in some pure, "unblemished" state Jefferson's status as "Founding Father," it seems an unthinkable proposition that Jefferson could have *loved*, or as Wills puts it, "cherished" Sally Hemings. Ultimately, this particular controversy goes beyond these two figures to strike at the heart, if you will, of cultural assumptions about emotion, in general, which assumptions have been historically vectored through ideologies and theories of racial difference. Thomas Jefferson contributed his own share to this controversial archive.

Jefferson's famous statement about blacks and love in Query 14 of *Notes on the State of Virginia* bears remembering here. There he mentions "that immoveable veil of black" (a reference to black skin perhaps) that "covers all the emotions of the other race." Then, turning specifically to the subject of blacks and love, he writes, "They are more ardent after their female, but love seems with them to be more an eager desire than a tender delicate mixture of sentiment and sensation."[27] As he progresses through this query, Jefferson goes on to qualify this assertion, but, in the end, he commits himself staunchly to establishing racial difference on the ground of emotional constitution and capacity. Because such capacities were qualifications for virtuous citizenship in the early Republic, not surprisingly blacks' supposed "incapacity to *feel* properly," notes Peter Coviello, placed them outside the bounds of citizenship. Jefferson's problem with blacks, Coviello adds, "is not exactly that they cannot feel, but that they do not feel with the proper proportion, regulation or intensity. Africans in America, he claims, do not love like the whites; they do not feel attachment like the whites . . . they do not suffer bereavement like . . . whites."[28]

I should rush to concede here that Jefferson's ideas about the comparative inadequacy of African Americans' emotional capacities cannot be easily mapped onto William Faulkner, not least because slavery and Jim Crow were worlds apart, but the writings of both men provide particularly stunning examples of the degree to which their ideas about racial difference were largely articulated through the language and rhetoric of emotion. Faulkner clearly inherited a discourse that racialized epistemologies of emotion, although he wrestled with the salient assumptions of that inheritance: Did blacks exhibit a greater capacity than whites for feeling and attachment, or were they, as Jefferson claimed, possessed of limited capacities to feel?

In the famous exchange between Ike McCaslin and his cousin, McCaslin Edmonds, in *Go Down, Moses* Faulkner stages this very debate. Ike echoes the sentimental canards of romantic racialism in his theory that Negroes are "better than we are. Stronger than we are." Their virtues are "pity and tolerance and forbearance and fidelity, and love of children." McCaslin counters that blacks are given to "Promiscuity. Violence. Instability and lack of control," but more, the very emotional virtues that Ike attributes to blacks, are, to McCaslin, no more, no less than can be found in mules and dogs (282). The deputy in "Pantaloon in Black," falls on McCaslin's side of the ledger in declaring, "When it comes to the normal human feelings and sentiments of human beings, [Negroes] might just as well be a damn herd of wild buffaloes" (149, 150).

As many have argued, "Pantaloon in Black" is a brilliant study in the misreading of emotion, specifically the misapprehension of grief. The deputy assumes that Rider does not show signs of grief at the passing of his wife: "His wife dies on him. All right. But does he grieve? He's the biggest and busiest man at the funeral. Grabs a shovel before they even got the box into the grave . . . and starts throwing dirt onto her faster than a slip scraper could have done it" (150). That the "effortless fury" with which Rider flings the dirt on the mound might be read as a sign of acute grief simply never occurs to the deputy. Rider's grief is no more readable to the deputy than are the "shards of pottery and broken bottles" (132) that surround Mannie's grave. I agree with John Limon that, in "Pantaloon," Faulkner "invites us to join an interpretive community on the model of Yoknapatawpha County. This Southern community, he continues, "cannot make sense of Rider (or all too easily makes of him its own kind of sense)."29

At least here in "Pantaloon" Faulkner demonstrates a profound understanding of the ways in which the deputy's reading of Rider's grief and, by extension, the broader landscape of his emotional life and disposition is but the product of a discourse that had historically explained, classified, and exiled blacks from the domain of the human, based on misunderstandings of how they feel (or don't feel, for that matter). Faulkner makes clear that the intensity of Rider's grief is inextricably connected to the intensity of his love for Mannie, which expression symbolizes his full personhood, but these are the signs "no white man could have read" (132). As this passage suggests, Faulkner roots that unreadability in assumptions about racial difference, assumptions that, at least in this case, grant to blacks the greater capacity for feeling, even if that feeling is misrecognized.

Loving Black Women

While, in "Pantaloon," Faulkner can imagine a love relationship between a black man and a black woman, he struggled to imagine such a relationship either between black men and white women or between white men and black women. The former configuration of cross racial relationships has received more than its share of discussion, especially as it has been historically presumed to be more socially transgressive. While relationships between white men and black women are presumably less so, I agree with Adrienne Davis that these unions provide perhaps the "greatest insight into racial fissures within southern ideology."[30]

How would we/how could we begin a discussion of the affective components of interracial relationships in Faulkner, with a particular emphasis on black women and white men? The challenges of such a task are readily apparent, Leslie Fiedler emphasizes, not least because of Faulkner's much-noted "dis-ease with sexuality."[31] As Irving Howe has written, "[S]o persistent [was] Faulkner's distaste for the doings of 'woman-flesh'" that he could treat with respect only those characters "beyond the age of sexual distraction."[32] Of course, Caroline Barr was such a woman. As numerous scholars have suggested, Faulkner's most profound sense of interracial love derived from his relationship with this woman whom he called "Mammy Callie," to whom he dedicated *Go Down, Moses*. In his eulogy, he praised her as "a fount of active and constant affection and love" and saw her "fidelity to a family which was not hers, devotion and love for people she had not borne."[33]

While Faulkner could sentimentalize his relationship with Callie Barr, drawing on the "family circle" rhetoric much beloved by advocates of slavery, he is at a loss to imagine how to represent those black women in whom the "magical powers of sexuality" are still alive. These women, literal and potential love objects, figure in Faulkner's writings as the parentheses of syntax, as the margins of narrative, where they exist mainly as "nameless, illicit hybrid female flesh" (GDM 289). This passage, from the dense and clotted fourth section of "The Bear," introduces us to Uncle Hubert's so-called cook, whose status as "cook" is belied by her appearance in a silk gown and glinting earrings. That the gown she wears belongs to Ike's mother, Sophonsiba, and is brazenly donned in *her* mother's house, pretentiously named Warwick, compounds the outrage. The woman's attire evokes for Ike, who recalls the scene in flashes and fragments, something "tawdry and illicit" yet "breathless and exciting." When his mother drives "the nameless face" from the house, Ike watches her "hurrying down the lane," the "once-hooped dress ballooning and flopping below a man's overcoat" (290).

The "overcoat" here functions not merely as an article of clothing, but also as an example of the vocabulary of euphemisms that have historically cloaked or "coated" over, if you will, the actualities of interracial sex. If only through her clothing, the black woman impersonates the white woman here, which impersonation is presumably the gateway to and precondition for any possible role as love object, but Sophonsiba, as the culture's agent, emblem, and carrier of Southern tradition, has the power not only to annul that possibility, but in so doing, to deny the nameless woman a place in the "citadel of respectability."

Of course, this turn of events is by now familiar, restaging as it does the central tropes in discourses of Southern "womanhood," from which construct black women have been historically excluded. "Respectability," Southern women's crowning virtue, is synonymous with their sexual virtue, which black women allegedly (and inherently) lacked. The black women who crop up in Faulkner's corpus (Joe Christmas's Northern ebony woman and the unnamed, gang-raped girl in *Light in August*, the "doe" in "Delta Autumn"), figure as sex objects blurring into each other, their very sexuality, evidence of their disgrace and moral dereliction. In gossiping about Hightower's female "cook" in *Light in August*, who quits because he allegedly "ask[ed] her to do something which she said was against God and nature," some of the younger townsmen quip, "If a nigger woman considered it against God and nature, it must be pretty bad" (66). Here, we confront the limits of the discourses surrounding interracial relationships, the limits of gossip, of slander, of epithets, of conjecture. Perhaps "love" resides only in that space between hearsay (the community) and the inner private spaces to which the community has no access.

If the black woman as possible love object has been banished from the house (or certainly from the domain of cultural respectability), as well as exiled from the bounds of narrative proper, the forbidden desire she represents reemerges, like the return of the repressed, to haunt Ike McCaslin's story as it unfolds in *Go Down, Moses*. In other words, while there are spaces the black woman cannot enter or inhabit (at least not to stay), there are simultaneously spaces she cannot leave (or spaces that cannot leave her). The black woman's comings and goings into the so-called sacred spaces of white patriarchy, even disgraced white patriarchy, as well as its privileged discursive domains, constitute among the most resonant passages of this book, the scenes in the commissary most especially. Here, she appears in Ike's first attempt to decipher the ledgers' fading entries, written in the near illegible and alternating hands of his father and uncle.

I agree with David Wyatt that "The Bear" is about "the epistemology and morality of reading, for which hunting is his ambitious and complex analogy."[34] I would add that it is also about the limits and morality of storytelling. There in the commissary Ike is attempting to decipher just what Eunice, the slave woman, meant to his grandfather, Old Carothers. In the famous passage, from which I borrowed the title and epigraph, Ike begins, *"So I reckon that was cheaper than saying My son to a nigger he thought. Even if my son wasn't but just two words. But there must have been love he thought. Some sort of love. Even what he would have called love: not just an afternoon's or a night's spittoon"* (258).[35] Here, Ike's speculations about the nature of his grandfather's relationship to Eunice evoke Addie's "shape to fill a lack," a lack in his knowledge of what they actually meant to each other. The point of his failed attempts at knowing is perhaps to emphasize how elusive is the definition of love, especially when one is trying to grasp its meanings, to trace its beginnings and burgeonings from a ledger clearly misnamed "Allknowledgeable." Ike attempts nonetheless to fill a historical gap, to *make* love, if you will, engaging in a form of retroactive affective reparations. But this process is not as easy as it might appear. Each of the component phrases of Ike's halting, uncertain utterance—"must have been," "some sort," "what he would call"—appears affirmative without actually being so. That his phrasing is halting and bespeaks uncertainty is inevitable, for the entries in the ledger that Ike struggles to decipher have been written by his slaveholding ancestors. Relying on their records for signs and documentation of interracial affection is useless, not least because each in his own way has denied, discounted, and made a mockery of Eunice's feelings.

While recording Eunice's suicide, Ike's uncles ridicule its very possibility: *"Who in hell ever heard of a niger drownding himself"* (256). Ike's repetitive questions—"But why? But why?"—implicitly grant to Eunice an interior life that might explain her suicide, but because the details of her life are so sketchy, he must create for her (as well as his grandfather) a narrative, a feeling life, from the fragments of the ledger. His narrative—a blend of fact and fiction, freighted with the terms and tones of compassion—imagines not just why she might have commited suicide, but also how she did it. Indeed, he focuses more on the how than the why: "He seemed to see her actually walking into the icy creek on that Christmas day six months before her daughter's and her lover's (*Her first lover's*, he thought. *Her first*) child was born, solitary, inflexible, griefless, ceremonial, in formal and succinct repudiation of grief and despair who had already had to repudiate belief and hope" (259).

Even as Ike seeks to construct for Eunice an emotional life missing from the ledgers, he ultimately and ironically circumscribes it. While he can later judge and condemn his grandfather, "this unregenerate old man who could summon, because she was his property, a human being because she was old enough and female, to his widower's house and get a child on her and then dismiss her because she was of an inferior race" (281), he can only imagine Eunice as "griefless." And in failing to imagine Eunice's grief, in casting her as "formal" and "inflexible," he diminishes her pain and suffering. Further, he fails to imagine the possibility of her love, even for this "unregenerate old man." At least here in "Go Down, Moses," Ike anticipates the man he will become in "Delta Autumn," a version of this "unregenerate old man," recapitulating not just the failure to acknowledge the possibility interracial affection, but the possibility of love.

It is tempting to read "Delta Autumn" as an answer to Ike's quandary there in the commissary, to see in the relationship between Roth and the "doe" the belated confirmation of interracial love that Ike was seeking in the yellowed pages of the ledger. It is further tempting to see this later generation fulfilling, even in the Jim Crow South, the interracial love that the law of slavery perverted in turning persons into property, into the objects of exchange. But ultimately "Delta Autumn" denies the reader such a progressivist interpretation, and in that denial illuminates Faulkner's ambivalence about the forms of interracial loving that could not be simply sentimentalized or stereotyped.

The relationship between Roth and his unnamed cousin is the veritable reenactment of that between Carothers and Eunice, right down to Roth's attempt to mediate his passion for the "doe" in monetary terms. Carothers's original $1,000 bequest to his and Eunice's son, which Ike likens to a "cast-off hat or a pair of shoes" (258) becomes Roth Edmonds's sealed envelope containing a "neat sheaf of bound notes" (341). But perhaps more telling than these obvious parallels is the fact that Ike becomes the broker, delivering to his distant kin a new iteration of history's script: she is for Roth effectively the "night's spittoon," who can be discarded and their offspring disowned.

Thadious Davis argues that, because Eunice's descendant "is complicit in Roth's sexual use of her body," she is thus "not finally a victim of his will."[36] In this sense, she recalls Harriet Jacobs, who stoutly claims "It seems less degrading to give one's self than to submit to compulsion.

There is something akin to freedom in having a lover who has no control over you."[37] Indeed, Roth controls neither the body nor the affective life of this distant cousin with whom he begets a child. The story of the affective lives of her female ancestors has been erased from the historical record, suppressed by her male kin, who can only record this story in the fragmentary, elliptical language of the ledger.

Erik Dussere terms theirs the language of accounting and numerical worth, a language, he argues, "ill suited to the work of representing and understanding the enormous complexity of history." But more, it amounts to a "reductive and amoral form of narrative," the inadequacy of which Faulkner establishes by setting it in counterpoint to the baroque articulations in the fourth section of "The Bear."[38] But Faulkner's aim seems not merely to set the "ledger's poetic brevity" against the "language of excess" (Dussere, 337), but to restore to the complex history of slavery and its legacies the language of the heart. In contrast to Roth's male ancestors, "the doe" is left to articulate and lend dimension to this language of the heart.

Eunice's descendant, from the black McCaslin line, is alone allowed to speak the language of love, which Faulkner sets against the vague locutions and interrupted phrasings assigned to Ike and his cousin, Cass: "here," "nothing," "this," "that," and then the sting of "You're a nigger" (344). But her brief cameo-like appearance in this scene fills in the gaps of a story of incest and betrayal, on the one side, and love, on the other. She describes the six-week interval in New Mexico, where "[she] cooked for him and looked after his clothes" (GDM), with no expectation of marriage, for she understood the McCaslin code "would forbid him forever to do" (342). When Ike urges her to "Go back North. Marry a man in [her] own race" (346), she voices that famous resounding passage: "Old man . . . have you lived so long and forgotten so much that you don't remember anything you ever knew or felt or even heard about love?" (346). There is no doubt that she is the story's emotional and moral center, that she represents an expression of emotion of which Ike and his white male ancestors are incapable, an expression moreover, that lies outside the ideological scripts of history. Undoubtedly, her relationship with Roth conforms to the sexual and racial codes of the antebellum economy that made black women's bodies readily available for white-male consumption, but she views that relationship in terms that this code can neither capture nor control. In explaining her decision to travel back to the Delta in hopes of reuniting with Roth, she importantly distinguishes between "believ[ing] him" (presumably as concerns the nature of their relationship) and "listening to" and "believ[ing] [herself]" (342). Despite his talk of "code" and "honor," what she feels for/about Roth is not bound by a discursive history that would cast her solely as the victim of rape and concubinage, nor one that would bind her to the empty, meaningless symbolism of Southern honor.

Here in "Delta Autumn," Faulkner seems implicitly critical of this Southern legacy in which interracial sex was sanctioned and interracial love denied except in its most sexless, sentimental forms. If he could only visualize interracial relationships as being situated in dishonorable places, on the outskirts of the emotional landscape, cast out and abjected like the unnamed "cook" and the "doe," it was because "the curse of his fathers . . . descended to him" (*Go Down, Moses*, 11), and, like Edmonds and the other white men of his imagining, he ultimately, "entered that heritage [and] ate its bitter fruit" (110).

The Truths of the Human Heart

Somehow Faulkner seemed to know that it would fall to a later generation of writers, those to whom he alluded in the Nobel Prize Address, to confront the difficult, yet necessary work, of representing the "old verities and truths of the heart," most importantly, love. It is significant that, although love comes first in Faulkner's list of the "old verities," when he next refers to them, there in the same address, love has fallen away and only "courage and honor and hope and pride and compassion and pity and sacrifice" remain (Nobel Address, 120). It could be argued that love is always gradually disappearing in Faulkner's oeuvre—from Ike's initial modifications ("must have been," "some sort of love," "his idea of love") to his inability to remember love in his old age. It is perhaps a testimony to Faulkner's understanding of the specific complexity (and exceptionality) of interracial love in the narratives of his generation that he chose to represent it as not fully formed, as if the plentitude of love in that domain lay not in its full actualization, but in unfinished form. We now know that Faulkner was prophetic, for Toni Morrison was among a host of writers who would go on to stand, decades later, where Faulkner stood in 1951 to receive the Nobel Prize.

Comparisons are often drawn between these two titanic writers, and some critics even argue that, in the literary sphere, Morrison is Faulkner's lineal descendant. It may come as a surprise for some that, at least as regards the subject of interracial affections, Morrison shares more with Faulkner than might readily be supposed. In her second novel, *Sula*, for instance, the title character is condemned for being "guilty of the unforgivable thing—the thing for which there was no understanding, no excuse, no compassion. The route from which there was no way back, the dirt that could not ever be washed away. They said that Sula slept with white men," which rumor "filled [the townspeople] with choking disgust.

There was nothing lower she could do, nothing filthier. . . . They insisted that all unions between white men and black women be rape; for a black woman to be willing was literally unthinkable."[39] This attitude toward interracial union is reiterated in *Tar Baby*, in which Son tells Jadine, "White folks and black folk should not . . . eat together or live together or sleep together. Do any of these personal things in life."[40] Of course, one should not assume that such views accord with Morrison's but, at least in these novels interracial relationships are no more representable (or "presentable") than they are Faulkner.

Throughout the 1970s and '80s, as black American women writers turned more and more frequently to what has come to be called "the neo-slave narrative," they revisited the history of slavery in fiction, particularly the thematic taboo of interracial love. But perhaps more than the representation of interracial love, sexual and otherwise, that we find in such works as Octavia Butler's *Kindred*, Shirley Anne Williams's *Dessa Rose*, and Gayl Jones's *Corregidora*, is the effort to confront the social construction of desire, along with its troubling intersection with abuse and exploitation.[41] Gayl Jones provides one of the most insightful explorations of the complexities of interracial relationships during slavery as well as their destructive historical legacies.

Early reviewers of *Corregidora* often pointed to the novel's Faulknerian themes and overtones, and critics ever since have delineated the parallels between the two writers.[42] It could be argued that Ursa Corregidora is Ike McCaslin's counterpart in questioning the nature of affective relations between a slave-owning male ancestor and his female captive. But whereas Ike's questions lead to speculation that "there must have been love," Ursa's question opens more broadly onto the complexities of emotion, in general, onto the ambivalence, the fluctuation, the fluidity of feelings, including those that may have obtained between slave masters and enslaved women.

The question Ursa seeks to answer is left stranded in the narrative's inquiry: "What is it a woman can do to a man that make him hate her so bad he wont to kill her one minute and keep thinking about her and can't get her out of his mind the next?"[43] She concludes that "It had to be sexual . . . it had to be something sexual that Great Gram did to Corregidora. . . . In a split second . . . of hate and love I knew what it was. . . . A moment of pleasure and excruciating pain at the same time" (184).

Significantly, like Faulkner's "doe," Great Gram is no mere victim here: she *does* something to Corregidora; she acts. In attempting to make sense of her great-grandmother's mysterious act, Ursa approaches an understanding of the complex character of emotional expression and its effects. It is significant that both "hate and love," "pleasure and excruciating pain" are conjoined in her conjecture about just what Great Gram did to the man who held her chattel. And hate and love are conjoined when Martin puts the impossible question to Ursa's mother: "How much was hate for Corregidora and how much was love" (131)? Instead of offering answers to this question about an experience to which she has no access, Ursa provides broader commentary on the nature and character of emotion. Such seeming antitheses and contradictions (hate versus love) enable us to understand how Corregidora could be slave master and lover, how Great Gram could be lover and enslaved, how an institution defined by physical brutality, sexual abuse, and domination could also generate possible affections between the races. Jones might thus agree with Freud, to take but one example, that "almost every intimate emotional relation between two people which lasts for some time . . . contains a sediment of feelings of aversion and hostility."[44] That we are not commonly inclined to make such allowances, owes greatly to the power of emotional patterns, which, the novel, suggests, are taught and learned.

Early in the novel, Ursa is asked, "How were you *really* taught to feel about [Corregidora]?" "How I told you," I said, "angry." She then follows with "Maybe I should ask you how you were taught to feel" (113). The emphasis here on being taught to feel raises implicit questions about whether that teaching took, about whether the anger passed down from Great Gram to her female descendants was all there was to "know," or all there was to learn, all that was absorbed, all that was "teachable" about feeling, whether hers or theirs. Ursa must not only learn to distinguish between "knowing" Great Gram's teachings and "feeling[s] of her own" (103), she must know (and feel) the ways in which "hate and desire [are] two humps on the same camel" (102). In other words, she must feel and understand, to borrow from Faulkner here, "the human heart in conflict with itself."

Jones takes up Faulkner's challenge to expose and explore these conflicts and, like him, she concedes to the limits of "knowing" whether and to what extent love could exist in slavery across the color line. She takes the more interesting course of exploring why such affection became unspeakable to those on both sides of that line and how history's emotional patterns were learned and thus might be unlearned.

Conclusion

While Faulkner offered his advice to future writers, some of whom, like Jones, accepted his challenge, it is perhaps in the realm of the visual arts that slavery's complex legacies have been perhaps most explosively and controversially explored. Kara Walker comes most immediately to mind.

Walker is a black female artist famous for her black paper cutout silhouettes in which she satirizes and vexes the primness of the form itself as
well as our notions regarding interracial intimacies and intergenerational
relationships during the Civil War era. In her image are two figures in
profile that bear much resemblance to one another. On the right side
is a sculpture of Thomas Jefferson, whose profile will remain instantly
recognizable to me for how strangely ubiquitous his image seems to be
at the University of Virginia, where I teach. On the left side of the Walker
silhouette, at first appears to a *prima facie* iconographic figure of a white
man. A close look shows what Darby English describes as a "female black
'primitive' standing back to back with him [with her] 'natural' hair, grossly
exaggerated and parted lips, West African neck extension rings, naked
breasts, and a short wavy skirt of wide bands."[45] This optical illusion not
only has us seeing double, but for many it may also have us seeing red for
the ways in which it could be said to stoke flames of anger by reminding
us of the forbidden emotions of desire and love, which would have made
such attachments possible in the first place.

As English argues, by exploiting what Mary Anne Doane has called
the "representational intensity" of miscegenation to comment on the
much-debated recent speculations about the consorting with female
slaves imputed to the "fathers of our country," the Walker silhouette
"first models and then mocks a widespread habit of [showing regard for]
these men." Relegated to the background or his backside as if secreted
away and consequently left behind, the black woman does not so much
participate in or partake of the respectability and regard that the man
warrants as she challenges it and begins to redefine it. His respectability
can be predicated on his acknowledgment of her. Her parted lips stand
ready to articulate her worth and presence.

I want to conclude by putting some pressure on an interesting observation that English's fine analysis ultimately fails to exploit. According
to English, "The impetus behind [an *amalgamated* cameo such as the
silhouette you see before you] was sentimental: it commemorated and
was thought to immortalize a pair's willing linkage to one another, and
to whatever noble institution their relation participated in" (emphasis
added). It seems to me that the place where love is made and can be
found is in the amalgamation, a point Annette Gordon-Reed makes in
The Hemingses of Monticello. There, she challenges those who perpetuate the familiar argument that "blacks and whites can have sex and
produce children (a basic, biological function) but they can never experience together higher-order emotional responses; they can never love
each other."[46] Such arguments, she continues, leave "no room for the
feelings, obsessions, and strategies of females" (313). Not just in this

book, but also in her *Thomas Jefferson and Sally Hemings: An American Controversy*, Gordon-Reed does not equivocate. She replaces Ike's "must have been" with her assertion that there *was* an intimate relationship between Jefferson and Hemings. Ike's choice of tense constitutes the violence of discursive suppression, which masked the sexual politics of white supremacy. Unlike Ike, Cass Edmonds, and Faulkner's other descendants of the planter class, the black women artists who came after Faulkner have elected not to "enter [*their*] heritage," at least not *in toto*. They have sought instead to quarrel with that heritage, particularly with the affective grammar and patterns it sought to inscribe and legislate. In so doing, they have given themselves both the right and permission to narrate anew the strange and unstable meanings of sex and love cross the color line.

NOTES

1. William Faulkner, *Go Down, Moses* (New York: Random House, 1940), 258. Subsequent references are cited parenthetically in the text.

2. George E. Kent, "The Black Women in Faulkner's Works," *Phylon* 35.4 (1974): 433.

3. See "Many Thousands Gone," in James Baldwin, *The Price of the Ticket: Collected Nonfiction, 1948–1985* (New York: St. Martin's Press, 1985), 77.

4. Peter Coviello, *Intimacy in America: Dreams of Affiliation in Antebellum Literature* (Minneapolis: University of Minnesota Press, 2005), 143.

5. *Vision in Spring* (Austin: University of Texas Press, 1984), 24.

6. Although Kent is writing specifically about "Delta Autumn" here, his assessment can be applied to Faulkner's writings in general. See "The Black Women in Faulkner's Works," 438.

7. "Anti-Miscegenation Law and Southern White Rhetoric," in Ted Ownby, ed., *Manners and Southern History* (Jackson: University Press of Mississippi, 2007), 110. See also Mary Frances Berry, "Judging Morality: Sexual Behavior and Legal Consequences in the Late Nineteenth-Century South," *Journal of American History* 78 (December 1991): 835–56, as well as Patricia Morton, ed., *Discovering the Women in Slavery* (Athens: University of Georgia Press, 1996). In the introduction to the volume Morton writes, "the racist taboo against miscegenation was fundamentally against those interracial sexual relationships that, because based on love and desire rather than on force, inherently challenged the integrally related sexual and racial controls of slavery and racism (15).

8. See Judith Sensibar, *Faulkner and Love: The Women Who Shaped His Art* (New Haven: Yale University Press, 2009).

9. "Address upon Receiving the Nobel Prize for Literature," in James B. Meriwether, ed., *William Faulkner: Essays, Speeches, and Public Letters* (New York: Random House, 1965), 120.

10. "On the Difference between Prevailing and Enduring," in Michael Millgate, *New Essays on "Light in August"* (Cambridge: Cambridge University Press, 1987), 138.

11. William Faulkner, *As I Lay Dying* (1930; New York: Random House, 1964), 164, 165.

12. William Faulkner, *Light in August* (1932; New York: Random House, 1959), 456.

13. See Jan Lewis, "Commentary," in Winthrop Jordan, ed., *Slavery and the American South* (Oxford: University Press of Mississippi, 2003), 113. Dawn Davis argues similarly that "love is the basis for a benevolent rhetoric of the West dutifully marching alongside the imperialist project and justifying its systems of information gathering and domination—the ideological foundation for moral and economic salvation." See "(Love is) the ability of not knowing: Feminist experience of the impossible in ethical singularity" *Hypatia* 17.2 (Spring 2002): 145

14. George Fitzhugh, *Cannibals All or Slaves without Masters*, ed. C. Vann Woodward (Cambridge: Harvard University Press, 1960), 205.

15. Here the tradition of "domestic workers" in and out of fiction also comes to mind. Many a novel or play has been written about the loyalty and devotion of the servant who is supposedly treated "like one of the family." Such sentimental language masks the low wages, the degrading and unfair labor practices suffered by the house worker, who is the veritable equivalent of a bound servant.

16. Angela Y. Davis, *Women, Race, and Class* (New York: Random House, 1983), 26.

17. Lewis, "Commentary," 115. Diane Miller Somerville concurs with Lewis. In "Moonlight, Magnolias, and Brigadoon; or 'Almost Like Being in Love': Masters and Sexual Exploitation in Eugene D. Genovese's Plantation South," Somerville discusses Genovese's *Roll, Jordan, Roll: The World the Slaves Made*, arguing that "Genovese crafts a discussion of the sexual abuse of slave females that at once minimized suffering and brutality or coerced sex between master and slave." She charges Genovese with euphemizing "the sex act between master and slave" and with suggesting that "sexual relations between master and slave were general consensual, innocuous." See *Radical History Review* 88 (2004): 70.

18. Adrienne D. Davis, "The Private Law of Race and Sex: An Antebellum Perspective," *Stanford Law Review* 51.2 (January 1999): 230, 227.

19. Peter Parish, *Slavery: History and Historians* (New York: Harper and Row, 1989), 3, 4.

20. William Safire, *New York Times*, 2 November 1998, A27.

21. Annette Gordon-Reed, *Thomas Jefferson and Sally Hemings: An American Controversy* (Charlottesville: University Press of Virginia, 1997).

22. Lucia Stanton and Diane Swann-Wright, "Bonds of Memory: Identity and the Hemings Family," in Jan Ellen Lewis and Peter Onuf, eds., *Sally Hemings and Thomas Jefferson: History, Memory, and Civic Culture* (Charlottesville, University Press of Virginia, 1999), 176.

23. Drew Gilpin Faust, *New York Times*, 9 November 1998, A28.

24. Garry Wills, *New York Times*, 7 November 1998, A17.

25. Gordon Wood, *New York Review of Books*, 44.10 (12 June 1997). Andrew Burstein is so intent on denying that a loving relationship could have existed between Jefferson and Hemings that he explains Jefferson's sexual appetite in exclusively medical terms, arguing that Jefferson engaged in sex for therapeutic reasons, solely for the benefits of health. See *Jefferson's Secrets: Death and Desire at Monticello* (New York: Basic Books, 2005).

26. Dan Jordan, *New York Times*, 11 February 2000, B29.

27. *Notes on the State of Virginia*, in *Jefferson's Political Writings*, ed. Joyce Appleby and Terrence Ball (Cambridge: Cambridge University Press, 1999), 416. Of this passage, Annette Gordon-Reed supposes that Jefferson's reference here could amount to a complaint that he could never know or access what blacks were "really thinking and feeling." See *The Hemingses of Monticello* (New York: W. W. Norton, 2008), 288. Well over a century ago, William Dean Howells makes a similar point in an essay praising Booker T. Washington as "an exemplary citizen." Part of what made Washington exemplary, Howells suggests, was his "proud tenderness," his "loving loyalty to family and race." Howells goes on to second-guess

that assessment, however, by posing the question, "What if upon some large scale [blacks] should be subtler than we have supposed? What if their amiability should veil a sense of our absurdities, and there should be in our polite inferiors the potentiality of something like contempt for us." See "An Exemplary Citizen," *North American Review*, 173:2 (August 1901): 281, 284.

28. Peter Coviello, "Agonizing Affection: Affect and Nation in Early America," *Early American Literature* 37.3 (2002): 448.

29. John Limon, "The Integration of Faulkner's *Go Down, Moses*," *Critical Inquiry* 12.2 (Winter 1986): 425.

30. Adrienne Y. Davis, 228. I should note here that in her consideration of interracial liaisons, Davis's primary objective is to pursue the economic and material consequences of these relationships, particularly as they are manifested in postmortem transfers of wealth. She is not inclined to approach such transfers as "romantic ruptures in the racist fabric of southern enslavement," even as she concedes that degrees of interracial affection could have existed (226).

31. Leslie Fiedler, "Appendix I: Notes and Comments," in Robert Penn Warren, ed., *Faulkner: A Collection of Critical Essays* (New Jersey: Prentice-Hall, 1966), 284.

32. Irving Howe, "Appendix I: Notes and Comments," in Robert Penn Warren, ed., *Faulkner: A Collection of Critical Essays* (New Jersey: Prentice-Hall, 1966), 284.

33. "Funeral Sermon for Manny Caroline Barr," in *William Faulkner: Essays, Speeches, and Public Letters*, 117.

34. David Wyatt, "Faulkner and the Reading Self," in Donald Kartiganer and Ann J. Abadie, eds., *Faulkner and Psychology* (Jackson: University Press of Mississippi,1994), 280.

35. The reference to "spittoon" here calls to mind a similar reference to "spit cup," in Zora Neale Huston's *Their Eyes Were Watching God*, a text that also recounts the history of sexual violation in its basest, most scatological terms. When Nanny says to Janie that she does not want men making a spit cup out of her body, she means, that she doesn't want them to use her body as a receptacle into which they can empty the spill of their lust.

36. *Games of Property: Law, Race, Gender, and Faulkner's "Go Down, Moses"* (Durham: Duke University Press, 2003), 175.

37. *Incidents in the Life of Slave Girl*, ed. Jean Fagan Yellin (Cambridge: Harvard University Press, 1987), 55.

38. See "Accounting for Slavery: Economic Narratives in Morrison and Faulkner," *Modern Fiction Studies* 47.2 (Summer 2001): 336, 337.

39. Toni Morrison, *Sula* (New York: Knopf, 1973), 112, 113.

40. Toni Morrison, *Tar Baby* (New York: Knopf, 1981), 210.

41. The poetry and essays of Alice Walker should be added to the discussion of works by African American women that strive for a more complex treatment of race and emotion in the 1970s and '80s. In "The Black Writer and the Southern Experience," for example, Walker writes, "No one could wish for a more advantageous heritage than that bequeathed to the black writer in the South. . . . We inherit a great responsibility as well, for we must give voice to centuries not only of silent bitterness and hate but also of neighborly kindness and sustaining love." See *In Search of Our Mother's Gardens* (New York: Harcourt, 21).

42. See Casey Claybaugh, "Toward an All-Inclusive Structure: The Early Fiction of Gayl Jones," *Callaloo* 29.2 (Spring 2006): 634–57.

43. Gayl Jones, *Corregidora* (1975; Boston: Beacon Press, 1988), 173.

44. Sigmund Freud, *Group Psychology and the Analysis of the Ego* (1921; New York: W. W. Norton, 1959), 41–42.

45. Darby English, "This Is Not about the Past: Silhouettes in the Work of Kara Walker," in *Kara Walker: Narratives of a Negress*, ed. Ian Berry, Darby English, Vivian Patterson, and Mark Reinhardt (Cambridge: MIT Press, 2003), 156.

46. *The Hemings of Monticello* (New York: W. W. Norton, 2008), 367.

All Mixed Up:
Female Sexuality and Race in
The Sound and the Fury

Kristin Fujie

This paper is part of a larger project that explores the interrelationship of gender and race in a selection of William Faulkner's novels from *Soldiers' Pay* (1926) through *Absalom, Absalom!* (1936). My reevaluation of Faulkner's career proposes that the author's turn toward the issue of miscegenation in the thirties should be understood not as a moment of division, as Eric Sundquist has powerfully argued,[1] but of transformation, when race explodes within an established landscape of sexual anxiety that takes the female body as its troubled matrix. The motivation for this project has come from my repeated encounter with passages in Faulkner's novels in which racial and sexual panic, black bodies and female bodies, seem strangely, even perversely, conflated. We see this in the grammatical aberration of the "womanshenegro" thrown up by the crucible of Joe Christmas's mind,[2] and in the haunting vision that Rosa Coldfield gives us of black and white bodies "twin sistered" to one another by an umbilical cord.[3] We see it as well in the intertextual confusion that arises between the image of Temple Drake "watch[ing] something black and furious go roaring out of her pale body,"[4] and the image of Joe Christmas's "black blood . . . rush[ing] out of his pale body" (465). In these moments, issues of gender and issues of race emerge, to borrow a phrase from the Quentin Compson of *The Sound and the Fury*, "all mixed up,"[5] speaking through and over one another in ways that defy explanation in their immediate contexts, and yet, like that "fierce rigid umbilical cord" that forces itself upon Rosa's consciousness, seem to expose interdependencies that are not only tortured, but also intimate, fundamental and abiding (112).

It is not surprising that criticism on gender and on race in Faulkner's writings has tended to focus primarily on one issue or the other.[6] As Deborah Clarke argues in her reading of the mother in Faulkner, the author himself exhibits "deep uneasiness with the combination of racial and sexual otherness, a possibility too threatening and too foreign for him to contemplate."[7] His career might be read as an extended negotiation

of the conflicting urges to confront and to repress this, the most threatening combination of threats. If we look at *As I Lay Dying* (1930), for
example, we can see that if the structure of the novel is, like Addie's own
coffin, carefully calculated to contain the maternal body going to pieces
within it, it also seems calculated to exclude; the precise economy of the
text's chapters coincides with a near absence of race as an active element, a feature which only merits attention given the intense build-up of
racial anxiety in the novels immediately surrounding it.[8] These combined
strategies of control and exclusion seem to have provided the necessary
conditions for Faulkner to articulate for the first, and perhaps only, time
in his career a psychologically complex and coherent maternal subject,
as though it were only by sealing the mother within the walls of a coffin "tight as a drum and neat as a sewing basket,"[9] that he could let her
"speak" her despair and her bitterness toward patriarchal society with
such impunity, pathos, and clarity.

    Light in August, in contrast, courts rather than eschews the problem-
atic combination of racial and sexual otherness. Carolyn Porter suggests
that the novel "deliberately, as it were, bit[es] off more than it seems able
to chew,"[10] and nowhere is this principle of consumption outstripping
comprehension more immediately felt than when the text's radical inclu-
siveness confronts, and seems to swallow whole, the compound threat of
femaleness and blackness—in a word, "womanshenegro." By deliberately
subjecting the reader to a great deal of unprocessed material, Faulkner
forces us to experience the novel's most abiding insight firsthand, which
is that the world gets into the subject long before the subject becomes
conscious of the world, and that consciousness is, itself, a coming-into-
awareness of the fact that something has already "happened" to the self,
and that the world has gotten under its skin in ways that it can now only
understand through indirection. The socioeconomic forces at play in
the novel are multiple, but nothing works upon Joe as immediately and
definitively as gender and race. His self-awareness arrives in the moment
when, hidden within the "pinkwomansmelling obscurity" of the dieti-
tian's closet at the age of five, mechanically eating from a tube of pink
toothpaste, he finds himself beset upon violently both from within and
without; when the woman-in-him vomits itself up, bringing the words,
"you little nigger bastard" down upon him, Joe thinks to himself "with
complete and passive surrender: 'Well, here I am'" (122). If, later, his
mind can only register the combination of "woman" and "negro" as a
failure to process, a jamming of the psychological apparatus, it is because
the nexus of sexual and racial otherness marks the absolute limit of intelligibility, the place where all coherence breaks down because it is the
locus of his initial, traumatic articulation.

Probing the interrelation of gender and race in Faulkner's career requires that we pay careful attention to such moments of fracture or dissolution in his writing, places where, to borrow Philip Weinstein's words, "the project of subjective coherence is under maximal stress."[11] Any reader who seeks out the margins of intelligibility in Faulkner's writing risks becoming stranded in what constitutes a Frenchman's Bend of textuality, a region at once fecund and abject, rich with meaning buried deeper than the author himself seems capable of excavating. Physically characterized by black morasses, ditches, odors, mud, blood, vomit, and other fluids, this backwater of consciousness holds little promise of bringing forth the issues subsumed within its indefinite boundaries. And yet, any study of gender or race in the author's career must inevitably traverse this landscape, where the paths of sexual identity and racial identity break down and, in moments of extreme crisis, become indistinguishable from one another.

Tracing these paths has brought back me back, predictably, to the text that remains for many of us the beginning of everything. The author's fourth published novel, *The Sound and the Fury*, has achieved the status of a seminal work, a view which Faulkner himself advocated. The account he gave of the story's genesis is by now well known—how he wrote his first three novels with "decreasing ease and pleasure," how frustrations surrounding the publication of the third drove him into mental isolation, and how he discovered therein a state of creative rapture so pure and moving that the subsequent novels would be measured in his mind by their failure to recapture it.[12] With seven published novels behind him, he wrote in 1933, "I seemed to have a vision of [*Light in August*] and the other ones subsequent to *The Sound and the Fury* ranked in order upon a shelf while I looked at the titled backs of them with a flagging attention which was almost distaste, and upon which each succeeding title registered less and less, until at last Attention itself seemed to say, Thank God I shall never need to open any one of them again" (227). This vision casts *The Sound and the Fury* as both origin and apex; nothing that precedes it appears on the shelf of Faulkner's memory, and nothing that follows matches, much less transcends, its place therein.

If we compare the fates of these twin convictions in the critical response to Faulkner's writings, we find that whereas the novel's primacy has been largely conceded with respect to the preceding works, it has been increasingly challenged with respect to those that follow. In short, most readers continue to regard *The Sound and the Fury* as Faulkner's "first great novel," but fewer characterize the novels leading up to *Absalom, Absalom!* in terms of steady diminishment. If we more readily accept the author's dismissal of his truly early novels, it is because the gesture confirms our conviction that *The Sound and the Fury* is the product of a markedly different and better writer than the one who penned *Soldiers' Pay*, *Mosquitoes*, and *Flags in the Dust*. Irving Howe succinctly articulated this sentiment when he asked, in one of the earliest studies of Faulkner's career, "What happened to Faulkner between *Mosquitoes* and . . . *The Sound and the Fury*? What element of personal or literary experience can account for such a leap?"[13] The characterization of the novel as jumping away from the earlier works, whether in spontaneous departure or active repudiation, has thoroughly shaped discussions of the novel's place in Faulkner's career. André Bleikasten echoes Howe's query and closes it off when he describes the novel as "an astonishing leap, unheralded and unpredictable, an almost miraculous performance that no amount of comment will ever explain away."[14] Even as he points to the tantalizing gap between the third and fourth novels, Bleikasten suggests that there is ultimately no real point in reading into it, for, while "[h]ints may be found in Faulkner's early works of what he was to achieve in *The Sound and the Fury* and in his other major novels," they are "promises only for having been kept."[15] In other words, the early novels can, at best, only reinforce what we already know, and know better, from *The Sound and the Fury* and the later novels; they have little or nothing new to teach us on their own.

When Eric Sundquist sets out to dethrone *The Sound and the Fury* in his book on Faulkner and race, he relies upon a similar line of argument. *The Sound and the Fury*, he writes, "is not Faulkner's best novel, but the paradox is this: its importance only appears in the larger context of novels to which it gives rise, and at that point it comes to seem indispensable" (9). It is this conviction—that *The Sound and the Fury* is, on its own, deeply flawed, and yet when considered within the context of the novels that follow, deeply profound—that leads him to his most remarkable claim, and the claim to which this essay primarily responds, which is that miscegenation not only provides the explicit motivating theme for Faulkner's truly "great" novels (*Light in August*, *Absalom, Absalom!*, and *Go Down, Moses*), but can be furthermore understood to tacitly or "unconsciously" inform *The Sound and the Fury*. "One might say," he suggests, "that *The Sound and the Fury* . . . *contains* the repressed that returns with increasing visibility over the course of Faulkner's career as he discovers the lost dimension of Southern experience *Sartoris* had failed to find" (26). The most fascinating facet of Sundquist's reading is the way its privileging of race as "*the* issue that determines and defines all others" for Faulkner, the South, and the nation, both evacuates *The Sound and the Fury* of any intrinsic significance, and also redeems it within the economy of the larger career (9). For Sundquist, the novel does not add up on its own, because "the 'mind' it does not have—and will not have until Faulkner's career develops—the mind of 'the South,' is paradoxically the only one that fully explains Quentin's incestuous fascination with Caddy's purity and the novel's strange obsession with her" (9). In short, Caddy's virginity carries within it the "myth of [Southern] innocence," an idea of purity that was projected *against* the miscegenation emancipation supposedly guaranteed, but could only be imaginatively sustained through "the supression of the miscegenation" that slavery had already sanctioned (24). Because the novel reproduces this repression nearly to perfection, however, *The Sound and the Fury* becomes, in Sundquist's reading, divided from its own mind, a text that, not unlike Benjy Compson, is moved to tortured figures of expression by something that it is trying to "say" but cannot, something that will remain "hidden" and "speechless" until Faulkner revisits Quentin Compson by way of regional and national history in *Absalom, Absalom!* In this respect, Sundquist argues, "the greater context of [Faulkner's] career may be said virtually to create the significance of *The Sound and the Fury*" (17, 21). Or, to apply Bleikasten's terms, whatever significance we see in the novel, it is only a promise for having been kept.

All of this is to suggest that while Sundquist's assessment of *The Sound and the Fury* as a not-so-magnificent failure is everywhere informed by his understanding of Faulkner's relationship to history, and of the centrality of race to that history, it also relies upon a perspective more endemic to Faulkner criticism, in which our readings of the early texts are shaped by our knowledge of what lies ahead. A corrective to this far-sighted view might be found in Gary Stonum's early attempt to theorize the relationship between Faulkner's poetry and what follows, in which he asks us to "suspend our capacity for hindsight a little and see the poetry on its own terms," such that we can understand "the path that Faulkner followed in order to reach the point of being able to write [the novels]."[16] The value of this approach lies in its commitment to keeping one eye focused on the larger trajectory of Faulkner's career, while remaining sensitive to the path itself, which is neither so wayward as to be indiscernible except from some future vantage point, nor so fixed as to resemble what Stonum cautions us against reading as "a gradual evolution of its own latent tendencies" (25). To see the early novels "on their own terms," is, I would argue, to recognize that the texts that Sundquist sees engaged in a "search for a way to say things" that will not be said until he discovers the issue of miscegenation are also the works in which the author is most explicitly fluent on the themes of women and sex (6). It is to acknowledge that *The Sound and the Fury* does have a "mind" in 1929—several in fact—and they are all clearly obsessed with the problem of Caddy's sexuality, a problem that proves at once too troubling and not indeterminate enough to be read as symptomatic of a deeper, unspeakable anxiety centered on race. The novel's central trauma, after all, is neither "hidden" nor "speechless"—we see it all too clearly in the image of Caddy's "muddy drawers" and we hear it, I would argue, in Mr. Compson's detailed description, whether real or imagined, of the "delicate equilibrium of periodical filth" (128). Indeed, what is so striking about *The Sound and the Fury* with respect to what follows is that it is everywhere haunted by the specter of contaminated blood, and yet menstruation, not miscegenation, seems to inform that anxiety. This is not to say that race is irrelevant to the novel's worries; indeed, we will see that racial transgression pierces the heart of its sexual drama. This emergent racial discomfort can only be approached, however, in relation to the atmosphere of extreme sexual anxiety that not only precedes and surrounds, but seems to actually *precipitate* racial anxiety's materialization at the novel's center. Race in this way acquires its powerful charge by becoming, like the smell of honeysuckle in Quentin's mind, "all mixed up" with female sexuality.

Recognizing how miscegenation emerges in Faulkner's writings from within an established problematic of gender will eventually require us to abandon the idea that *The Sound and the Fury* is the first of Faulkner's novels that really matters. It is thus ironic that in order to restore the text to the context of the early career we must return to an image Faulkner repeatedly identified as the novel's moment of transcendent genesis, and thus to a scene that has perhaps contributed more than any other to the dismissal of his previous writings. The image of Caddy's muddy drawers, seen from below, as she ascended the tree to gaze upon death was, Faulkner repeatedly suggested, the origin of the entire novel, an idea that Sundquist has called its "genetic myth," one which has "so overwhelmed the novel itself that one no longer questions its relevance, even though there is good reason to do so" (10). The critique is valid, for while the image dominates Faulkner's comments on the novel, as John T. Matthews has pointed out, it "appears only fragmentedly in Benjy's section and hardly at all thereafter, as if the novel advances by losing the initial image in its own writing."[17] The "loss" of the image relates of course to the "loss" of Caddy herself, who physically disappears from her brothers' lives, but also recedes, psychologically, from the reader as she is absorbed into their consciousnesses—a vanishing act that, as Sundquist notes, seems to be acted out within the progression of the scene itself: "[Versh] went and pushed Caddy up into the tree to the first limb. We watched the muddy bottom of her drawers. Then we couldn't see her. We could hear the tree thrashing" (39). From the perspective of her brothers and the servants on the ground, Caddy seems to disappear *behind* her muddy drawers, a detail that will prove prophetic for while she will thereafter emerge, herself, only in sporadic, ethereal snatches, the dark stain that subsumes her in this scene will prove less ephemeral, and more relevant than has been thus far recognized.

The tension between the image's recession and its persistence is most pronounced in relation to Quentin, to whom the scene is literally lost because he is not present to see it, but who nonetheless remains wholly within its shadow.[18] Quentin is of course the one who pushes Caddy into the branch to begin with, and the deep effect of this incident upon his psyche can be seen in the meticulous cleanliness he maintains around his own person, as if trying, like Lady Macbeth, to outwardly rid himself of a contamination etched into the very paths of his consciousness. His encounter with the "little dirty child" is particularly telling in this respect, for while the "moist dirt ridged into her flesh" immediately recalls Caddy's naked backside, onto which the mud has "soaked clean through" (125–26, 74), it also gestures more broadly to an entire contaminated atmosphere that seems to grow out of her soiling, as if the drawers have, as Mrs. Compson suggests about Caddy herself, "corrupt[ed] the very air" that Quentin breathes and taken not just the Compson name, but Quentin's entire world and "drag[ged] [it] in the dirt" (104). Even Caddy's loss of virginity—which would seem to constitute the seminal catastrophe of the novel—seems to affect Quentin by drawing him back to the earlier moment of her fall; he recalls, or perhaps imagines, asking her on the night he meets Dalton Ames, "do you remember the day Damuddy died when you sat down in the water in your drawers," and then again, "Caddy do you remember how Dilsey fussed at you because your drawers were muddy" (151–52). Whatever Quentin sees in Caddy's muddy drawers, it is clearly something that he is compelled to relive over and over again until he takes his own life.

Accessing what Quentin "sees" in this image requires a broader context than the novel provides, but it is crucial to recognize that the abstract significance of the drawers, or what Faulkner called their "symbology," ultimately stems from their stubborn materiality, a fact which criticism has tended to elide in its interest, on the one hand, in underscoring Caddy's invisibility and, on the other, in rescuing her presence from within the novel's masculine economy. Both arguments read Caddy in terms of a fundamental indeterminacy, figured either as absence or excess; for Bleikasten, she is a "blank counter, an empty signifier, a name in itself void of meaning and thus apt to receive any meaning" (*Splendid*, 56), whereas for Minrose Gwin, she is "*something more* than we can say," something which lies "beyond sound and syntax, between the lines."[19] However, like the "long and fading smear" of cow dung that Ab Snopes leaves on Mrs.

De Spain's blond rug in "Barn Burning,"[20] the stain on Caddy's drawers is, itself, a sign, and its meaning is less open to interpretation than critics have tended to assume. Given the persistence in Quentin's mind of Mr. Compson's descriptions, whether real or imagined, of the "periodic filth" and "liquid putrefaction" that lie mysteriously concealed beneath the "outward suavity" of the female body (81), it seems necessary to read the stain on Caddy's drawers as an image not simply of "something 'dirty,'"[21] but of a *specific* filth, a contamination that originates, significantly, from within the female body, rather than entering it from without. It seems critical to me that we distinguish between the dirt of menstruation and the dirt of sex because what is at stake in the distinction is precisely what Mr. Compson tells Quentin when he suggests that women are "never virgins," and that "virginity is a negative state and therefore contrary to nature." To believe, as Quentin's father asks him to believe, that "nature is hurting [him], not Caddy," is to accept that women are physically hard-wired for impurity, their virginity always already lost to the internal corruption of menstruation (116).

It is this unbearable truth that seems to torture Quentin in the image of Caddy's muddy drawers, for *more* distressing than the violation of his sister's virginity by all the Dalton Ameses of the world is the possibility that her virginity never mattered to begin with, that the "tragedy is second-hand," because Caddy's purity was always already lost. What the novel asks us to believe is that Quentin's loss of virginity *as a meaningful concept*—as something that "matters"—threatens him with nothing short of annihilation, because it seems to render everything not only, as we have already seen, irredeemably dirty, but also utterly meaningless. It is precisely this sense of self-nullification that haunts him when, following his escapade with the dirty little girl in town, he sees "a piece of torn newspaper lying beside the road," and begins to laugh and cry at the same time, thinking, "I thought about how I'd thought about I could not be a virgin, with so many of them walking along in the shadows and whispering with their soft girlvoices lingering in the shadowy places and the words coming out and perfume and eyes you could feel not see, but if it was that simple to do it wouldn't be anything and if it wasn't anything, what was I" (147). In other words, if virginity is no more significant than a torn piece of paper, its loss as simple and unmomentous as passing another person in the dark, then Quentin's own existence must, by extension, be utterly without consequence. But why must this be so?

It is at this point that the early novels prove enlightening because the question that Quentin's chapter raises, but doesn't really answer, is why his sense of integrity is so intimately bound up with the idea of virginity to begin with, and thus why the possibility of its negation is so profoundly disturbing. We might note that the novel's reticence on this point—its failure, or refusal, to provide a definite explanation for Quentin's obsession with his sister's purity—is precisely what makes it possible to read a great deal of significance into Caddy's virginity, and, indeed, for Faulkner himself to later rewrite that virginity via the Quentin Compson of *Absalom, Absalom!* as a meditation on the unspeakable truth of miscegenation. The early novels tell a different story, however, one that suggests that Quentin's investment in his sister's purity originates not in the historical past, but in the psychosexual history which comes down to him through Horace Benbow of *Flags in the Dust*, Gordon of *Mosquitoes*, and, most importantly, Elmer Hodge of the unfinished novel *Elmer*.

While the author will not identify his protagonist as a "commonwealth" until *Absalom, Absalom!*, he already possesses a considerable and burdensome inheritance from these figures of the artist, each of whom chooses a different medium, but who all cultivate a virgin ideal as an alternative to the perceived threat of a contaminating reality linked to female sexuality. Quentin's fate seems sealed from the moment that the "vague shape somewhere back in [Elmer's] mind" crystallizes into the definite image of "a Dianalike girl with an impregnable integrity, a slimness virginal and impervious to time or circumstance."[22] This perfectly sealed body finds its perfect opposite in Elmer's nameless first lover, who he remembers as "a full red mouth never quite completely closed, a young body seemingly on the point of bursting out of its soiled expensive dress in soft rich curves" (378). This strict dichotomy between the pristine virgin and the dirty whore will persist in the character of Gordon, who puts his ideal into marble as "the virginal breastless torso of a girl," "simple and eternal in the equivocal derisive darkness of the world."[23] Gordon insists that his medium of choice is "pure" only because "they," by whom he means women, "have yet to discover some way to make it unpure." "They would if they could," he speculates, "God damn them!" (329). For all their abstraction, Horace's blown glass vases exhibit the same prejudices; he keeps one vase on his night table, calls it by his sister's name, and apostrophizes it, in his "realization of the meaning of peace and the unblemished attainment of it, as Thou still unravished bride of quietude."[24] His mistress, by comparison, is thoroughly ravished and by no means unblemished. Her presence is associated in his mind with shrimp, the smell of which "invariably rouse[s] in him a faint but definite repulsion" and seems to "cl[i]ng about his clothing" for hours after he has carried it home to her (403).

While the virgin ideal is clearly a response to, and repudiation of, the perceived contamination of the sexual woman, *Elmer* suggest that the impurities that the virgin ideal functions to deny, and which return so forcefully in the fact of menstruation, are rooted not in female sexuality, but in sexual difference. The soiling effects of Caddy's drawers upon Quentin's psyche find a precedent in the following scene, in which Elmer suffers a great disillusionment on the playground of his childhood:

> Elmer was bitterly shocked. I wont never get married he swore, having fled like a hurt beast. Boys and girls ran and shouted on the playground just as yesterday, just as on all yesterdays. But was it the same? wasn't there something beneath it that he hadn't seen, hadn't been told about? Boys and girls. . . . Things that Elmer had heretofore accepted without question now had a terrible soiled significance: why there were different urinals for boys and girls, why boys herding touching each other shouted over nothing, why girls clumped giggling and sibilant; . . . The schoolhouse dull and ugly in brick, the playground ungrassed by generations: trees, light: his mother and father, his own body all become sinister, dirty . . . Elmer fled not even getting his books. That night he undressed in the dark. (370)

Prior to this revelation Elmer possesses a "lack of self-consciousness" that is "beautiful," through which the world appears as a "continuous succession of happy astonishments" in which "all mankind including Elmer [is] admirable" (369). The "shock" that he receives on the playground explodes this blissful continuity from within, for what it exposes seems now to have always been there, lurking beneath the surface of things and just out of sight. The scene clearly anticipates Joe Christmas's discovery of menstruation in *Light in August*, but it is significant that Faulkner represses the specific content of Elmer's shock, because the effect is that it becomes a discovery not of sex or menstruation, but the fact of division itself, which cleaves "all mankind" into boys and girls, herds and clumps, and makes everything—his surroundings, his family, his own body and memories—"sinister and dirty." If female sexuality is not the root of the problem here, it swiftly becomes the scapegoat. Elmer sutures his innocence back together by resolving to be "through with women," "even his mother," and to "never get married," and he emerges the following morning, "clean again," his "temporary atomized oneness, coalescing again" (370). His world is in this way partly redeemed, split between the odorous, stale, clinging spaces inhabited by women, and the cool, clean, expansive spaces of solitude.

However, as Quentin, too, will discover, the male subject can never be "through" with women, because the "hurt" and the "dirt" that he displaces onto her flesh are the very conditions of his own existence; men, it turns out, are also "never virgin" in the sense that their integrity is violated from the start. As he will do for Joe Christmas and Thomas

Supten, Faulkner attaches this founding "shock," of which all others are but reverberations, to a specific incident in Elmer's life, in this case, to his earliest memory in the novel, of the night that his family's home burned down when he was five years old. "Dragged out of sleep into a repressed fearful Sound composed of the disintegration of wood and stone which his young mind had accepted as being stable and impervious to sudden change," Elmer finds the foundations of his world in dissolution, all familiar, stable things rendered strange and frightening. Even his mother becomes unrecognizable to him, the "loving querulous busy creature" replaced by a "stark un-human face" (345). He finds himself rushed into a "mad crimson world where things hurt his feet and one side of him seem[s] to curl bitterly," and here, caught between the bitter recoiling of his own body against an alien, persecuting world, and the conviction that his family has "deserted him," clinging to the skirt of a strange woman beside him, Elmer "we[eps] for himself, for man, for all the sorrows of the race" (345–47). The scene is an early instance of Faulkner's interest in imagining and probing those unknowable moments when the subject emerges into self-consciousness, plucked from oblivion and installed into a body which, pried away from its environment by duress, confronts a newly alienated world with unmediated terror and sadness. It is this injury, and all its associated feelings of fear, grief, shame, dissolution, and vulnerability, that Elmer repudiates anew when he flees the "shock" on the playground or, later, the atomizing proximity of the sexual female body, experiences which acquire their particular horror by calling him back to the bitter anguish of his own becoming.

It is this same injury, I would argue, that Quentin confronts in Caddy's muddy drawers and relives in his compulsive return to their traumatic memory. François Pitavy beautifully articulates this idea of a psychic wound when he describes "the tear by which Quentin lets out his being and his life." For Pitavy, the "tear" in Quentin's psyche is "the distance between the reality of a world he denies and must nevertheless inhabit, and the ideal which is his reason for living." What ultimately destroys Quentin, he argues, is the reality, or the "certainty of Caddy's destruction," which he can neither accept nor ignore.[25] I suggest that it is rather the collapsing of this distance between the real and the ideal that destroys Quentin. For as I have suggested, it is not "the certainty of Caddy's destruction" that seems to haunt him, but the suspicion that there was, after all, nothing there to destroy, because Caddy was "never virgin," a statement which we are now in a position to better understand as a recognition that she was always already implicated in the corrosive effects of time and circumstance, always already vulnerable to the "derisive darkness of the world," in a word, always just human.

By putting the "dirt" and the "hurt" of the world back into the virgin ideal, menstruation reopens the founding injury at the core of the male psyche, as evident in the dissolution that steadily undoes Quentin's mind and his entire chapter. He remembers lying in bed, wondering "when will it stop when will it stop," repeating the words over and over until "the honeysuckle got all mixed up in it the whole thing came to symbolize night and unrest I seemed to be lying neither asleep nor awake looking down a long corridor of gray halflight where all stable things had become shadowy paradoxical all I had done shadows all I had felt suffered taking visible form antic and perverse mocking without relevance inherent themselves with the denial of the significance they should have affirmed thinking I was I was not who was not was not who" (170). As Dana Medoro argues, the "scent of mud and honeysuckle—of the 'liquid putrefaction' with which they become intimately connected—literally invades his sense of coherence" and "contaminates the very syntax of his narrative, distorting its rules and eventually turning his "I" into a diminished 'i.'"[26] Indeed, menstruation seems to inform Quentin's chapter right down to the psychic pattern of repetition which, as we've already seen, compels him to relive the trauma of Caddy's soiling over and over. If "[a]gain" is "[s]adder than was," and "[s]addest of all," it is because Quentin, too, is a victim of "periodical filth" in the sense that his violation is not only ineradicable, but ongoing (95). It is what Bleikasten has called the "hemorrhage of being," that "ceaseless movement of becoming,"[27] which, like the smell of honeysuckle, that "saddest odor of all," keeps "coming and coming" (133). It is his awareness of this fate that Quentin ultimately cannot stand, and which leads him take his life.

It is a good thing that the topic of this conference is "Faulkner's Sexualities" and not "Faulkner and Race," because I have not left myself much room to comment on the latter. But this is, in a sense, the whole point— that any conversation about race in *The Sound and the Fury* needs to be preceded by a rather lengthy conversation about female sexuality. What I have attempted to demonstrate thus far is that Quentin's suicide and the obsessions that drive him to it become much more meaningful when restored to the context of the early career, where Faulkner actively explores the virgin ideal as a figure of repression within the male psyche. Caddy's muddy drawers, I have suggested, undo this repression by exposing the impurities that the virgin ideal functions to deny, impurities rooted not in sex or female sexuality but in the very condition of being, and thus reopening the founding injury which lies at the core of the male psyche. What I would like to suggest now, by way of a closure that points forward, is that the "tear" that menstruation opens up in Quentin's psyche creates a point of entry for the problem of race that will become so central to his later novels.

Race, we should note, is a part of Faulkner's fictional landscape from the very beginning of his career as a novelist, but less as a theme than as a fictional device. In novels like *Soldiers' Pay* (1926) and *Flags in the Dust* (1929), black characters play neutral or stabilizing roles, functioning almost without exception as figures of nostalgia for the imagined order and peace of a prewar, or premodern world. In the earlier novels, we repeatedly find images of black bodies in stasis, as when Faulkner describes "[t]he same negro in the same undershirt dron[ing] up and down the lawn with his mower,"[28] or "a negro lad lean and fluid of movement as a hound, lounging richly static nearby" (*Flags*, 24). As characters, this physical viscosity translates into a resistance to historical momentum, such that in *Soldiers' Pay*, when Loosh salutes Donald Mahon, his mother, Callie, reprimands him until he "lo[ses] his military bearing and . . . bec[omes] again that same boy who had know Mahon long ago, before the world went crazy."[29] It is not until *The Sound and the Fury* that race begins to acquire and hold a detectable charge—a capacity to disturb order rather than simply preserve or create it—and it seems to do so by moving into the orbit of female sexuality.

As John Duvall argues in his paper for this volume, black sexuality is present from Faulkner's early writings, but as a kind of "figurative blackness," which "unhinged" from black characters, resurfaces in white male characters like Gordon, Horace, Quentin, and Popeye; black characters by comparison seem to exist in a kind quarantine from this libidinal blackness. When, in *The Sound and the Fury*, the black child Versh unbuttons the white child Caddy's dress, this quarantine seems to be broken, not because Versh exhibits any sexuality—he is literally coerced into doing it—but because he becomes the first black character I have found in Faulkner's novels to participate in a sexually charged scene with white characters. The heightened tension that his participation adds to the exchange between brother and sister—"'Unbutton it, Versh.' Caddy said. 'Don't you do it, Versh.' Quentin said" (18)—may anticipate the kind of racial dynamics Faulkner will explore in his later novels, but it seems to say much more about the ways in which race relations first begin to acquire their explosive potential by becoming "mixed up" with the problem of female sexuality. That Caddy is undressed by a black character is provocative in its own right,[30] but what is even more striking is the way in which this act pierces the novel's central trauma by setting in motion the series of events leading to her fall into the branch. Indeed, that racial transgression is bound up with menstruation in Quentin's mind is implied in his description of black people as "sharp black trickles" that come into white people's lives; race penetrates white consciousness through the charged trope of blood (170).

One need not believe that racial anxiety has any hold on *The Sound in the Fury* in order to recognize the legacy of this "black trickle" in the novels to follow, where miscegenation becomes increasingly central, and where the fear of black blood thoroughly complicates the fear of female blood inherited from the earlier novels, but never replaces or wholly "explains" it. The brown/black, excrement/blood-covered phallus/corn cob that has attracted so much attention at this conference is an apt example of the principle of accretion that seems to define Faulkner's imagination—nothing is left behind; rather, new meanings are acquired. As Michael Zeitlin has argued with respect to *Elmer*, the early novels take on "psychosexual issues that Faulkner [will] subdue in his greatest fiction," where he "assimilates the most intimate psychological and intertextual material to a broader sense of history, social reality, and the place he would soon designate as Yoknapatawpha."[31] Much of the material foregrounded in the earlier works are, indeed, subdued in characters like Quentin, Joe Christmas, and Thomas Sutpen, but their psychological insights are, as Zeitlin argues, not "abandoned," but "assimilate[d]," "elaborate[d]," and "disguise[d]" (220). The early novels are thus indispensable in two senses: firstly, because they lay down the paths for, and thus make possible, Faulkner's eventual turn toward history not as an abstract concept but as a feature of psychic life (consider that both Joe Christmas and Thomas Sutpen take on historical consciousness in the form of deeply personal, psychological injuries suffered in childhood); secondly, because they help us understand why Faulknerian male subjectivity remains, throughout Faulkner's career, so unstable, and why female sexuality, in particular, poses such an abiding threat to male coherence. Like Elmer and all his successors, Faulkner was never "through with women," and we must therefore keep in mind the problematic of gender put forth in the early novels, even as race expands and transforms that problematic in the novels to follow.

NOTES

1. Eric J. Sundquist, *Faulkner: The House Divided* (Baltimore: Johns Hopkins University Press, 1983), 5.

2. William Faulkner, *Light in August:* The Corrected Text (New York: Vintage International, 1990), 156.

3. William Faulkner, *Absalom, Absalom!:* The Corrected Text (New York: Vintage International, 1990), 112.

4. William Faulkner, *Sanctuary:* The Corrected Text (New York: Vintage International, 1993), 223.

5. William Faulkner, *The Sound and the Fury*: The Corrected Text (New York: Vintage International, 1990), 128. All subsequent references are to this edition, unless otherwise noted.

6. Notable exceptions are to be found in the work of Philip Weinstein. See *Faulkner's Subject: A Cosmos No One Owns* (New York: Cambridge University Press, 1992). For full-length studies of Faulkner and race, see Thadious Davis, *Faulkner's "Negro": Art and the Southern Context* (Baton Rouge: Louisiana State University Press, 1983); James A. Snead, *Figures of Division: William Faulkner's Major Novels* (New York: Metheun, Inc., 1986); and Sundquist, *Faulkner: The House Divided*. For full-length studies of Faulkner and gender, see Minrose Gwin, *The Feminine and Faulkner: Reading (Beyond) Sexual Difference* (Knoxville: University of Tennessee Press, 1990) and Deborah Clarke, *Robbing the Mother: Women in Faulkner* (Jackson: University Press of Mississippi, 1994).

7. Clarke, *Robbing the Mother: Women in Faulkner*, 17.

8. Although *As I Lay Dying* was published before *Sanctuary*, the latter novel was actually written first, and then later revised and published.

9. Faulkner, *As I Lay Dying*: The Corrected Text (New York: Vintage International, 1990), 88.

10. Carolyn Porter, *William Faulkner* (New York: Oxford University Press, 2007), 91.

11. Weinstein, *Faulkner's Subject: A Cosmos No One Owns*, 2.

12. "An Introduction to *The Sound and the Fury*," reprinted in William Faulkner, *The Sound and the Fury*: An Authoritative Text, Backgrounds and Context Criticism, ed. David Minter, 2nd ed. (New York: W. W. Norton & Company, 1994), 230.

13. Irving Howe, *William Faulkner: A Critical Study*, 3rd ed. (Chicago: University of Chicago Press, 1975), 20–21.

14. André Bleikasten, Introduction to *William Faulkner's "The Sound and the Fury"*: A Critical Casebook (New York: Garland Publishing, Inc., 1982), xi.

15. André Bleikasten, *The Most Splendid Failure: Faulkner's "The Sound and the Fury"* (Bloomington: Indiana University Press, 1976), 5.

16. Gary Lee Stonum, *Faulkner's Career: An Internal Literary History* (Ithaca: Cornell University Press, 1979), 40–41.

17. John T. Matthews, *The Play of Faulkner's Language* (Ithaca: Cornell University Press, 1982), 21.

18. I thank Peter Lurie for pointing out Quentin's absence in the scene during my reading of this paper at the conference. This interesting detail has also been noted by François L. Pitavy in his essay "Through the Poet's Eye: A View of Quentin Compson," in *William Faulkner's "The Sound and the Fury"*: A Critical Casebook (New York: Garland Publishing, Inc. 1982), 79–99.

19. Minrose Gwin, *The Feminine and Faulkner: Reading (Beyond) Sexual Difference* (Knoxville: University of Tennessee Press, 1990), 36, 47.

20. William Faulkner, "Barn Burning," in *Collected Stories of William Faulkner* (New York: Vintage Books, 1977), 12.

21. Sundquist, 10–11.

22. William Faulkner, *Elmer*, ed. Dianne L. Cox, *Mississippi Quarterly*, 36:3 (1983: Summer), 378.

23. William Faulkner, *Mosquitoes* (New York: Liveright, 1997), 11.

24. William Faulkner, *Flags in the Dust* (New York: Vintage Books, 1973), 190–91.

25. Pitavy, "Through the Poet's Eye: A View of Quentin Compson," 85.

26. Dana Medoro, *The Bleeding of America: Menstruation as Symbolic Economy in Pynchon, Faulkner, and Morrison* (Connecticut: Greenwood Press, 2002), 84.

27. Bleikasten, *Splendid*, 136.

28. William Faulkner, *Soldiers' Pay* (New York: Liveright), 151.

29. P. 167. The one exception I can think of to this pattern in the early novels is Simon's son, Caspey, who comes home from the war, refuses to go back to his former role in the Sartoris clan, and must be beaten into saddling Bayard's horse.

30. Diane Roberts points out that "the picture of a black boy undressing a white girl in front of her brothers goes to the very heart of southern sexual taboos."

31. Michael Zeitlin, "Faulkner and Psychoanalysis: *The Elmer Case*," in *Faulkner and Psychology: Faulkner and Yoknapatawpha, 1991*, ed. Donald M. Kartiganer and Ann J. Abadie (Jackson: University Press of Mississippi, 1994), 220, 236.

Faulkner's Black Sexuality

JOHN N. DUVALL

In the latter half of the 1990s, two prominent African Americans from the world of arts and entertainment made startling and basically identical claims about the President of the United States. On the eve of the 1996 presidential election in which William Jefferson Clinton won a second term by defeating Bob Dole, comedian Chris Rock made the following observation on *Saturday Night Live*: "So we got a big election coming up. Who's gonna win? Bill or Bob? Bob or Bill? I like Clinton. Know why I like Clinton? Because he's got real problems. He don't got president problems. He got real problems like you and me, like running out of money, his wife's a pain in the ass, all his friends are going to jail. I know Bill Clinton. I *am* Bill Clinton!"[1] Two years later, Nobel Prize–winning author Toni Morrison, tongue in cheek, made explicit what Rock broadly implied:

> African-American men seemed to understand it right away. Years ago, in the middle of the Whitewater investigation, one heard the first murmurs: white skin notwithstanding, this is our first black President. Blacker than any actual black person who could ever be elected in our children's lifetime. After all, Clinton displays almost every trope of blackness: single-parent household, born poor, working-class, saxophone-playing, McDonald's-and-junk-food-loving boy from Arkansas. And when virtually all the African-American Clinton appointees began, one by one, to disappear, when the President's body, his privacy, his unpoliced sexuality became the focus of the persecution, when he was metaphorically seized and body-searched, who could gainsay these black men who knew whereof they spoke?[2]

In 2002 Rock and Morrison's shared conception of Clinton's blackness becomes institutionalized when Clinton became the first (and so far only) white inductee into the Arkansas Black Hall of Fame.[3]

This outing of Bill Clinton's "true" black identity speaks directly to the kind of thinking about racial impersonation and figuration that my essay engages. There are two ways of thinking about Clinton's relation to blackness. One could say, dismissively, that Clinton was engaged in a kind of cultural blackface, a bad faith appropriation of blackness. Such a

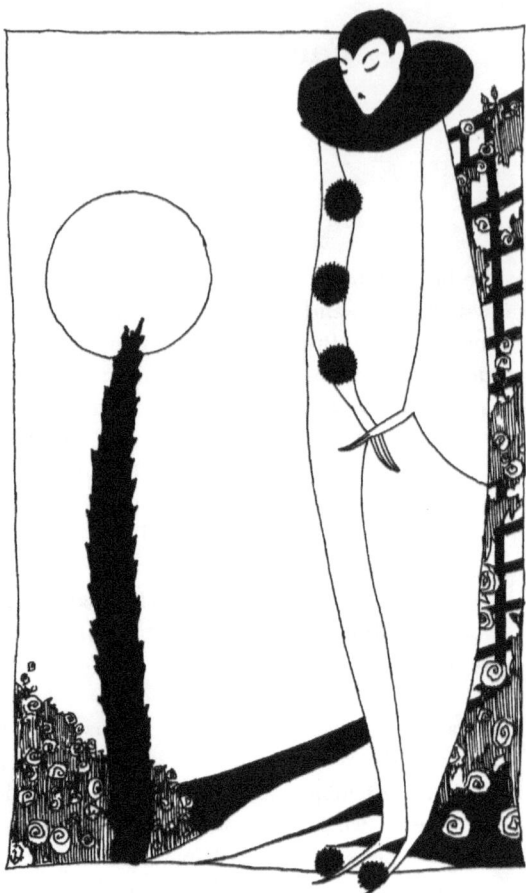

Fig. 1. "Pierrot Standing."
From William Faulkner, *The Marionettes*. Introduction and textual apparatus by Noel Polk. Charlottesville: Bibliographic Society of the University of Virginia by the University of Virginia Press, 1977. Between pages 6 and 7. By permission of the Bibliographic Society of the University of Virginia.

claim, however, presumes that there is an authentic white Southern identity lurking beneath a calculated performance of blackness by the man from Hope, Arkansas. Moreover, such a claim overlooks the reality of Bill Clinton's upbringing. As a poor white who lived among poor blacks, Clinton could never engage in a metaphorical blackface minstrelsy because there was no conscious intent to parody or demean black culture. This leads us to the second way of thinking about Clinton's racial performance. Rather than blackface, Clinton's racial enactment was (and still is) a pastiche performed in whiteface. As president, Clinton projected a white face to America while performing cultural blackness. Or perhaps more accurately, he performed the culture of impoverished rural Southerners, black and white, where his class difference as "white trash" meant that he was never truly a White Southerner in the first place. It is then this whiteface performance that fascinates me because of its potential to generate all sorts of cultural misrecognitions. It is precisely this liminal space of "Caucasian but not White" that is the focus of my discussion of Faulkner's black sexuality.

As I see it, Bill Clinton's relationship to blackness plays out in the full light of postmodern media culture the masked presence that William Faulkner almost obsessively developed in his modernist fiction from the 1920s to early 1940s. That trope is the whiteface minstrel, the individual who appears white even as he performs cultural blackness. (I use the masculine pronoun here and elsewhere because I see Faulkner's white-face minstrels primarily as male.) Faulkner's creation of racially inverted white characters almost always complicates a Southern worldview that quite literally would see the world in terms of black and white. I would therefore like to make a claim that, in light of Rock's and Morrison's, makes perfect sense: America's first black Nobel Laureate wasn't Toni Morrison—it was William Faulkner. Faulkner's blackness, however, is not the result of his embodying stereotypes of blackness. It emerges instead from his imagining a realm of sexual identity that serves ultimately to detach blackness from the Southern concept of the Negro.

Let us begin with a metaphorically masked figure, a minor charac-ter who nevertheless is strikingly present in Faulkner's second novel, *Mosquitoes*, where a young woman, Jenny, recalls meeting a funny lit-tle "black man" whom she finally remembers is named Faulkner. Her friend is confused, since "black man" doesn't really signify in 1920s par-lance, and asks if he was "a nigger."[4] Assuring her friend that he was white, Jenny implies that Faulkner's blackness is associated with his crazy performance of gender, one in which he stands ready to couple with either male or female partners on the dance floor. Fictional Faulkner's "blackness" models subsequent minstrel performances of masculinity in Faulkner's fiction; the excessive libidinality of fictional "Faulkner," which opens nonheteronormative possibility, signals the way that the Caucasian loses white identity and shades toward blackness.

This figuration of a black "Faulkner" is anticipated in *The Marionettes*, Faulkner's hand-letter play with a series of pen and ink drawings that he wrote in 1920 while attending Ole Miss. [Fig. 1] Working within the modernist Pierrot tradition, Faulkner imagines a psychologically divided figure: two of the main characters are Pierrot and Shade of Pierrot.[5] While Pierrot is a drunken dreamer, Shade of Pierrot is the successful seducer of Marietta. The first drawing of Pierrot in *The Marionettes* shows him passed out at a table with a bottle and an overturned glass. In Faulkner's second drawing, Pierrot is a tall clown, but in a later drawing, Shade of Pierrot, playing his lute for Marietta in the background, appears

Fig. 2. "Marietta by
the Fountain." From
William Faulkner, *The
Marionettes*. Introduction
and textual apparatus by
Noel Polk. Charlottesville:
Bibliographic Society of the
University of Virginia by the
University of Virginia Press,
1977. Between pages 45
and 46. By permission of
the Bibliographic Society of
the University of Virginia.

perspectivally as a little black man.[6] Faulkner's Pierrot is a minstrel figure.
[Fig. 2] First developed in commedia dell'arte, Pierrot was reimagined
in French pantomime by Jean-Gaspard Deburau in the early nineteenth
century. The forerunner of the whiteface circus clown, Deburau's Pierrot
established the character as the ineffectual lover, always represented on
stage in baggy white clothes and whiteface makeup. And this is how
Faulkner draws Pierrot: from his stylized cupid's bow lips to his caplike
hair, Pierrot is not simply white; rather he is in whiteface makeup, which
means his identity is masked. Whiteface Pierrot, who is asleep, cannot
act, certainly not sexually, and as he stands, his hands crossed in front
of him suggest a kind of impotence, if not a symbolic castration. It is
only the dream figure of the unconscious, the silhouetted black Shade of
Pierrot, that is capable of sexual performance. What Faulkner suggests

through these drawings is that the real artist is not the one who presents a white face to the world but rather resides in the poet's interiority, which turns out to be black. The duality of Pierrot/Shade of Pierrot is crucial to understanding Faulkner's subsequent development of a whiteface minstrelsy that implicitly racializes white male sexuality. The limitation of Faulkner's portrayal of figurative blackness is that it draws on stereotypes of African American sexuality but at the same time significantly unhinges blackness as form of unlicensed sexuality from a biological or essentialist notion of race: in other words, Caucasians as well as Negroes can perform blackness.

"Black" Caucasians recur throughout Faulkner's major period: in *The Sound and the Fury* the sexually tortured, feminized Quentin Compson, always followed by his black shadow, is identified by the boys fishing by the bridge as enacting the linguistic performance of a "colored man" from the "minstrel shows"[7]; in *Light in August* Joe Christmas's sexual inbetweenness, aside from his unknowable racial identity, would be sufficient to mark him as black. Even Ike McCaslin, whose repudiation of his patrimony also terminates his performance of heterosexuality and leads to his retirement into the extreme homosociality of the hunter's world, is marked as his text's secret black man. Unlike his good-old-boy father and uncle, Uncle Buck and Uncle Buddy, who under the appropriate social circumstances can be Mr. Theophilus and Mr. Amodeus, Uncle Ike can never be a mister. Having repudiated his patrimony at the age of majority, Ike has also repudiated his proper white identity, and so tracks along the path of the pliant African American male, who is always "boy" until old age finally grants him the honorific "uncle."[8]

All of these characters are in a sense blacks in whiteface; they present a white face to the world, but their being (through primitivist art or sexuality) at some deeper level is marked as black, which leads to all sorts of social misrecognitions because this blackness usually goes unremarked (except for the occasional confused comments of a young woman). Faulkner's deployment of a figurative blackness, I believe, should be read in light of Havelock Ellis's work on sexual inversion. Faulkner, as we know, read widely in Phil Stone's library in the 1910s and early 1920s and almost certainly read Stone's copy of Ellis. The artists in *Mosquitoes* at one point discuss Freud and Ellis. Ellis's famous study, *Sexual Inversion* (originally published in 1903 but which went through a series of editions throughout the 1910s and 1920s) is at pains to show the universality of homosexuality—that it occurs in other animal species, throughout human history, and in all cultures. But Ellis singles out certain groups as having particularly high incidences of homosexuality: geniuses ("homosexuality is especially common among men of exceptional intellect"), literary artists, and primitives.[9] As Ellis elaborates on his claim regarding literature as one of the chief avocations of inverts, it is almost impossible not to speculate on how Faulkner might have experienced such an assertion, especially in light of his pose as the failed poet: "[homosexuals] especially cultivate those regions of *belles-lettres* which lie on the borderland between prose and verse. Though they do not usually attain much eminence in poetry, they are often very accomplished verse writers" (294). Ellis's first two categories, geniuses and artists, would seem to overlap, which makes his third category all the more anomalous. If homosexuality in European nations is practiced by a discrete (and discreet) minority, Ellis speaks of the commonness of inversion in a variety of primitive peoples, from American Indians and Tahitians to Africans: "Among the negro population of Zanzibar forms of homosexuality which are believed to be congenital (as well as acquired forms) are said to be fairly common. . . . Among the Bangala of the Upper Congo sodomy between men is very common, especially when they are away from home, in strange towns, or in fishing camps" (19). "On the whole," Ellis summarizes, "the evidence shows that among lower races homosexual practices are regarded with considerable indifference, and the real invert . . . generally passes unperceived or joins some sacred caste which sanctifies his exclusively homosexual inclinations." Ellis's following paragraph significantly adds class to the mix: "Even in Europe today a considerable lack of repugnance to homosexual practices may be found among the lower classes. In this matter . . . the uncultured man of civilization is linked to the savage" (21). What Ellis misses here is that his extremes meet, for it is not just the uncultured man of civilization who is paired with the primitive (lower races/lower classes) but also the overcultured man (genius/artist) who takes his sexual pleasure in primitive fashion.

In keeping with Ellis's views of homosexuality, Faulkner's self-portraits in *Mosquitoes*, both ironic and idealized, seem to merge the under- and overcultured. If "Faulkner," the professional liar, seems like the author's wry gesture toward one of his youthful poses as the tramp, the sculptor Gordon represents Faulkner's serious artistic ambition.[10] The tall Gordon, who we are repeatedly told has a hawk's face, is the 5–feet 5–inch Faulkner's idealized version of himself as a hardworking masculine artist. Gordon (hawk-man/falconer/Faulkner), the dedicated artist as genius, seems opposed to the licensed fool "Faulkner"; however, they share a similar ambiguous relationship to whiteness, since both are merely Caucasians in whiteface. This ambiguity is signaled by the very space in which we meet Gordon. Accessible only by a "darkling corridor" (*Mosquitoes* 13) leading to "dark tortuous stairs" (21), Gordon's attic studio/apartment, one learns, "had housed slaves long ago" (11).

Early in the novel, Mrs. Maurier, accompanied by her niece Patricia and Mr. Talliaferro, drops by Gordon's studio to try to persuade the sculptor to join her yachting party. Patricia openly admires the statue of the female torso and asks Gordon if he will give or sell it to her. When he refuses, she asks, "Why are you so black?" Since Gordon clearly does not understand her meaning, she tries to elaborate: "Not your hair and beard. I like your red hair and beard. But you. You are black. I mean . . ." (25). Although Patricia is unable to fully identify what constitutes Gordon's blackness, she, like Jenny, identifies the white male artist as black. Like "Faulkner," then, Gordon is not white, which places him in implied relationship to racial otherness. At the same time, as a starving artist, Gordon oddly combines both of Ellis's extremes for inverted tendencies: he is simultaneously overcultured (as artist) and undercultured (economically lowerclass). Living in poverty in a space where blacks had lived, Gordon is perceived by Mrs. Maurier in a way that oddly suggests Southern attitudes toward race. Because he's an artist, he must be "so spiritual": "He's one of these artists who never have much, lucky people." Mrs. Maurier's attitudes reveal that the dark artist is little different than the happy-go-lucky darkies, who must be equally lucky not to have much either. When Gordon walks out on her, Mrs. Maurier tries to blame Patricia's behavior, but Patricia points out that in fact it is her aunt who has been rude by barging into his studio unannounced. Mrs. Maurier's response is telling: "These people are different," her aunt told her coldly. "You don't understand them. Artists don't require privacy as we do: it means nothing whatever to them" (30). What I hope my discussion to this point has made clear is how easily one might, in the context of the South in the 1920s, substitute "Negroes" for "artists" in the previous sentence. Mrs. Maurier's fascination with artists, her desire to decorate her party with them, reveals that she's slumming for the primitive in much the same way that wealthy New Yorkers went to Harlem's Cotton Club. For Faulkner's whiteface males, their association with blackness queers their white identity.[11]

If the "little black man" named Faulkner serves a comic function in *Mosquitoes*, the little black man in *Sanctuary* is a nightmarish figure of terror. At the center of *Sanctuary*'s figurative blackness is the gangster Popeye, who although Caucasian, activates a Southern hysteria over black male criminality and sexuality. Doreen Fowler recently has argued that "the bootleggers and prostitutes in *Sanctuary* function as substitutes for a nearly invisible black community" by suggesting "the racial segregation that historically characterizes Faulkner's South."[12] Given my previous discussion of *The Marionettes* and *Mosquitoes* as a context for thinking about Faulkner's use of figurative blackness, I wish to develop Fowler's claim in order to argue that *Sanctuary* can be read as a coded meditation on racial otherness, one that once again cuts close to the bone of Faulkner's authorial identity. In the logic of whiteface minstrelsy that I have been articulating, I believe that in *Sanctuary* the social and psychological processes of becoming black map the limits of representational thinking; the race changes effected by the text blur the boundary between the figural and the real.

For many readers today, Popeye, who rapes the Ole Miss coed Temple Drake with a corncob and gets away with it only to be executed for a crime he does not commit, is the very embodiment of racial blackness. In fact, the last few times I have taught *Sanctuary*, most undergraduates and even many graduate students have been certain that Popeye is African American. Such a misreading, of course, forgets historical context. Seeing Popeye as African American fails to grasp that even in an illegal bootlegging operation, it would be simply unthinkable for a black man to have a position of authority over white men. This contemporary misrecognition oddly enacts the stereotypes of the Negro of the 1930s, but a reading that sees Popeye as African American is not simply an error since it leads to the very ambiguity created by the text's deployment of blackness.

There are, in other words, some very good reasons why readers today process Popeye as African American. Students who have studied other Faulkner novels remember that his fiction often turns on complex issues of miscegenated identity embodied by racially ambiguous characters. Even for those students for whom *Sanctuary* is their first encounter with Faulkner, their skills as close readers lead them to make a racialized sense of repetition. "He smells black," thinks Horace during his encounter with Popeye in chapter 1, a detail that resonates with a clichéd racist sentiment that Negroes smell funny.[13] "Popeye's black presence" (121) looms over the Old Frenchman place; Horace Benbow tells his sister, Narcissa, and Miss Jenny about "that little black man" (109) with this threatening pistol; and most specifically, Temple Drake twice contemptuously refers to Popeye as "that black man" (42, 49). Oddly, Popeye's size and physical prowess become confused when Horace refers to Popeye as "that gorilla" (128), a term that seems to belie Popeye's diminutive build, but which is consistent with the figurative blackness that links the character to racial otherness. "Black" Popeye is a primitive—unevolved and subhuman—an implication that is present in white racist attitudes toward African Americans.

Even the way Popeye's skin is described creates ambiguity with its oxymoronic "dark pallor" (5). How can paleness be dark? This ambivalent description of Popeye's skin is no more helpful in fixing racial identity than the description that tells us that his "face had a queer, bloodless color"

(4). Like "queer" Gordon from *Mosquitoes*, "queer" Popeye is not neces-sarily sexually identified by this word, though "queer" was by the 1930s used to name homosexuality. What is queer about Popeye is his combina-tion of violence and nonheteronormative voyeuristic libidinality.

While the mentally challenged Tommy does at one moment refer to Popeye as "the skeeriest durn *white* man I ever see" (19), this identifica-tion is overwhelmed by the references to Popeye's blackness. It is inter-esting, however, what Tommy's emphasis of the word "white" implies about the Southern racial imaginary, namely, that Popeye's whiteness is anomalous, so much so that it is more like what African American mas-culinity was imagined. On the one hand, Popeye is not manly, since he is scared, it seems, of his own shadow. On the other hand, Popeye inspires fear because he is scary. One never knows when he will draw his gun and kill something or someone. Popeye thus effectively enacts two conflict-ing stereotypes of the black man: he is seen as an object of derision for his comical cowardice but he is also known as an unthinking, danger-ous brute that white men should fear. Even while identifying Popeye as white, therefore, Tommy names the gangster's difference in a fashion that queers Popeye's white identity.

Popeye's whiteface performance of blackness does not operate in a vacuum. Just as the relationship between tall Gordon and fictional little "black" "Faulkner" in *Mosquitoes* can trace its genealogy in whiteface minstrelsy to the Pierrot-Shade of Pierrot relationship in *The Mari-onettes*, the relationship of the two central male characters in *Sanctuary* is similarly hinged, signaled as it is in the opening scene of the novel in which the reflected faces of Horace and Popeye merge in such a way that Horace appears to be wearing Popeye's hat.[14] If the misrecognition of Popeye's racial identity is in part a function of his clothes, this startling visual image of transvestment suggests the way in which blackness will descend on Horace during the course of the novel. Stated in terms of Pierrot/Shade of Pierrot, Popeye is Horace's black shadow. Horace and the client he represents, Lee Goodwin, experience cultural and psycho-logical forces that suggest their becoming black.

Just as "Faulkner" and Gordon represent aspects of Faulkner's artistic identity and ambition, so too do Popeye and Horace. Diminutive "black" Popeye is a nightmare version of that funny little black "Faulkner" from *Mosquitoes*.[15] If fictional "Faulkner" represents William Faulkner's tramp persona, Popeye eerily suggests Faulkner's dandyism. One of the first details suggesting Popeye's "blackness" is sartorial: "His suit was black, with a tight, high-waisted coat" (4). Temple's sense of Popeye's blackness surely comes in part from the skin-tight black suit he wears. Taunting Popeye after he calls her a whore, Temple asks: "What river did you fall in with that suit on? Do you have to shave it off at night?" (50). This detail also eerily links Popeye with Faulkner. As Joseph Blotner has noted, the young Faulkner's dandyism included having his mother, Maud, alter his new suits to make the legs tighter, so much so that his pants were "close to skintight."[16] Beyond the matter of clothing, Faulkner's description of Popeye's face suggests a feared and fantasized authorial self-representation: "His nose was faintly aquiline, and he had no chin at all" (5). While the gangster's physical delineation seems to point toward the author, Faulkner's representation of Popeye, as James Polchin has noted, parallels 1920s popularizations of Freud and Ellis that would position Popeye within the psychopathology of homosexuality.[17]

Both Popeye and Horace are linked by nonheteronormative performances of masculinity that place them in groups that Havelock Ellis saw as having a disproportionate number of homosexuals. Horace, the Oxford educated lawyer who even in running away from his loveless marriage takes along a book, represents Ellis's overcultured man, while Popeye, a child of the underclass, suggests the undercultured. As Faulkner's earlier presentation of Horace in *Flags in the Dust* makes clear, Horace is an artist figure. His glass blowing equipment that he brings home with him from World War I allows him to pursue his artistic impulses; working in the garage he produces after several tries "one almost perfect vase of clear amber, larger, more richly and chastely serene and which he kept always on his night table and called by his sister's name."[18] Horace's bedside ornament, of course, bespeaks at one and the same time his incestuous desire for Narcissa and his sublimation of that desire in his art. Despite the displacement, Horace's desire is marked as transgressive and primitive (precultural); if he transgresses in one fashion, he is liable to have other nonnormative desires. In *Sanctuary*, Horace remains the artist figure and one moment in particular strongly recalls a gesture the sculptor Gordon twice makes in *Mosquitoes*. Speaking to Ruby about his psychological limitations, Horace reaches out and places a hand on her face, "touching the flesh as though he were trying to learn the shape and position of her bones and the texture of her flesh" (17). Art in *Mosquitoes* is a kind of "dark" perversion, yet it is art that allows Gordon in effect to pass as a heterosexual even as his interiority produces all manner of transgressive sexual behavior. Horace thinks of his transgression as his incestuous thoughts about his stepdaughter, Little Belle, but as in *Mosquitoes*, the more profound prohibition is against a darkly figured same-sex sexuality.

If Popeye's blackness is queerly positioned between figurativeness (after all, he's really white) and literalness (nevertheless, other characters identify him as black), Horace's relationship to the racial other begins as unambiguously figurative, constructed by simile. Twice Narcissa articulates what she finds troubling in Horace's leaving his wife, Belle: "But to walk out just like a nigger," Narcissa says, "And to mix yourself up with moonshiners and street-walkers" (108). A few pages later she elaborates her dismay: "When you took another man's wife and child away from him, I thought it was dreadful, but I said At least he will not have the face to ever come back here again. And when you just walked out of the house like a nigger and left her I though that was dreadful too, but I would not let myself believe you meant to leave her for good" (117). Narcissa's racialized complaint against her brother, of course, bespeaks her outrage at his compromising her sense of white respectability and gentility, but her words say much more. What makes Horace "like a nigger" is that he cannot be confined to heteronormative domesticity. Narcissa unreflexively invokes the specter of the presumed unchecked, primitive libidinality of the African American male to name her brother's relation to difference.

Two crucial moments link blackness and nonheteronormativity. The first, strikingly, is generated by a presumptively heterosexual coupling of Temple and Red. Since Red is brought in by Popeye to have sex with Temple while he watches, Red is most often viewed as Popeye's surrogate, a move that tends to read Popeye's desire into a heterosexual paradigm. But Temple says Popeye is "not even a man," certainly not a "real man" (231) and in childhood his doctor says that the delicate, undersized boy "will never be a man, properly speaking" (308). In the sexological world of the late 1920s, to be less than or other than a man implies inversion, and certainly the slight Popeye who never develops secondary male sexual characteristics fits this model. How then does one read Popeye's voyeuristic participation in this sexual threesome? As Temple and Red engage in coitus "nekkid as two snakes," Popeye, fully clothed in his black suit, stands at the foot of the bed "making a kind of whinnying sound" (258). The critical presumption of Popeye's heterosexuality is not supported by his nonsignifying noise. Wherein lies Popeye's identification while he watches—as the penetrator or as the penetrated? His sound does not distinguish. His whinnying expresses but does not represent a jouissance that operates beyond the pleasure principle. The second key moment in the figurative linking of blackness and nonheteronormativity occurs when Horace visits Temple in Miss Reba's establishment. The story Temple tells of her violation is explicit in its detail but is fantasy, a fabrication that operates with its own symbolic logic that may nevertheless speak the truth of her night of terror at the Old Frenchman place. We know that Popeye was never in the room with Temple long enough for the scenario she describes to have occurred and that moreover Popeye rapes her the next morning, not that night. What is of interest, then, is Temple's racially and sexually imagined attempts at avoiding her violation. I am particularly interested in her penultimate and final ruses. On the verge of being raped, she imagines herself as an unattractive middle-aged school teacher disciplining "a little black thing like a nigger boy" (219). This reversal of the power relation turns threatening "black" Popeye into an African American boy who can be controlled.

Temple decides she needs to go one step further and performs a sex change: "So I was an old man, with a long white beard, and the little black man got littler and littler and I was saying Now. You see now. I'm a man now" (220). By becoming a man, she hopes to unman Popeye and this funny "little black man" is no longer the African American boy but a kind of reverse metonymy, the whole standing (or rather failing to stand) for the part, where the part is the flaccid phallus. And though Temple's words describe Popeye's impotence, the imagined moment of sexuality that ensues is between two men: "Then I thought about being a man, and as soon as I thought it, it happened. It made a kind of plopping sound, like blowing a little rubber tube wrong-side out. It felt cold, like the inside of your mouth when you hold it open" (220). Although Temple describes the dreamlike transformation of her vagina into a penis, what "it" in fact represents is the experience of Popeye penetrating her with the corncob. She may have avoided the literal phallus of the "little black man" but this moment, as will become clear in the trial of Lee Goodwin, constitutes a different kind of black phallus.

Temple's fantasized, sex-changing version of her violation finds its completion in Horace's own sex-change fantasy of violation. When he returns to Jefferson after hearing Temple's story, Horace vomits up a "hot ball" of black coffee that recalls the "hot ball" that Temple had described as part of her anticipation of being raped. In this moment of literal physical abjection, Horace experiences the psychological abjection of non-normative desire. As he vomits over the toilet, Horace relives Temple's story about her violation but as the pronouns shift from male to female, it is not so simple as his incestuous desire for his stepdaughter. As James Polchin has argued, "like Temple Drake's story of her rape in which she creates her physical and mental state as a man, Horace projects himself into a female position in his own recollection of the rape. For Horace, the image evolves as an erotically charged act of anal intercourse" (154). Far from simply an imagined penetration of Little Belle, Horace instead experiences the violation of his own "black tunnel" (223). In this moment, when Horace's desires "go primitive," he ceases to be merely "like a nigger" and begins to become symbolically black.

Popeye, the figure of black male criminality (despite quite possibly being a white "invert"), commits the crime that occasions the need for Jefferson's primitive form of justice, a mob vengeance that entails mutilation and lynching. Although on trial for killing Tommy, Lee Goodwin is convicted and punished for violating Temple, who identifies him as the murderer and her rapist. Rape in the Southern imaginary of the 1920s and 1930s is a racialized crime committed almost exclusively by the Negro who lusts after white women. How is it, then, that the victim of the lynching is a white man, Lee Goodwin? The Southern practice of castration and lynching of the black sexual offender (whether the offense was real or imaginary) would be inflicted on no white man and Lee, it turns out, is no white man. But how exactly is Lee stripped of his whiteness during the trial in such a way that he serves as another instance in Faulkner of whiteness becoming black?

Clearly Lee's relationship to whiteness is already tenuous because of his class position as a poor white. Moreover, as a bootlegger, he operates outside of the law and provides an illicit product that was understood to corrupt social values by lowering inhibitions. One of the reasons for Prohibition was to promote sexual morality. Perhaps most tellingly, in an otherwise segregated South where work itself was often raced (some menial jobs would not be performed by whites), bootlegging was an equal opportunity venture—both poor whites and African Americans produced corn liquor.[19] Nevertheless, Lee's complete racial reassignment requires a prosthetic intervention.

What performs perhaps the oddest moment of race change in all of Faulkner is the corncob surrogate phallus that Popeye used to rape Temple; it is her "little black thing like a nigger boy" writ large. As such, the cob is not Lacan's "little otherness" (the unconcretizable *object petit a*, that fantasy of desire) but rather what we might call Faulkner's very concrete "little blackness"—the *object petit noir*.[20] When the district attorney, Eustace Graham, introduces the cob into evidence, "it appeared to have been dipped in dark brown paint" (283). The cob, then, overtly marked as the unnatural instrument of violation, is also implicitly raced: in its dark brown coloring, the cob is the disembodied (thus already disciplined and castrated) African American phallus. The effect of the courtroom scene recalls Frantz Fanon's description of the experience of reading a passage from Michel Cournot that carnivalizes the size of the black penis: "one is no longer aware of the Negro but only of a penis; the Negro is eclipsed. He is turned into a penis. He *is* a penis."[21] Or perhaps it is Fanon's point with a twist: *Sanctuary*'s surrogate penis *is* Negro. The criminality of the mute black phallus is reassigned in the courtroom, anticipating the mutilation and lynching of Goodwin's body. At the same time, the district attorney's own whiteness and linguistic authority (in Lacanian terms, his phallic authority) derives from his ability to speak the meaning of the black phallus.

As such, the black phallus is the uncannily appropriate object of the white male gaze and white vengeance; it is the object that makes Goodwin's alleged crime "no longer the matter for the hangman [a fit end for a white murderer] but for a bonfire of gasoline [a warning to other would-be black rapists to leave white women alone]" (284). This free-floating surrogate black phallus, while implying the castration of the black man, simultaneously reminds the all-white male jury of the imagined primitive sexual power of the Negro male.

This is why Lee Goodwin can become the object of the white community's peculiar brand of mob justice. In the Southern imaginary, the libidinously primitive black phallus, when linked to Goodwin, has the effect of erasing his claim to whiteness, and as he blackens, Temple Drake becomes yet another instance of Southern Womanhood violated by the Negro. The cob suggests a kind of transubstantiation—the blood of the violated white virgin constituting the surrogate black phallus. Through Temple's testimony that names Lee rather than Popeye as the "owner" of the black phallus, we witness the construction of another unrecognized artificial Negro. The crime effectively becomes a black crime and so more readily fits the established Southern narrative of white punishment of black primitive libidinality. Symbolically de/reraced, Lee is thus made available to serve the communal role of the black male in a ritualized lynching. The blackened cob effectively merges all the text's funny little blacknesses, from Popeye and Horace to Uncle Bud (the African American boy who lives at Miss Reba's whorehouse) and Temple's black fantasy retelling of her rape.

Together, then, these three characters in *Sanctuary* instantiate once again Faulkner's whiteface minstrelsy—individuals who present a white face to the world but who beneath the mask of whiteness subliminally function as culturally black. Crime and punishment, taken in this fashion, is about the social construction of whiteness. I have outlined the way Lee stands in for Popeye but there is also a complex relation of substitution between Lee and Horace. Sometimes a cigar is just a cigar, but Horace's corncob pipe is hardly just a pipe when read in light of the racial and sexual context of the blackened cob. During the trial, Horace in a legal sense "represents" Goodwin. But in the white male community's act of violent retribution that follows, Lee symbolically represents Horace. Effectively switching roles from the courtroom matinee to the open-air evening performance, these two whiteface characters are the odd men out in what Faulkner portrays as the blackface minstrelsy of Jefferson's lynching.

Focalized through Horace's angle of vision, the lynching of Lee Goodwin embodies multiple racialized misrecognitions and appropriations.[22] Approaching the jail, Horace sees a bright fire in the vacant lot next to the jail, which renders the events that he witnesses in "savage silhouette" (295), which turns whiteness black. In lynching Lee, the white men (who appear as though in blackface) literalize Fanon's point that such acts are sexual revenge revealing the psychopathology of white men and their feelings of "sexual inferiority . . . in relation to the Negro, who is viewed as penis symbol" (159). The lynchers appropriate their stereotype of black sexual primitivism to punish the white-faced black, Lee. The text reveals that before dousing him with coal oil and setting him on fire, the black-face lynchers sodomized their victim; one of the men says when Horace is recognized: "Do to the lawyer what we did to [Goodwin]. What he did to her. Only we never used no cob. We made him wish we had used a cob" (296). Strikingly, the homosexual act is performed in the name of preserving nonmiscegenated heterosexuality and the superiority of the white over the black penis. Here too is Horace's imagined anal rape, fantasized while vomiting, made all too real. But this sexual deviancy that links Horace and Lee is color coded: "black" (to the extent that his desire is "inverted" and thus primitive) Horace is metaphorically lynched and sodomized by the mob. The crowd's vengeance may be performed on Goodwin's body, but Horace unconsciously processes the scene as if he were the victim. Horace's brush with the blackface mob completes the transformation of the qualifying simile (Horace is "like a nigger"), turning it into the full-blown identity of metaphor (Horace is another black man who is available for lynching).

The defeated Horace Benbow who returns to his wife, Belle, in Kinston, is a decidedly queer heterosexual white man, his whiteness and heterosexuality called into question by his relationship to that scary little black man named Popeye. Horace's very nearly fulfilled fantasy of anal penetration disciplines him so completely that he returns in the world's view to presumptive heteronormative domesticity. Horace, however, is merely passing along the color (and sex) line. Psychologically impotent, Horace again instantiates Faulkner's ineffectual, dreamer Pierrot, while "black" Popeye (even though physically impotent) embodies Shade of Pierrot's transgressive libidinality that once again points to primitivism and racial otherness.

What I hope to have suggested is that, in Faulkner's Yoknapatawpha, African Americans are not the only ones who lead "black" lives and that a whole range of issues surrounding whiteness and sexual identity comes into sharper focus if one recognizes the closeted blackness of so many of Faulkner's troubled white characters. Faulkner's whiteface minstrelsy uncouples blackness and the Negro, which means that cultural blackness may reattach itself to racial whiteness. To make this claim is neither to cast William Faulkner as a forerunner of critical whiteness studies nor to see him as a traitor to whiteness. Faulkner the man, as we know, was quite capable of racist articulations. Whatever one finally thinks about Faulkner's appropriation of blackness, his texts remain sites of proliferating misrecognitions in which Faulkner repeatedly risks grotesque self-exposure, whether as that funny little black man named "Faulkner" or as that scary little black man named Popeye. But it is precisely Faulkner's foolhardiness that means that his fictions are never merely personal but always open outward to larger social and historical issues of the inevitably raced and gendered body. It is, finally, a Pierrot-like mask that enables Faulkner's depiction of a black sexuality through a minstrelsy of whiteness.

NOTES

1. Saturday Night Live: *The Best of Chris Rock*. Videocassette. Vidmark/Trimark, 2000.

2. Toni Morrison, "The Talk of the Town," *New Yorker* (5 October 1998), 32.

3. The extend to which Clinton's induction into the Arkansas Black Hall of Fame signals his cultural blackness can be found in the ABHF's mission statement: "Throughout its history, the annual induction ceremony has sought to correct the omissions of history and to remind the world that Black history is a signification part of American history. The foundation seeks to further the impact of the annual induction ceremony by providing an environment in which a future generation of African American achievers with Arkansas roots will thrive and succeed" (www.arblackhalloffame.org/foundation/).

4. William Faulkner, *Mosquitoes* (1927; New York: Liveright, 1997), 144.

5. Judith Sensibar places Faulkner's use of Pierrot in the context of other modernist uses of this figure and sees Pierrot speaking to Faulkner's own fragmented sense of self. See Sensibar's introduction to her edition of William Faulkner's *Vision in Spring* (Austin: University of Texas Press, 1984), xiv–xix.

6. All of Faulkner's drawings are available in the facsimile edition of *The Marionettes*, intro. Noel Polk (Charlottesville: University of Virginia Press, 1977). I direct the reader's attention particularly to Pierrot as a tall whiteface clown (between manuscript pages 6 and 7) and to Shade of Pierrot as a black minstrel (between manuscript pages 45 and 46).

7. *The Sound and the Fury* (1929; New York: Vintage International, 1990), 120.

8. My thinking here grows out of Philip Weinstein's discussion of property, propriety, and the proper in relation to Southern honorifics in his *What Else But Love? The Ordeal of Race in Faulkner and Morrison* (New York: Columbia University Press, 1996), 87–97.

9. Havelock Ellis, *Sexual Inversion*, vol. 2, *Studies in the Psychology of Sex*, 3rd ed. (Philadelphia: F. A. Davis, 1924), 26.

10. Appendix A of Ellis" *Sexual Inversion*, "Homosexuality among Tramps," posits that an unusually high percentage of American tramps engage in homosexuality. As a particular instance of the lower class, this obviously fits Ellis's scheme, but casts a curious light on Faulkner's self-fashioning posture as the tramp.

11. For a fuller treatment of the ways in which Gordon instantiates Faulkner's black sexuality, see my essay "'Why Are You So Black?' Faulkner's Whiteface Minstrels, Primitivism, and Perversion," in *A Companion to William Faulkner*, ed. Richard C. Moreland (Oxford: Blackwell, 2007), 148–64.

12. Doreen Fowler, "Faulkner's Return to the Freudian Father: *Sanctuary* Reconsidered," *Modern Fiction Studies* 50 (2004): 422.

13. William Faulkner, *Sanctuary* (1931; New York: Vintage International, 1993), 7.

14. As Noel Polk has pointed out in "The Space between *Sanctuary*," in *Intertextuality in Faulkner*, ed. Michel Gresser and Noel Polk (Jackson: University Press of Mississippi, 1985), this opening scene in which the two characters merge constitutes Popeye as Horace's double: "he is at once Horace's twin, his alter ego, at the same time his id and his superego; he is at once the reductio ad absurdum of Horace's darker sexual impulses" (23).

15. In "Faulkner's Self-Portraits," *Faulkner Journal* 2.1 (1986), Michel Gresset also notes that "Popeye shares exactly the same characteristics as Faulkner in *Mosquitoes*: he is little, and he is black—at least from the suit he wears" (5). Gresset, however, does not pursue the sexual connotations (beyond impotence and voyeurism), suggesting instead that there seems to be "a double evil potential in undersize linked with blackness" (5).

16. Joseph Blotner, *William Faulkner: A Biography*, vol. 1 (New York: Random House, 1974), 180.

17. See James Polchin's "Faulkner's *Sanctuary* as Psychosexual Text," in *Faulkner and Gender*, ed. Donald Kartiganer and Ann J. Abadie (Jackson: University Press of Mississippi, 1996), 148–51. In addition to Popeye's homosexuality, Polchin sees Temple's account to Horace of her imagined moment of sex change "as a psychological case of psychosexual inversion that grounded so many discussions in the popular psychology texts and confession magazines of the time" (153) and reads Horace's erotic projection of himself into the scene of Temple's rape as his fantasy of anal intercourse (154). For Polchin, what Horace represses is not incestuous desire (of which he is aware) but homosexual desire.

18. William Faulkner, *Flags in the Dust* (New York: Random House, 1973), 190.

19. One of the stories Faulkner knew was the 1908 lynching of the African American bootlegger Nelse Patton, who was lynched for raping and killing a white woman. An account of this history is in Joel Williamson's *William Faulkner and Southern History* (New York: Oxford University Press, 1993), 157–61.

20. As Lacan describes it in *The Four Fundamental Concepts of Psycho-Analysis*, ed. Jacques-Alain Miller, trans. Alan Sheridan (New York: Norton, 1978), the *object petit a* "is something from which the subject, in order to constitute itself, has separated itself off as organ. This serves as a symbol of the lack, that is to say, of the phallus, not as such, but in so far as it is lacking. It must, therefore, be an object that is, firstly, separable and, secondly, that has some relation to the lack" (103).

21. Frantz Fanon, *Black Skin, White Masks*, trans. Charles Lam Markmann (1952; New York: Grove, 1967), 170.

22. For Fowler, who also sees the racial implications of the lynching, the punishment ultimately signifies an instance of the Freudian primal scene wherein "miscegenation replaces the prohibition against incest" (421).

Popeye's Impersonal Temple

Michael Wainwright

Naturam expellas furca, tamen usque recurret.[1]

The setting is a basement nightclub in Liverpool, England. A giant glitter ball throws down spasmodic motes of light across a litter-strewn dance floor. Prospective dancers search for partners as "The Look of Love" begins to play from the sound system

HIM:[*shyly*]You dancin'?

HER:[*guardedly*]I'm dancin'. You askin'?

HIM:[*just as shyly*]I'm askin'.

Courtship, as the opening credits to the popular British television sitcom *The Liver Birds* indicates, can be awkward. Broadly speaking, this difficulty is transhistorical and transcultural, as prevalent in twentieth-century America as in twenty-first-century Britain. For, ninety years ago, the young William Faulkner (1897–1962) experienced this common difficulty in courting (Lida) Estelle Oldham (1896–1972). His initial approach, sealed when Estelle married Cornell Franklin (1892–1959) on 18 April 1918, failed.[2] Nevertheless, a second opportunity arose with the breakdown of the Franklins' marriage and their subsequent divorce. Faulkner seized his chance and within less than two months—on 20 June 1929, to be precise—he and Estelle married. Even so, believes Louis Daniel Brodsky, "the humiliation of having to accept his formerly pedestalled lady, a divorcee now with two children, tainted whatever passion and exuberance he might have had for the presumably virginal Estelle."[3] Did Faulkner harbor any bitterness alongside this supposed chagrin? His earliest publications offer an insight in this regard. His first novel, *Soldiers' Pay* (1926), closes with the awkwardness and disappointment of a defeated courtship. Joe Gilligan has helped Margaret Powers to marry the ailing Donald Mahon. Then, soon after Donald's death, Joe proposes to Margaret. "I couldn't marry a man named Gilligan," she replies. Having inherited the powers ("Powers") of man ("Mahon"), now embodying each side of the sexual divide, Margaret knows that she must never become a Gilligan—or girl again.[4] Faulkner's second novel,

148

Mosquitoes (1927), adds resentment in victory to the maladroit aspects of courtship. Dawson Fairchild is undoubtedly a caricature of Sherwood Anderson (1876–1941), but is there also a touch of Faulkner himself in Fairchild's attitude to the mating game? Courtship, Fairchild lectures the sexually incompetent (but ardent) Ernest Talliaferro, is less a matter of tactics and more the "illusion that you can seduce women. Which you can't," he declaims, because "[t]hey just elect you."[5] Fairchild's vision of contemporary women is shattering. He sees them as "merely articulated genital organs with a kind of aptitude for spending whatever money you have" (201). They are synecdochic animations of valued parts that cost men dear. The sheer unpleasantness of Fairchild's remark has had serious critical repercussions. Two responses are illustrative: Gail Mortimer rebukes the author for his oblivion to the female sex except as gestational carriers;[6] Frederick C. Crews concludes that Faulkner retained a "saturnine resentment of women."[7] A cursory reading of the sexual politics—defined herein as sexuality, secondary selection, and sex within a sociobiological context—in Faulkner's sixth novel, *Sanctuary* (1931), would appear to confirm such accusations. This validation, however, would be a mistake because Mortimer and Crews typify a selective criticism that fails to appreciate Faulkner's rapid maturation not only as a man but also as an artist. In marrying Estelle, an event in the interstice between *Mosquitoes* and *Sanctuary*, Faulkner willingly became a stepfather. This act was nothing less than a form of altruism. As evolutionary critic Joseph Carroll insists, adoption is often symbolic of the ability "to abstract from one's reproductive interests and to devote oneself to some disinterested social good," and this impersonal sensibility soon began to enhance Faulkner's literary output too.[8] An authorial disinterest would hereon distinguish his literature. Hence, not a personal expression of virulence or indifference toward the sexual status of women, *Sanctuary* rather illustrates how sexual politics is conditioned by, and mediates between, the biological base of human nature and the cultural superstructure of society. If heated criticism continues to surround the novel, then this contentiousness emanates from Faulkner's prescience concerning sexual politics rather than from his personal feelings.

Heretofore the plantation belles of John Pendleton Kennedy (1795–1870) and associated authors had haunted American literature. Nineteenth-century artistic representations of female behavior in deference to male proprieties of race (European American), class (patrician), and upbringing (exclusive) fulfilled a phallocentric standard. Furthermore, modest females selecting their desired mate for a life of spousal fidelity resounded to the evolutionary tenets of sexual selection propounded by Charles Darwin (1809–82). *Sanctuary* violently dislocates the Faulknerian

aesthetic from these patterns of literary and scientific influence. The figures of Temple Drake and Popeye, in particular, expedite this trauma. At
the opening of the narrative, Temple is a mere seventeen, but her tender
years do little to palliate family expectations. Temple's immediate relations—her mother being dead—are a traditional Southern patriarch and
four brothers in their father's mold. Each of these men wishes Jefferson
to reverence their demure Temple as an exemplar of Southern womanhood. The male Drakes, like Anatidaen protectors of their female charge,
carefully guard Temple's reputation while circumscribing her freedom.
As a circuit judge, her father is socially empowered to oversee this vigil,
and courtship becomes his especial focus. In one incident, the shotgun-
brandishing judge confronts a suitor he deems unworthy. Youngest
brother Buddy is also an officious sentinel in this regard; Temple affirms
"that if he ever caught me with a drunk man, he'd beat hell out of me."[9]
The male standards of the House of Drake are stiflingly rigid in both
principle and practice.[10] If Scarlett O'Hara in *Gone with the Wind* (1936)
by Margaret Mitchell (1900–49) "had lived too long among people who
dissembled politely" while projecting their codes of propriety onto her,
then so has Temple.[11] Reacting against conformity, Temple turns toward
rebelliousness for the first time. This tactic secures her some leeway.
Judge Drake allows his daughter to attend the University of Mississippi,
satisfied that the relevant authorities carefully supervise coeducational
status. The dormitory for women is known as "the Coop"—freedom for
female undergraduates appears ostensible rather than actual (*Sanctuary* 198). For Temple, though, Ole Miss nonetheless offers a tangibly
looser domain. Faulkner carefully designates the distance between Jefferson and Oxford as a two-stage railway journey. Now Temple can enjoy
the sexual economy from a biological basis far less restrained by familial
strictures.

   Faulkner's Oxford offers two fields of play for young women interested
in heterosexual courtship: locals constitute the first sort, undergraduates comprise the second type. Since Faulkner portrays the early years
under the Butler Act during which Chancellor Alfred Hume (1866–1946)
had relaxed some nonacademic restrictions, each division offers certain
advantages.[12] On one side, town males can exploit their automobile ownership because "students in the University were not permitted to keep
cars." On the other side, university males can enjoy exclusive Ole Miss
events specifically arranged for the purposes of intersexual politics such
as "the Letter Club dances" held "on alternate Saturday evenings" and
"the three formal yearly balls" (198). The automobile as a detached modern appendage, or impersonal twentieth-century display tool, thereby
comes up against the intimacy of the courtship dance. Faced with these

competing fields, Temple chooses to sample both kinds coextensively. "I am on probation" (216), she admits, "for slipping out at night. Because only town boys can have cars" (217). Yet, she remains "cool, predatory and discreet" while participating in life on campus (198). Does this split mentality propound a "cruelly selfish lust which makes her completely disregard the well-being of any other person," as critic Sally R. Page insists?[13] No, her teenage response to the Oxford environment is Faulkner's rendition of a de facto case of biologically fostered and culturally conditioned behavior.

Late-twentieth-century amendments to sociobiology, especially those forwarded by British geneticist Richard Dawkins (b. 1941) and English biologist John Maynard Smith (1920–2004), enable the literary critic to appreciate Faulkner's subtlety in this portrayal.[14] The relevant refinements concern the basic asymmetry in gamete size, that is reproductive cell size, that Darwin analyzed in the *Mammalia* class of vertebrates. Females produce large eggs while males form far smaller spermatozoa. As a corollary, female production of gametes is scarce in comparison to the superabundance of sex cells carried by males. This relative rarity makes females the more valuable members of mammalian species, males the more expendable. Sexual difference therefore affords females a choice of partners. In honing this first principle, contemporary theorists understand the politics of mammalian breeding to be a conflict between male and female interests. Hence, the fundamental sexual difference in gamete production results in the predominance of male promiscuity. All courting males aspire to the *strategy of selfish exploitation* to which females respond with their *he-man strategy*. Female sexual selection in this instance is a matter of recognizing prospective mates whose hereditary characteristics augur well for breeding. Those males that suffer intrasexual disadvantage in terms of manifest robustness are left to employ the *strategy of fidelity*. The female *strategy of domestic bliss* has evolved to assess these signs of faithfulness with the prospect of securing a trustworthy suitor. By extracting a prenuptial investment from each potential partner, females can attempt to foster qualities of domesticity in advance. The demand for a long period of celibacy will induce casual males to give up in frustration with perseverance certifying devotion.[15]

These two courtship domains, selfish exploitation relaying with the he-man strategy and fidelity interacting with that of domestic bliss, are unlikely to exist in isolation from one another. Females will tend to employ the he-man strategy when faced with a preponderance of male *philanderers*, using the strategy of domestic bliss when dependable males predominate. Females resorting to the he-man strategy in an environment of male philanderers are *fast*, and those employing domestic bliss in response to *faithful* males are *coy*. Over numerous generations, an environment develops in which *x* percent of females are fast and (100–*x*) percent remain coy while a respective *y* percent of males philander as (100–*y*) percent stay faithful. When any population implementing such a mélange of fixed individual behaviors becomes resistant to invasion from mutant strategies, then an evolutionarily stable state has developed. However, cautions Smith, an entire intrasexual community is unlikely to consistently practice a single strategy; concomitantly, two different types of individual within each sex are improbable. The courtship behavior of a particular female is more liable to switch between her two available modes depending on the frequency with which she encounters the corresponding male strategies. A mixed *evolutionarily stable strategy* would then be achieved if each female spends *x* percent of her time being fast and the remaining (100–*x*) percent being coy, with each male a philanderer for *y* percent of his time, spending the remaining period in faithful mode. Inconstant mating behavior can be consistent with an established set of mating strategies.

Having asserted this, however, one must sound another cautionary note. Such modeling makes no presumption that philandering is more likely than faithfulness in male practice. Genetic causation must work in an environment, and, as Dawkins plainly states in *The Extended Phenotype* (1982), "there is no general reason for expecting genetic influences to be any more irreversible than environmental ones." Although genes are significant factors in behavior, the effects of genetic variation "may be overridden, modified, enhanced or reversed by other causes."[16]

Returning to Faulkner's text with this caveat in mind, not the whims of lust, but the long-established mixed evolutionarily stable strategy at Oxford underlies Temple's switches in courtship behavior. The he-man strategy recommends itself when courting the philandering complement of Oxonian youths and the strategy of domestic bliss when probing the dependability of undergraduates. Only when Gowan Stevens enters the courtship scene does her bifurcated fast-coy response appear to near resolution. Here is a man who combines a robust biological basis for sexual selection with an aristocratic command over the cultural superstructure. Furthermore, as a graduate of the University of Virginia, Gowan is allowed to attend social events at Ole Miss while simultaneously enjoying the freedom of car ownership. Temple enjoys this seemingly all-encompassing combination of attractions but fails to investigate his provenance. Gowan's history in the sexual economy is less innocent than Temple assumes. Narcissa Benbow, "with that serene and stupid impregnability of heroic statuary," is, in fact, Gowan's archetype of Southern womanhood (*Sanctuary* 253). He only turns to Temple for solace when rejected by this reification of his dreams. What is more, he holds resentment toward his previous setback.

An intrasexual component to male behavior during sexual selection, the *assessor strategy*, draws this emotion from Gowan. Smith defines this exclusively male behavior as a capacity to rank rivals in natural and sexual selection according to a perceived level of threat. When an individual believes he holds primacy over an antagonist, the assessor strategy suggests the employment of aggressive tactics, but if an individual deems himself inferior, then assessment advises passivity. One tactic of intrasexual evaluation often conducted during courtship is the *parallel walk* in which rivals concurrently display a particular ability. This reciprocal test soon unmasks any difference between the contestants. If no distinction is apparent, then the ensuing contest is usually protracted. To signal a high value for a contested ability tends to be an expensive exercise. "Otherwise," as Smith explains, "assessment strategies would be vulnerable to cheating."[17] Under normal conditions, then, assessed ability and fighting success correlate (the paradoxical inferior victory is the rarest of exceptions). Although the gradations of behavior are more refined than implied by this précis, a courtship evaluation of resource-holding power takes place between males in most mammalian species, including *Homo sapiens*.

Sanctuary presciently tracks these ramifications in the case of Gowan and his rivals for Temple following a formal dance at the University of Mississippi. After taking Temple home, Gowan must drive past the Oxonians excluded from the event. One of them breaks an empty liquor bottle, "propping the jagged shards upright in the road" (*Sanctuary* 199). The desire to burst the tires on Gowan's car—or deflate his ego—is aggressively apparent. Gowan, aware of the intrasexual politics at play, thwarts the scheme by pulling to their side of the road before reaching the debris. He invites his competitors to join him for a drink in town. Defeated at this initial stage of assessment, one of Gowan's competitors acknowledges the fact by warning him that "somebody broke a bottle there" (200). Having bought some illicit whiskey from a local "confectionery-lunchroom," the antagonists embark on a second phase of intrasexual evaluation: a drinking contest as a parallel walk. Bragging that the liquor "hasn't got much kick," Gowan seals victory by significantly outdrinking his opponents (201). Nevertheless, the contest has been squalid, as his overnight convalescence in the toilet at Oxford Station confirms.

On her way to Starkville by rail the next morning, Temple is to join Gowan on the platform at Taylor for a secret assignation. They plan to spend some hours together before Gowan drives her to Starkville to coincide with the arrival of the train. Because of his hangover, however,

Gowan only reaches Taylor as the service pulls away. To fulfill their plan, Temple must jump from the moving vestibule, springing down and running beside the car while an official shakes his fist at her. But the ire of this male "conductor" is the least of Temple's worries, because Gowan, taking over the directorial role, and recalling her scrawled name on the lavatory wall at Oxford, subjects her to a verbal attack. That women can employ a double courtship strategy has been an unpalatable discovery. "Think you can play around all week with any badger-trimmed hick that owns a ford, and fool me on Saturday, don't you?" Gowan fumes. Temple's sexual politics appears to be a massive obstacle to their future together. The prospect of alcoholic oblivion proffers Gowan an immediate remedy. Touring the backwoods for liquor, though "apparently looking straight ahead," he drives "into the tree at twenty miles an hour" (205). The collision damage suffered by his car and the hazard entertained by the occupants not only echo the impact imparted on his consciousness by the revelation of Temple's nature, but also foretell the trauma to be inflicted on her when their search for help leads to the perverse sanctuary of the "Old Frenchman place" (184). This refuge "for crimps and spungs and feebs" accommodates the mentally arrested Tommy, the decrepit old Pap, and various hoodlums (185). Moreover, Temple will discover a courtship trajectory here, as advanced by the gangster Popeye, to which her rebelliousness makes her perceptive, but for which she has no biologically engendered response.

A peculiar aura invests Popeye as an exception to the regular type of male circulating in the sexual economy. Faulkner was determined to locate the initiation of this difference in terms of biological inheritance and some of his late alterations to *Sanctuary*, as Philip Cohen affirms, concerned the "addition of Popeye's childhood biography."[18] These emendations posit a twofold betrayal at conception. Popeye's mentally deranged maternal grandmother points to an infirmity on the distaff side of his lineage, while his father taints the spear side with syphilis. His mother, pregnant with Popeye before her marriage, begins to ail within three weeks of her wedding. The prognosis for her fetus is not hopeful. Even being born on "Christmas day" offers little prospect of a miracle, because, as Faulkner must have known, syphilis during pregnancy can cause physical deformity, mental illness, and infant mortality. "At first," the doctors attending Popeye's birth, "thought he was blind. Then they found that he was not blind, though he did not learn to walk and talk until he was about four years old" (*Sanctuary* 389). Having "no hair at all until he was five," his physical development remains excruciatingly slow. "With care," specialists advise his mother, "he will live some time longer. But he will never be any older than he is now." Struggling more than most to survive childhood, Popeye proves his doubters wrong. Only the fact that "he will never be a man, properly speaking" is incurable (392). Hence, a cruel irony undermines the Freudian conjunction between eye and penis that associates the nickname Popeye with machismo. Indeed, when Horace Benbow first meets Popeye, he notes that his guide to the Old Frenchman place "smells like that black stuff that ran out of Bovary's mouth and down upon her bridal veil when they raised her head" (184). Popeye's very breath seems laced with a syphilitic legacy that leaves the masculinity of his mien and build diminished. His sobriquet therefore holds a second irony—the gangster displaying a severe diminution of the physical prowess secreted in the comic strip hero.[19] Horace concurrently notices that Popeye's "face had a queer, bloodless color, as though seen by electric light" (181). Even the "feeb" Tommy comments on "them gal's hands of hisn" (210). Certainly, one can interpret Popeye in effeminate terms, but his face "like a mask carved into two simultaneous expressions" suggests otherwise (182). Another aspect of this alterity surfaces when Popeye visits his mother. "Prosperous, quiet, thin, black, and uncommunicative in his narrow black suits," he is recognized by his mother immediately (393). Successful in capitalist terms, despite his challenged biological inheritance, Popeye's demeanor and dress nonetheless imply that he remains reticent according to the criteria of courtship communication. Blackness does not proclaim the vivid colors so readily associated with a mastery of the sexual economy. Even so, this supposedly undistinguished specimen, aware that he is outside the patriarchal norm, has developed a culturally dominated approach to the politics of sex, a trajectory that bespeaks alterity.

With her rebellious inclination, Temple will find this difference tempting. Coming face to face with the gangster for the first time, she cannot help but flash that "grimace of taut, toothed coquetry." Intriguingly for Temple, as Popeye walks by, he offers no relay to her signal—"the finicking swagger of his narrow back did not falter" (211). Temple next cajoles Popeye to take her and Gowan back to Jefferson. The gangster's "soft, cold voice" issues a sharp reply. "Make your whore lay off of me, Jack" (212). Temple's response is to goad Popeye further. This reaction establishes a reciprocal temptation that predicates Temple as a possible inductee into Popeye's particular sexual economy. Gowan breaks this hiatus, intervening in the developing interplay by forcing Temple into the Frenchman house. Gowan's maneuver initiates the last courtship dance between the graduate and his belle: "their feet scraped on the bare floor as though they were performing a clumsy dance, and clinging together they lurched into the wall" (213). Disorienting conditions have broken down the formalities of a university ball into a leaden-footed shambles.

This dance, more an abysmal performance than an intimacy, anticipates a macabre dénouement.

Gowan starts drinking again, this time embarking on a parallel walk with the owner of the Old Frenchman place, Goodwin, and the mysterious Van. Forsaken by her desultory protector cum suitor, Temple continues to focus her attention on the seemingly disadvantaged Popeye. Women, *Sanctuary* implies, can learn to expose any pretence of sexual vitality. As a corollary, men with palpable honesty tend to win their favor. Through her Oxford experiences, Temple appears to have developed this ability. Popeye, who has survived and prospered despite his obvious deficiencies, must embody a singular kind of evolutionary fitness. Withheld from Temple for the present, the perverseness of this successful adjustment and correspondence to some niche in modern living allures her via mystery, singularity, and enforced ignorance.

Popeye's particular response to biological inferiority has been to exploit the detached and impersonal twentieth-century possibilities for secondary selection to create the mutant courtship *strategy of impersonal gratification*. The automobile and the gun become his phallic signaling tools of choice: his yellow car stands out against the black background of Model T Fords (which one assumes the "hicks" of Oxford drive), while his reputation with a pistol is second to none. Excluded from the standard biological and patriarchal constructions of courtship, Popeye situates himself at the forefront of a culturally directed sexual selection. Being at the vanguard of this revolution, Popeye exerts a sexual fascination over Temple, drawing her into his unfamiliar territory. Only Ruby Lamar, Goodwin's lover and mother of his child, appreciates the teenager's growing sense of disorientation. Ruby has known Popeye since her whorehouse days in Memphis. An escapee from that particular sexual economy, one in which men use money to subvert the biological determinant of female choice, she impresses on Temple that her goading of Popeye is a case of "riding" too far (217). Furthermore, "playing at it" in sexual terms with the gangster is a dangerous game (220). This, however, is the extent of the older woman's warning. For, as Diane Roberts makes plain, "even though she speaks to Temple in the traditionally female space of the kitchen, her child at her feet, Ruby's voice oscillates between feminine and masculine situations."[20] There is a sense of female accommodation to male impositions, intimated in Ruby's "naked ankles" above "a worn pair of man's brogans" (*Sanctuary* 184) that are constantly "unlaced" (219), which Temple would do well to escape. Unsurprisingly, the youngster's first night in the backwoods augurs ill. Sitting in bed, with her "hat tilted rakishly upon the back of her head," she presumably awaits Gowan (227). Beset with three domains rampantly contesting for her choice of sexual dominion—selfish exploitation interacting with the he-man strategy, fidelity relaying with that of domestic bliss, and impersonal gratification expecting a correspondingly detached response—Temple's inconsistent behavior intensifies. "A raincoat and a khaki-covered canteen" hanging on the wall symbolize this confused state of mind (226). Although she contemplates the canteen as a metaphorical chastity belt, she also puts on the raincoat as a form of rubber protection. This latter act answers for her decision to have sex. That Temple then produces "a compact from somewhere," arranges her hair, and powders her face, compounds this implication (227). When the comatose body of Gowan accompanies Van's declaration of resource-holding power, "we're bringing you a customer," her preparations have been to no avail (229). Despite and in contrast to Gowan's state, however, the sexual atmosphere does not dissipate.

By the following morning, the presence of Temple's fear-induced instability has started to destabilize Ruby's relationship with Goodwin. "Motionless, facing one another like the first position of a dance," the couple confront one another "in a mounting terrific muscular hiatus" (245). When the impasse breaks, Goodwin strikes, and Ruby suffers. Having acted heroically in offering her "own body as sacrifice," as Roberts asserts, Ruby can do nothing more to protect Temple.[21] The teenager, abandoned by Gowan, who has admitted intrasexual defeat in walking alone toward town, must face her coming ordeal with only Tommy for a guard. Faulkner's text now becomes rampant with intimations of danger. For, in her attempt to hide that evening, Temple chooses to enter through the "trap" (*Sanctuary* 243) into the "crib" (237) of the "broken-backed" barn (207). Here, caught in the ironic embrace of the crib, Popeye will succeed in breaking Temple. Awaiting her fate, Temple's inability to control her usually amicable body, testifies to the self-alienation to come. She thinks of her legs, all that "I'd done for them," all the "dances I had taken them to," but they do not repay her in staying Popeye's intent (329). The gangster murders the gallant Tommy. Then, realizing his strategy of impersonal gratification, he penetrates Temple's reserve in a manner detached from common expectations by raping her with a corncob. The "loose hulls," or empty husks, of the maize seeds on the crib floor have foretold this device (243). The impersonal dildo has replaced the personal flesh. Both impotent and infertile—the woody cylindrical stem substituting for an erect penis, the maize seeds for semen—Popeye's tool of choice nevertheless confirms his position in the vanguard of a revolution, a traumatic transformation of sexual politics from which Temple will never recover.

Popeye, immune to the personal suffering of his object, intends to continue enjoying this peculiar prowess. Thus, his relocation of Temple following her rape is less concerned with murder and more determined by his need for a salubrious sexual environment. The Old Frenchman place, some "twelve miles from town," is unsuitable for Popeye's predilection (262). "Set in the middle of a tract of land," Goodwin's house is the most substantial remains "of cotton fields and gardens and lawns long since gone back to jungle" (184). There is no "sign of husbandry—plow or tool; in no direction was a planted field in sight—only a gaunt weather-stained ruin in a somber grove through which the breeze drew with a sad, murmurous sound" (206). This is nature in the raw where even "what had once been a kitchen garden" is today choked "with cedar and blackjack saplings" (210). *Natura naturans*, or the Arcadian Great Mother, is on the verge of regaining her dominion through sheer fecundity. *Naturam expellas furca, tamen usque recurret*. While conveying the state of the former plantation, this apt proverb concurrently emphasizes the alienation of those without biological sympathy. Horace Benbow had glimpsed this lack in Popeye during their inadvertent backwoods trek. Led by the gangster along a peripatetic track, Horace asked why they could not take a short cut. "Through all them trees?" is Popeye's rejoinder. Sticking to the path, Popeye maintains the lead, "his tight suit and stiff hat all angles," startlingly out of place "like a modernist lampstand" (183). Only in the city, manmade and impersonal, does he feel at home. Memphis, specifically the brothel owned by Miss Reba Rivers on Manuel Street, is his destination with Temple.

Popeye feels immediately at home on entering the whorehouse with its "weary quality. A spent quality; defunctive, exhausted—a protracted weariness like a vitiated backwater beyond sunlight and the vivid noises of sunlight and day" (278–79). This is an environment where man has perverted the biological. Darwinian sexual selection does not come into play in Reba's place. "We dont stand on no ceremony here," she explains (280). A detached setting, "full of sounds" that are "indistinguishable, remote" (287), the bordello vibrates to the discordant jangle of "a mechanical piano" rather than to the intimate music of love (288). The naïve experience of Virgil Snopes confirms the impersonality of the house. Staying in the brothel without initially cognizant of its function, Virgil goes to sleep hearing "the whispers of silk that came through the walls and the floor, that seemed as much a part of both as the planks and the plaster" (314). The reification of women, not as marble statuary but as sex objects, appears complete. Reba's prostitutes are not so much *on the game*, as in the English expression, but *integers of impersonal gratification*. Here Temple remains, submerged by the violent repercussions of violation, in an impersonal state of unconscious submission; Popeye, though, feels safe. Instead of backwoods flora, Manuel Street merely offers "a forlorn and hardy tree of some shabby species—gaunt, lop-branched magnolias, a stunted elm or a locust in grayish, cadaverous bloom—interspersed by rear ends of garages" (277). When flowers do appear, as Reba's hat attests, they are "rigidly moribund" (279). Popeye has secured a perfect location for his impersonal needs.

Temple's boudoir, a room in which "the mantel supported a wax lily beneath a glass bell," may conform to Popeye's weird standard, but modern dissembling, shallow pretenses, and gestures to the natural economy cannot satisfy her (325). She finds this side of urban America a remote and godless prison; for, as soon as Temple relates critically to her surroundings, she feels "in as complete an isolation as though she were bound to a church steeple" (289). Popeye's power over Temple starts to evaporate hereupon. The sense of procreative sex still applies to Temple, the biological imperative perversely helping to break the stranglehold of bordello politics, while Popeye must translate that reproductive standard into the impersonal. Realizing that the gangster can never consummate their relationship helps to bring Temple back from her forced translocation as she begins to consciously relate to her initial rape and her continuing ordeal. In focusing on the gangster's impotency, the personal undermining the impersonal, her second rebellion gets under way. Reba, who has known Popeye far longer, articulates this feeling. "A young man spending his money like water on girls and not never going to bed with one," she declares. "It's against nature" (356). Even to the jaded eyes of a madam, Popeye's proclivities appear exceptional. The Manuel Street prostitute Minnie soon notes of the Popeye-Temple relationship "how he wasn't here hardly at all, gone about every other night, and that when he was here, there wasn't no signs at all the next morning." One of Reba's friends later advances a reason for his absences and the lack of sexual detritus. "Maybe he went off and got fixed up with one of these glands, these monkey glands," Myrtle opines, "and it quit on him" (357).[22] Ribald humor, yes, but Faulkner also intimates that Popeye, signaling himself as a nascent subspecies of *Homo sapiens*, is especially suited to testicular material transplanted from another species.

Popeye employs two tactics to compensate Temple for their lack of sexual congress. He derives the first from normal male standards. Mirrors, brushes, perfumes, and powders start to clutter Temple's dressing table. Beginning to resist her abuser, she throws these accoutrements aside. His approach fails because directing capital largesse along patriarchal lines cannot mask Popeye's alienation from the biological economy. From his perspective, therefore, a secondary tactic needs be, and is, more innovative. He employs a fellow hoodlum, named Red, to replace the dildo as his detached sexual tool; the surrogate male becomes the whole simulacrum that precedes the less-than-complete sinews of Popeyean flesh. In this manner, Popeye aims to assuage the incarnate rebellion of Temple and better satisfy his own impersonal needs (since there no longer exists a substantial connection between his body and that of his victim). Red enables Popeye to become a voyeur in the sex act, to remain apart from other flesh, and to enjoy a singular sense of consummation. Popeye's perspective, characterized by his grotesque "whinnying sound," is now that of another species (358).

The performances of others empower Popeye's climaxes, but they also seed a fatal tension. *Naturam expellas furca, tamen usque recurret.* On the one hand, Temple understands that she and Popeye will never stimulate each other personally. On the other hand, she now satisfies her need for personal human contact through her dubious interaction with Red. A relationship seemingly bordering on love springs up between the two active players in Popeye's sexual economy. Full of vitality, as his name implies, Red is in stark contrast to Popeye. Not only is he "almost a head taller than anybody else," but he is also a man who enjoys flaunting the sartorial plumage of "his gray suit and [a] spotted bow tie" (342, 341). He may not be a multicolored specimen, yet his grayness stands out against the white and black background associated with Gowan and Popeye, and his outstanding "Red" head adds to this impression by symbolizing an engorged phallic glans. In addition, as a town dweller who nonetheless "looked like a college boy," Red embodies the two courtship fields that Temple coextensively enjoyed at Oxford (341). No wonder, then, that her means of escape from the trauma of the impersonal involves the rejection of the master in favor of the master's erstwhile tool.[23]

The tension so engendered between Popeye, Temple, and Red comes to a head at the Grotto nightclub. Again, the courtship ritual of the dance comes to the fore, Popeye employing an assessor strategy overwhelmingly weighted in his favor by the presence of numerous henchmen. Red ought to back down in these circumstances, but he does not. Popeye initiates the proceedings by leading Temple to the dance floor. Fondling for the gun that lies "rigid" at his armpit, her partner's prosthetic manhood attracts Temple's impersonally tainted impulses. "Give it to me," she whispers as her hand begins "to steal down his body in a swift, covert movement." Suddenly, as consciousness synchronizes with natural sense, Temple withdraws her fingers "in a movement of revulsion" (342). Red, trying to seize the initiative, chooses this juncture to ask Temple for a dance. The presumption of his intervention is fatal. Popeye allows the pair to meet briefly in a private room. With his suspicions confirmed, Popeye has Temple returned to Reba's whorehouse and shoots Red dead outside the nightclub. Temple's enforced third rebellion, paradoxically a cultural one, but belonging to the well-established order, has achieved its aim. The opportunity repeatedly afforded her by Popeye—"'I'm giving him his chance,' he said. 'Will you go back in that house, or will you get in this car?' . . . 'I'm giving him his chance'" (338)—but left untaken is evidence to this effect. This refusal asserts Temple's rebellion against Red as another of her abusers (just as her contempt of court will later signal Goodwin's punishment too). The irony of Red's failure to secure a fare-well dance with his sexual victim soon becomes apparent after his death. At his wake, supposedly a teetotal event in keeping with the Volstead Act, there is a stash of whisky in the backroom liberally used to pep up the fruit punch. Drunkenness ensues, a scuffle breaks out, and the resultant jostling tips the coffin over. Red's final appearance is a dance macabre with his mourners as they maneuver him toward the empty casket.

Popeye's murderous actions at the Grotto repeat two ghastly incidents from his childhood. At a party, Popeye had locked himself inside the bathroom for some minutes before absconding. The adults only discovered what had happened in the interim on breaking down the door. They found "a wicker cage in which two lovebirds lived; beside it lay the birds themselves, and the bloody scissors with which he had cut them up alive" (392–93). The young Popeye later repeated this vendetta on another typical object of human affection, cutting up "a half-grown kitten" (393). These episodes evince a victimized child, an individual damned by reckless procreation, becoming a victimizer. In their turn, Temple and Red had become Popeye's tormenting lovebirds.

"He will never be any older than he is now," the doctors had said of Popeye, but his immaturity is of a different order than that exhibited by Dawson Fairchild in *Mosquitoes* (392). This difference signals Faulkner's complex and swift maturation as an artist. At one level, as Dawson's surname paradoxically implies, Fairchild remains a juvenile concerning sexual politics, but a blatantly unfair one. The female body confronts him as "merely articulated" parts rather than as an animated whole (*Mosquitoes* 453). At another level, Popeye becomes far more unbalanced at a similar stage of sexual development, the established relations that predominantly govern society continue to constitute a greater anguish, and his effect on Temple is physically and psychologically shattering in a manner to which Fairchild's synecdochic projection significantly palls. Temple and Red's closeness, the socially determined difference that enabled their ambiguous relationship, reiterated Popeye's exclusion not only from relations both sexual and social with women, but also from social relations with men (the Irigarayan hom[m]o-sexual). This was an all-inclusive rejection that Popeye did not wish to face. He therefore killed Red. Yet, because she continued to manifest his enigmatic ideal, he spared Temple. Worshipping her as an impersonal physical space has supplied him with proof of metaphysical perfection. Extending this critical inference helps to suggest Popeye's reasoning hereafter: he can only forsake the material and reach this spiritual goal via his own death. His calmness before execution would seem to concur with such a conclusion; his evasion of justice through passive suicide adds another disagreeable layer to his legacy.

A trap had closed to snare Temple in the barn loft; the opening of another such door signals Popeye's demise. One may be inclined to imagine his spasmodic last moments on the hangman's noose solely as an impersonal dance of death, but his kicking legs also signal the possibility of an inverted parallel of continuing distress. The prospect of carrying Red's child leads Temple into another trap rather than offering any hope of salvation from the wounds of a perverse society. Trying to convalesce, surrounded by Old World culture as she sits in the Luxembourg Gardens of Paris, attended by the stalwart Southern patriarch that is her father, but reminded of a new order from within, Temple remains "sullen and discontented and sad" (*Sanctuary* 398). A future, which she conceived in a perverted escape route masquerading as love, but one that the impersonal still hauntingly commands, beckons. Interwar Europe during "the season of rain and death," insists Faulkner, is fitting temporally and spatially for this singularly lost member of an American generation (398). A nascent form of twentieth-century sexual politics has generated incurable trauma, four deaths, and the probability of troubled lives to come. Cold impersonality has undone the solidarity offered by warm personal relations.

NOTES

1. This epigraph from Quintus Horatius Flaccus (65–8 BC) translates as "nature can be expelled with a pitchfork, but nevertheless always returns."

2. This early attempt to win Estelle's favor had started when both she and William were children. "Bill tried to attract her attention," recalls his brother John, "by being the loudest one, the daringest. But the more he tried the more mussed he got, and sweaty, and dirtier, and Estelle simply wasn't interested." John Faulkner, *My Brother Bill: An Affectionate Reminiscence* (New York: Trident, 1963), 85.

3. Louis Daniel Brodsky, *Life Glimpses* (Austin: University of Texas Press, 1990), 28.

4. William Faulkner, *Soldiers' Pay*, ed. Joseph Blotner and Noel Polk (New York: Library of America, 2006), 311.

5. William Faulkner, *Mosquitoes*, ed. Joseph Blotner and Noel Polk (New York: Library of America, 2006), 110–11. Hereafter cited parenthetically.

6. Gail Mortimer, "Evolutionary Theory in Faulkner's Snopes Trilogy," *Rocky Mountain Review of Language and Literature* 40.4 (1986): 197.

7. Frederick C. Crews, *The Critics Bear It Away: American Fiction and the Academy* (New York: Random House, 1992), xxi.

8. Joseph Carroll, *Evolution and Literary Theory* (Columbia: University of Missouri Press, 1995), 146.

9. William Faulkner, *Sanctuary*, ed. Joseph Blotner and Noel Polk (New York: Library of America, 1985), 216. Hereafter cited parenthetically.

10. In archaic terms, a drake is an ensign or standard depicting a dragon.

11. Margaret Mitchell, *Gone with the Wind* (London: Macmillan, 1974), 239.

12. Having, as historian Leslie H. Allen (1887–n.d.) records, "read in the papers that boys and girls were coming home from school and telling their fathers and mothers that the Bible was all nonsense," and having heard the Reverend W. J. Murray (1876–n.d.) sermonize that "the teaching of evolution in the schools ought to be stopped because it was attacking religion," local legislator John Washington Butler had determined to act. Leslie H. Allen, *Bryan and Darrow at Dayton* (New York: Russell & Russell, 1967), 1–2. The Tennessee Legislature passed his bill in 1925 and banned the study of evolution in the publicly funded institutes of Tennessee. The popular appeal of the Butler Act resulted in the Mississippi legislature's discussion of an antievolution statute, the passing of the bill by a vote of seventy-six to thirty-two, and the signing of the legislation by the fundamentalist Democratic governor, Henry Lewis Whitfield (1868–1927), on 11 March 1926. Hume made his changes to campus regulations during his initial tenure as Chancellor, which lasted between 1924 and 1930. His second period in office covered 1932 to 1935.

13. Sally R. Page, *Faulkner's Women: Characterization and Meaning* (De Land, Fla.: Everett/Edwards, 1972), 81.

14. Indeed, the general argument in the next paragraph develops that proposed in Richard Dawkins, *The Selfish Gene* (1976; Oxford: Oxford University Press, 1989), 140–65.

15. A female could ensure constant attention from her mate by concealing when she is fertile. "Women," notes geneticist Steve Jones, "are the only female primates who do not make it obvious when they are most fertile." Steve Jones, *The Language of the Genes: Biology, History, and the Evolutionary Future* (London: Flamingo, 2000), 155.

16. Richard Dawkins, *The Extended Phenotype: The Long Reach of the Gene* (1982; Oxford: Oxford University Press, 1999), 13.

17. John Maynard Smith, *Evolution and the Theory of Games* (Cambridge: Cambridge UP, 1982), 110.

18. Philip Cohen, "Faulkner by the Light of a Pale Fire: Postmodern Textual Scholarship and Faulkner Studies at the End of the Twentieth Century," *Faulkner and Postmodernism*, ed. John N. Duvall and Ann J. Abadie (Jackson: University Press of Mississippi, 2002), 176.

19. Popeye the Sailor, created by the cartoonist Elzie Crisler Segar (1894–1938), first appeared in January 1929.

20. Diane Roberts, *Faulkner and Southern Womanhood* (Athens: University of Georgia Press, 1994), 132.

21. Ibid.

22. Russian-born French surgeon Serge Voronoff (1866–1951) promoted the implantation of monkey gland material into human testes. This procedure was a 1920s prosthetic equivalent to the present-day drug sildenafil citrate (trademark Viagra).

23. One intends the English pun of "tool" for "penis."

Temple Drake's Rape
and the Myth of the Willing Victim

Caroline Garnier

William Faulkner worked on *Sanctuary* and *As I Lay Dying* within the same couple of years: He wrote *Sanctuary* in 1929, wrote and published *As I Lay Dying* in 1930, and then revised *Sanctuary* to publish it in 1931.[1] This may explain why these two novels, written at a time when Faulkner was himself concerned with matters of marriage, sex, and pro-creation,[2] can be seen as two sides of the same coin: They present different aspects of a Southern sexual culture that juxtaposes and merges abuse and respect, perversion and morality, deviance and norm, sanity and insanity, and private and public sexualities in ways that reveal the very thin line that exists between what we consider "normal" and what we judge as shocking.

The gruesome rape at the center of *Sanctuary* was, Faulkner said, "the most horrific idea I could think of"; however, the reality that inspired the novel was not only the "ghastly story he had heard in the night club a few years before about the girl who had been raped by the impotent gangster using a bizarre object," but also the sexual culture Faulkner witnessed around him.[3] Because Temple Drake's rape is presented as shocking, sensational, and a token of "abnormal" perversity, it tends to eclipse the more commonplace threatening presence of male sexual domination found at different levels of society in both *Sanctuary* and *As I Lay Dying*. Through an analysis of the sexual experiences of Temple Drake, Addie Bundren, and Dewey Dell Bundren, the following essay explores the interaction between obvious and hidden forms of sexual subordination as well as their resulting secret, insidious forms of psychic trauma.[4]

In *Sanctuary*, Popeye's sexual domination of Temple is anything but subtle. Early on in the novel, Faulkner establishes sex as a matter of power rather than pleasure: Popeye is impotent and it is unlikely that his victim, a seventeen-year-old college girl, derived pleasure from being penetrated with a corncob and later being held captive in Miss Reba's brothel for five weeks. As Jane Gallop reminds us, Freud likewise excluded questions of pleasure from his theory of sexuality in order to determine the active/passive roles of men and women in gender relations.[5] In *Sanctuary*, sex is a powerful tool Popeye uses to subdue Temple: gun, corncob, surrogate penis, as well as physical and psychological domination are all connected in the novel before, during, and after her rape. Sexuality throughout the novel has therefore less to do with sexual gratification than with objectification, control, and silencing.

In that power struggle, Temple has no chance of winning. In her account of the rape to Horace Benbow, she imagines a series of different ways her assault could have been prevented, had she not been a teenage girl. After she fantasizes being a boy, she imagines fastening herself up into an iron belt, being dead, being an unattractive teacher, and being "an old man, with a long white beard," until she virtually turns her genitals into male parts (217–20). Her account clearly establishes the adult male as dominant and confirms that she is devoid of power. Throughout the novel, her pleas and screams, her "aching, rigid" smiles and defensive body language, as well as her efforts to impress with her social status, her father's position as a judge, and her brothers' protectiveness are all in vain. Other readers have interpreted Temple's attitude at the Frenchman's Bend as teasing, but the text clearly expresses more uneasiness and nervousness on her part than glamour. Her smiles, for instance, are in fact a "grimace," and it is important to see them as an attempt to control the situation rather than as an invitation to assault. Michael Wainwright in this volume calls Temple's "courtship" of Popeye at the Frenchman's Bend a "dance," which I find quite adequate, even though we draw opposed conclusions on her goal: Temple clearly exercises the only power she has—her looks—to obtain favors of Popeye, namely that he would drive them back to town. Her little "dance" resembles that of a cute little girl asking her father a favor. However, her body language during the night she stays at the Frenchman's Bend leaves little room for interpretation: "She sat on the bed again. She sat with her legs close together, her head bent," then "lay, her hands crossed on her breast and her legs straight and close and decorous, like an effigy on an ancient tomb" (70–71). As she hears the men coming closer, she stands "in the corner, her arms crossed, her hands clutching her shoulders" (73); "She took the raincoat from the nail and put it over her own coat and fastened it" (70).

But it is not only the situation surrounding Popeye and his obvious sexual domination of Temple that indicates Temple is subordinated to men in *Sanctuary*. In the patriarchal society of the novel, the all-male institutions supposed to "protect" the "weak sex" seem to converge into a system that gradually objectifies that "most sacred *thing* in life: womanhood" (283, emphasis added). This sacred *thing*, this "temple" of sacrosanct womanhood, is, in fact, steadily desecrated into a sexual commodity by the institutional sanctuaries that pretend to put it on a pedestal to better "protect" it. Throughout her ordeal, Temple is in "complete isolation as though she were bound to a church steeple"; she is perpetually crushed by *Sanctuary*'s all-male institutions of family, gentlemanliness, prostitution, civil protection, medicine, and law (158).

Temple's familial sanctuary is made up of her father—"Judge Drake of Jackson"—and four brothers—"Two are lawyers and one's a newspaper man. The other's still in school. At Yale," boasts Temple (54). No mention is made of any female relative; Temple's family is a male space, where she leads the sheltered lifestyle of a privileged Southern college girl whose father typically "sit[s] on the veranda, in a linen suit, a palm leaf fan in his hand, watching the negro mow the lawn" (54). In *Sanctuary*'s patriarchal family, men control their daughters' and sisters' sexuality by choosing— and, if necessary, murdering—their suitors, and women who misbehave are locked up, sent away, put on probation, or even beaten by their male "protectors" (55–58).[6] And Temple *is* a misbehaving daughter. Escaping her familial protection, she jumps off the train to go to the ball game with Gowan, who promised to get her there faster than the train. In doing so, she puts herself in the hands of her first abductor, a so-called gentleman who forces her to go to the Old Frenchman's Bend, a place where she begs him not to go (26–27).[7]

On the way there, Gowan, who is drunk, crashes their convertible into a tree. The car accident is no small ordeal: She "felt herself flying through the air" from the convertible, she "scrambled to her feet, her head reverted"; "her bones turned to water and she fell flat on her face," "her mouth open upon a soundless wail behind her lost breath" (38). Shocked, hurt, and mute after this frightful accident, Temple is thrown into the Frenchman's Bend, the second male sanctuary encountered in the novel. Like Temple's family, this secluded bootlegging place is run by four men and an old "Pap." The men of this illegal sanctuary not only fail to care for her, but they instill in her a terror that further destabilizes her, as all four men start "pesterin her," as Tommy puts it: "[Van's] hard forearm came across her middle . . . [he] drew her toward him by the wrist. . . 'Right on my lap here,' Van said" (64–68). To reassure herself, Temple insists that these men and Ruby, the woman who cooks for them, are "just like other people" (56). Even though she is afraid of them, she does not leave because she is even more afraid of whom she might meet by entering the woods at dusk, as would many women: "'Let her go,' Goodwin said. Then she was free. She began to back slowly away. . . . Still smiling her aching, rigid grimace Temple backed from the room. In the hall she whirled and ran. . . . She ran to the road and down it for fifty yards in the darkness, then without a break she whirled and ran back

to the house and sprang onto the porch and crouched against the door"
(65). Although some critics have characterized her fear of the woods as
"ridiculously excessive,"[8] this fear of the woods and the many "wolves"
it might hide—a symptom of what I call the "Little Red Riding Hood"
syndrome—explains why she does not exchange the sanctuary of the
Frenchman's Bend for that of the woods.

Kali Tal explains that for many young women, such an awareness that
rape is an omnipresent risk, that any man can turn into an aggressor,
"makes growing up a recognition of subordination and life a state of
siege."[9] After a night at the frightening Frenchman's Bend, Temple has
a similar awareness: "I had been scared so long that I guess I had just
gotten used to being." Although her rape by Popeye the next morning is
horrific and shocking, it is not what struck her as most fearful. Horace
cannot help but notice from her description that the night that preceded
it was "the only part of the whole experience which appeared to have left
any impression on her at all: the night which she had spent in *comparative inviolation*" (215, emphasis added). After that night, Temple thinks
she can "stand just anything," and Popeye's presence is just another element of what she sees as a "converging threat" from all men (89, 148).

Sanctuary therefore mixes two dissonant voices: although the novel
points at Popeye as the main aggressor, pathologizing him as a "mon-
strous" anomaly through his mental retardation, his impotence, his psy-
chopathic tendencies, and his violent upbringing, Temple clearly sees
the threat as coming from all the *normal* men around her (121, 302–9).
This "comparative inviolation" calls attention to the presence of secret,
private sexual abuse and intimidation in a society where, as Laura Brown
explains, sexual abuse not only takes the form of violent physical assault,
but also more insidious verbal and psychological forms. We should
"stretch the definition of trauma," Brown says, "to include such daily
occurrences" of abuse.[10] To that end, Brown describes Maria Root's concept of "insidious trauma": "By this, [Root] refers to the traumatogenic
effects of oppression that are not necessarily overtly violent or threatening to bodily well-being at the given moment but that do violence to the
soul and spirit. Her model suggests, for instance, that for all women,
living in a culture where there is a high base rate of sexual assault and
where such behavior is considered normal and erotic by men, as it is in
North American culture, is an exposure to insidious trauma."[11]

Brown also explains that it is not only the assault per se that is potentially traumatic, but the very fear of it: "All of us know someone like our-
selves who was raped, more often than not in her own home by a man she
knew. In consequence, many women who have never been raped have
symptoms of rape trauma: we are hypervigilant to certain cues, avoid

situations that we sense are high risk, go numb in response to overtures from men that might be friendly—but that might also be the first step toward our violation" (107). This explains why Temple's deepest fear at the Frenchman's Bend comes from all men rather than from Popeye alone.

It should come as no surprise then, as Joseph Urgo also pointed out, that in the trial at the end of *Sanctuary*, Temple accuses Lee Goodwin instead of Popeye.[12] It is no accident that she points to the white, sane, paternal Goodwin rather than to the "black," impotent, childlike, and insane Popeye. In naming Goodwin, Temple names the patriarch. It is interesting that as a white father, within the novel as well and in most of its critical response, Goodwin manages to pass for an innocent victim, as if he could not be seen as the criminal Temple has revealed him to be: instead, he is turned into a martyr, "sacrificed by Temple's evil," as Page affirms (84). On the other hand, Duvall's new interpretation of Goodwin and Popeye's "miscegenated" identities, in this volume, possibly suggests that the "blackness" in Goodwin could explain his actions, as if Popeye and Goodwin would both have to have some "blackness" in them to be seen as criminals. To Temple, however, Goodwin is clearly a white man, and it is as such that he is found guilty. Furthermore, while Popeye is "not even a man," says Temple, Goodwin is "a real man," as Ruby tells her: "You don't know what it is to be wanted by a real man. And thank your stars you haven't and never will. . . . And if he is just man enough to call you a whore, you'll say Yes Yes and you'll crawl naked in the dirt and the mire for him to call you that" (231, 59). Temple's perjured testimony shows that on the bench of female justice, it is not the madman who performs irrational crimes that is found guilty, nor the fantasized black savage, it is the white father who beats his wife, kills, illegally makes and sells alcohol, and "pesters" the vulnerable Temple. By accusing Goodwin, Temple points to the "comparative inviolation" exercised by "normal" men rather than to the violent rape itself.

But sexual abuse does not seem to faze *Sanctuary*'s male characters: although men in *Sanctuary* publicly appear to be shocked by her rape and lynch Goodwin for it, privately they not only are *not* shocked, but actually condone it, as show comments such as "I saw her. She was some baby. Jeez. I wouldn't have used no corncob" (294). As John Duvall concludes, this type of comment "says, in effect, that any sane man would enjoy raping Temple."[13]

Behind patriarchal principles such as "we got to protect our girls," the novel's male characters represent more of a threat than a protection (298). Gowan, who appears to be a gentleman (26–27), is far from being a chivalric protector; instead, he actually puts Temple in danger by bringing her to the Frenchman's Bend and abandoning her there. In fact, none of the novel's male characters intend to protect Temple from harm. Over the five weeks Temple is sequestered at another illegal institutional sanctuary, Reba's whorehouse, looking for her and rescuing her is not an apparent priority for the men in her community any more than it is for the men in her own family. Even the men who know where Temple is held captive do nothing to rescue her: The doctor visits her at the whorehouse to "fix her up" so she can be further abused (149); Red is used as a surrogate penis by Popeye; and Clarence Snopes, the senator, only tells Horace where she is "for a price" (202–6). Horace even makes sure Temple *stays* in the whorehouse, verifying from time to time that she has not left, because he "may need her," he says, to testify at a trial— not to testify against the man who raped and abducted her, of course, but to *defend* Goodwin, the alleged murderer and well-known bootlegger who participated in her abduction (267–68).

Temple's sequestration is therefore far from the work of a single mad-man; it is made possible by the support of an entire male community. It is only appropriate that she is secluded at the very heart of that community, in its most secret, yet well-known, sanctuary, protected by police and law officials. This sanctuary provides refuge and immunity to the ashamed victim and the remorseless, venerated perpetrator (195, 268). In this third male sanctuary of prostitution, which is ironically called Miss Reba's "respectable house," everyone participates in Temple's subordination (255). The doctor who facilitates Temple's further abuse by Popeye and Red wears a Masonic ring, symbolic of the male fellowship from which women are excluded. He represents a male-dominated medical system that grants the gynecologist "authority" over "womanhood," as the judge proclaims (150, 283). When he enters Temple's room at the whorehouse, she adopts the same position as she did at the Frenchman's Bend: "lying on her back, her legs close together, she began to cry, hope-lessly and passively, like a child in a dentist's waiting room" (150). Com-plicit with the doctor are the prostitutes, whose normalizing discourse and obedient participation in Popeye's abuse distort Temple's perception of her surroundings: In that world, all women are whores, sleeping with Popeye is a lucrative privilege, and police and law officials respect Pop-eye's secrecy.[14]

Could this be why Temple telephones Red to plan her escape rather than her father the judge? For the law, the fourth institutional sanctuary of the story, clearly does not aim at protecting Temple any more than do its other sanctuaries. The courtroom is presented from the start as a male space made up of "fathers and husbands" (285).[15] The trial is sup-posed to "right her wrong for her," as the judge says, but it is a scene of overt corruption, perjury, and false accusations, where lawyers are easily corruptible, sex is exchanged for services, men are sentenced for crimes they did not commit, and judicial decisions are overpowered by mobs' lynchings.

Such an untrustworthy judicial system partly explains why women seldom say a word about sexual assaults of any kind: "Rape is probably the most underreported of all violent crimes," explains Patricia Cluss, and this was naturally even truer of the early decades of the twentieth century.[16] Part of that silence stems from the fact that too often women are seen as being the source of evil, as male and female characters in *Sanctuary* repeatedly imply. "Half the trouble in this world is caused by women," declares Snopes, implicitly excusing the other half, and "It's us poor girls . . . causes all the trouble and gets all the suffering," says Miss Myrtle (187, 255). The victim's partial responsibility in her abduction is also implied in Horace's question: "dont you know that putting yourself in the position of disaster is the surest way in the world to bring it about?" (272). Likewise, numerous critics have shared the view that Temple only got what she deserved, thereby exemplifying what Julie Allison and Lawrence Wrightsman see as one of the most prevalent myths about rape: the belief that "only bad girls get raped," and that "any healthy woman can resist a rapist if she really wants to."[17] "These falsehoods," explain Allison and Wrightsman, "create a climate hostile to rape victims, portraying them as often-willing participants in furtive sexual encounters, or even instigators of them" (98–99). And the common question becomes, in reality as in many of *Sanctuary*'s critical reviews, "What did the *girl* do which contributed to her being abused?"[18]

This kind of popular belief serves to protect patriarchy by directing the blame elsewhere. As Brown explains, "If we maintain the myth of the willing victim, whom we then pathologize for her presumed willingness,"—just as Temple has often been pathologized as a nymphomaniac—"we need never question the social structures that perpetuate her victimization" (106). Likewise, by misinterpreting Temple's complex reaction to her ordeal as instigation, willful participation, and enjoyment, many readers have failed to unmask the patriarchal structures that make that ordeal possible in the novel.

Trauma theories enable us to revisit Temple's experience and make sense of her actions in a radically different way. Described as "match-thin," "looking herself no more than an elongated and leggy infant," Temple, the "pore little critur," "small childish figure no longer quite a child, not yet quite a woman" is obviously unable to defend herself physically against rape and abduction (70, 59, 68, 89). She therefore needs to come up with other strategies to resist and eventually escape her abductor.

Thus, she uses her body as an instrument against Popeye through Red, the man he has hired to have sex with her. As Scott Yarbrough demonstrates, "Initially, Temple is *not* in control of her own sexuality (Popeye is), and it is only through control of her sexuality that she will eventually be able to gain independence from Popeye" (50). Through becoming "wild as a young mare," Yarbrough adds, and using Red to plan her escape, Temple tries to turn the tables on Popeye and uses the very tool he used to dominate her: sex (57, 60). Here again, sex is therefore to be seen as an instrument in the power struggle, and not as a source of pleasure.

Her vengeful sexual aggressiveness can also be interpreted as an example of what Freud calls the "repetition compulsion" that is one of the symptoms of "traumatic neurosis."[19] In the wake of a traumatic event, he explains, a possible "defensive measure" is the compulsive repetition of the traumatic event that "override[s] the pleasure principle" (11). Such a masochistic compulsion to repeat a traumatic experience can be explained by a need to *control* a situation the victim could not control before (25). This self-destructive mechanism implies turning "a *passive* situation" in which one is "overpowered by the experience" into a reenactment of the unpleasurable experience that is in fact a way to take on "an *active* part" (15).

Another way Temple "repeats" her traumatic experience to gain control over it is through language. As we have seen, when she talks about the event with Horace, she transforms her physically passive role into a verbally active, aggressive role, where, among other strategies, she fastens herself into an iron belt: "I was thinking maybe it would have long sharp spikes on it and he wouldn't know until too late and I'd jab it into him. I'd jab it all the way through him and I'd think about the blood running on me and how I'd say I guess that'll teach you! I guess you'll let me alone now! I'd say. I didn't know it was going to be just the other way" (218). Instead of telling Horace about her rape, she makes up a fantasized version of it: "suddenly Horace realized that she was recounting the experience with actual pride, a sort of naïve and impersonal vanity, as though she were making it up" (216). The way she twists the truth resembles Lisa Aronson and Robert Pynoos's description of the way children draw or narrate their traumatic experiences.[20] These children often alter the *proximity* of the event, the *lethality* of the instrument (a knife becomes a finger), the *intentionality* (a murder becomes an accident), the *object* of the violence, or the *seriousness* of the injury (the victim is "really hurt" instead of "dead"). They typically draw the event as they wish it had happened, and also create what is called "intervention fantasies": they alter the precipitating events, invent interrupting actions, reverse the lethal or injurious consequences, or gain safe retaliation through fantasies of revenge. Likewise, in her fantasized account, Temple clearly turns herself into the aggressor; she reverses the situation from victimization to aggression, which is not only a more bearable version of the event: it is actually therapeutic. Temple's linguistic sexual aggressiveness can therefore be seen as resistance to subordination.

It is also through language that she resists domination by testifying against Goodwin, and by extension against all the white patriarchal figures he represents. As we have seen, it is a form of revenge against patriarchal sexual domination—a significant gesture that Deborah Clarke sees as Temple's "sole exercise of power" (52).

But despite Temple's resistance, the above-mentioned male-dominated institutions are implacable, and there is in the end no way out for her, no sanctuary. Her escape drives her right back into her initial familial sanctuary: after the trial, Temple's return to her family merely seems like a transfer of power from Popeye to father, both of whom she calls "Daddy" (136, 139–141, 231, 236). Throughout the novel, at several key moments including the threatening approaches of Goodwin, Popeye, and the doctor, Temple is described as gradually "shrinking," "cringing," "disintegrating" (158, 159). The same language is used when she is returned to her father and approaches her brothers at the back of the courtroom: "Again the girl stopped. She began to cringe back, her body arching slowly, her arm tautening in the old man's grasp. He bent toward her, speaking; she moved again, in that shrinking and rapt abasement. Four younger men were standing stiffly erect near the exit. They stood like soldiers . . . in a close body, the girl hidden among them, they moved toward the door . . . the girl could be seen shrunk against the wall . . . she appeared to be clinging there, then the five bodies hid her again and again in a close body."[21]

By the end of the novel, Temple is reduced to a marionette in the hands of whichever male will get to control her: "Her face quite pale, the two spots of rouge like paper disks pasted on her cheek bones, her mouth painted into a savage perfect bow" (214, 284, 286). Temple has finally become what her entire community raised her to be: a doll, an object.[22] *Sanctuary* not only stages Temple's shocking desecration, it stages her gradual objectification—an objectification that starts *before* her rape and continues *after* her liberation. This situation resembles what Brown describes as "layers of trauma" as opposed to single traumatic events (110).

One of the most common effects of trauma is for the victim to feel dead even though she has survived the ordeal. Back in her father's hands, Temple is practically dead. In the last paragraph of the novel, sitting in the Luxembourg Gardens next to her father who "sat, his hands crossed on the head of his stick, the rigid bar of his moustache beaded with moisture like frosted silver," she seems "to dissolve into the dying brasses, . . . vanquished in the embrace of the season of rain and death" (317). The process of "disintegration" is now complete. She has returned to her family, and later to her initial abductor, Gowan, to whom she is eventually married in the novel's sequel, *Requiem for a Nun*. In the end, Temple's "comparative inviolation" remains largely unnoticed in contrast to the violent, sensational, "abnormal" expressions of male desire in the novel.

Although the story of Temple takes sexual domination to an unusual extreme, the more "normal" conditions under which other female characters live in Yoknapatawpha County are not all that different. What Dewey Dell and Addie Bundren describe in *As I Lay Dying* is quite representative of the "milder," everyday forms of sexual oppression that are often performed by trusted males and family members.

In the early-twentieth-century South of "country people," Dewey Dell's family is structurally similar to Temple's: she has four brothers and a father. Her agonizing mother is distant, and both of her parents' families are devoid of "womenfolks" (170–71). An adolescent, Dewey Dell is trapped by a pregnancy that comes "too soon too soon too soon" (60, 120). As such, she illustrates that for women in the rural South, sexual powerlessness started with a lack of control of their own bodies, whose properties seemed mysterious and inescapable. As Amy Wood explains, at the time, "menstruation, deflowering, pregnancy, and childbirth"— grouped in the novel under the term "women trouble" (200)—were "painful and often bloody experiences that women accept[ed] as intrinsic to their identity and destiny."[23] The widespread ignorance about bodily functions and reproduction mechanisms was the cause of many unwanted pregnancies.[24] All women could do was interpret the signs given by their body, as does Dewey Dell: "I know it is there because God gave women a sign when something has happened bad," she says of her pregnancy (58). Clueless and powerless over her femininity, Dewey Dell is the embodiment of uncontrolled sexuality and fertility: "I feel like a wet seed wild in the hot blind earth," she says (63), an image Faulkner used recurrently in some of his early poems about pregnancy, marriage, and loss.[25] She sees her sexual desire as an unavoidable trap that puts her at the mercy of Lafe, the young man who picks cotton into her sack to "get into the secret shade" of the woods with her. "And so it was because I could not help it," she says (27).

Reflecting on her life as a wife and mother of five in a single, central chapter at the heart of *As I Lay Dying*, Addie depicts marriage and reproduction in similar terms, in that marrying Anse has given him control over her body. She describes procreation in terms of violation: "my aloneness had been violated and then made whole again by the violation," she says (172). Her personal account parallels Nancy Theriot's findings about some women's view of conception and parturition as an aggression, which is in fact fairly common and often triggers "indifference or hostility to children and/or husbands."[26]

Addie describes her violation as a linguistic deception: "He had a word, too," she says about her husband, "Love he called it"; "it was as though he had tricked me, hidden within a word like within a paper screen and struck me in the back through it" (172). His words are described as a weapon, an instrument of coercion; "we use one another by words," she says (172). Likewise, Sheila Kitzinger explains that victims of sexual abuse "often have no legitimate way of describing personal experiences except in the terminology of the oppressor": "A teenager sexually abused by her schoolteacher said, 'All the words I had were the words *he* gave me. *He* called it *love*.'"[27]

Trapped in a system where it was commonly understood that women's primary responsibility, and the fulfillment of their nature, was the bearing of children, Addie exemplifies how at the turn of the twentieth century, it was terribly difficult for women to escape that condition of "breeders." She represents women's growing desire to limit the number of children they bore, at a time when family limitation was seen by social leaders as "shirking [one's] patriotic duty, committing 'race suicide,' sinning against nature," explains James Reed.[28] Like her contemporaries, Addie finds herself at the mercy of a husband who embodies that social drive to produce children, despite her resistance: "'Nonsense,' Anse said; 'you and me aint nigh done chapping yet, with just two'" (173). Conforming to her culture's expectations of her, Addie therefore unwillingly continues to "give Anse" more children (174).

Suzanne Lyons explains that in addition to resenting their unwanted pregnancies, many mothers also recall the ensuing childbirth experience in terms of "violation" and expose "the similarities between a traumatic obstetric experience and the experience of assault," where not only husbands but also children and doctors are seen as the "aggressor."[29] As Kitzinger explains, the experience of parturition poses another linguistic problem: alienated by the birth process, "Women can find no words in which to describe what happened. After childbirth everything may be 'explained' in medical terms—and the woman is silenced" (74).

The parallel made in *As I Lay Dying* between obstetrics and assault may be no accident. As Kitzinger argues, at the time the novel was written, the medical profession was increasingly taking part in the "widespread male violence against women" (76). The growing number of male doctors in obstetrics, as opposed to midwives, explains Kitzinger, started raising issues of trust, powerlessness, and abuse in Western society, where birth "has become an institutionalized act of violence against women, and post-natal depression is often grief that follows helplessness in the face of that violence" (77).[30]

In fact, the social drive to produce children was supported by a medical system that further oppressed and silenced women by failing to provide adequate medical care regarding "female trouble." Although by 1865 contraceptive methods existed and were described in medical manuals, women had little access to them, especially in rural areas. Reed explains that the practice of family limitation had become a subject of public debate as early as the 1830s, but that the issues of contraception, abortion, and fertility rates were still highly controversial a century later (124). Ignorance about the reproductive cycles prevailed, and birth control often ended up in the hands of irresponsible crooks, as doctors and pharmacists prescribed abortifacients or contraceptive pills that did more harm than good. Moseley, the pharmacist in *As I Lay Dying*, describes these contraceptive practices: "So I thought maybe her ma or somebody had sent her in for some of this female dope and she was ashamed to ask for it. I knew she couldn't have a complexion like hers and use it herself, let alone not being much more than old enough to barely know what it was for. It's a shame the way they poison themselves with it. But a man's got to stock it or go out of business in this country," declares Moseley, "It's a crime and a shame; but after all, they'll buy it from somebody" (200). Later McGowan, the other pharmacist, describes the treatment he gave Dewey Dell: "So I took a graduated glass and kind of turned my back to her and picked out a bottle that looked all right, because a man that would keep poison setting around in a unlabelled bottle ought to be in jail, anyway. It smelled like turpentine. I poured some into the glass and gave it to her . . . I went back and put some talcum powder into six capsules and kind of cleared up the cellar and then I was all ready" (247–48).

Many unwanted pregnancies, within marriage as well as outside of it, often resulted in abortions, which, although illegal, remained the main means of family limitation well into the 1930s.[31] In an effort to resist her condition, Dewey Dell chooses to pursue this option on the way to Jefferson, in a town ironically called "New Hope" (120). She asks McGowan, the pharmacist, to perform that illegal abortion. In lieu of medical treatment, however, what she gets is sexual assault. Again, she is "tricked" by his linguistic deception: He calls Dewey Dell's rape the "operation" that is part of the medical "treatment" that will rid her of her unwanted pregnancy.

"It won't hurt you," he tells her, "You've had the same operation before"; he then puts "some talcum powder into six capsules" and directs her to get "the rest of the treatment . . . Down in the cellar" (247).

What is quite remarkable here is that unlike Temple Drake's, Dewey Dell's rape is surprisingly a nonevent: She never says a word about it, and McGowan only alludes to preparing for it (246–48). The rape itself remains untold, secret, unnoticed—within the novel as well as in most of its critical response—which is another sign of a sexual culture that tends to ignore, normalize, and therefore perpetuate such forms of abuse. Dewey Dell's rape is never acknowledged as such—even by herself— and she has no other choice but to silently go on with her unwanted pregnancy.

Dewey Dell clearly sees this pregnancy as a threat: "I feel my body, my bones and flesh beginning to part and open upon the alone, and the process of coming unalone is terrible" (61–62). It was quite common at the time to see pregnancy as a potentially fatal "condition" that brought about a very real possibility of death, since, as Sally McMillen reports, "the whole country experienced high maternal and infant mortality," and this was even truer of Southern women.[32] Judith Leavitt and Whitney Walton also explain that at the time, "Women feared that the physical strain of childbirth would weaken them for long periods of time, make them lifelong invalids, or kill them."[33] As a life-threatening experience, it was not uncommon for pregnancy to trigger an array of psychic disorders in the pregnant woman, among which the "insanity of pregnancy."[34] Among these disorders, morbidity was quite common, a tendency exemplified by Dewey Dell: She tells Reverend Whitfield that she is "already dead" and repeats, "the dead, hot air breathes on my face again. . . . The dead air shapes the dead earth in the dead darkness, further away than seeing shapes the dead earth. It lies dead and warm upon me" (62–64, 121, 179).[35]

Given the circumstances, one can only imagine what kind of pregnancy, childbirth, and mothering will ensue for Dewey Dell, as her failed attempt to abort leaves her silenced, powerless, and terrified. It might be just as disastrous as her mother's experience, who saw childbearing as "terrible" (171). Trauma theories applied to childbirth shed a new light on Addie as a mother. This "lonely woman," without "living kin" besides her husband and children and unsupported by a community that is quick to blame her for the dysfunctional state of her family, can be seen as a "birth survivor" whose symptoms are similar to those of rape victims (22, 171).

Among the most common symptoms of traumatic childbirth is a sense of powerlessness within the birth experience, which can be perceived as "painful, humiliating, mutilating and occurring in an unsympathetic environment," says Lyons (101). Kitzinger adds that isolation, and the feeling of being "'abnormal,' 'unnatural' no longer 'whole,' different from other women" are other posttraumatic symptoms (76). These symptoms are also exhibited by Addie, who is unjustly seen by others, such as Cora Tull, as "not a true mother" (173). Another common symptom is what Lyons calls the "disappearance" or inadequacy of language, where emotions within the traumatic event outflank the simple syntax of speech, as it is the case for Addie. Although Addie's monologue has often been dismissed by critics as being unreliable because she is dead, mentally disturbed, hypocritical, ignorant, illiterate, or incoherent,[36] her linguistic struggle can be understood in terms of traumatic symptoms. In her chapter, Addie struggles with a male language that she feels "tricked" her and that cannot describe her experience (172). She tries to resist that language by twisting words and syntax to better express her distress. Like Temple's use of language in *Sanctuary*, Addie's linguistic struggle can therefore be seen as a form of resistance.

In addition to language, and similarly to Temple, who uses Red to escape Popeye, Addie also takes control of her sexuality by cheating on Anse with Reverend Whitfield and bearing his child, Jewel: "I gave Anse Dewey Dell to negative Jewel. Then I gave him Vardaman to replace the child I had robbed him of. And now he has three children that are his and not mine" (176).

But Addie's main exercise of power in the novel seems to be her decision to die. She decides early on that dying is the only way out of her marital subordination. At the time, women often had no choice but to marry and procreate, and "only the natural end of their childbearing years, a severe physical disorder, or death brought them surcease," says McMillen (182). In her account, Addie's successive pregnancies sound like steps towards death: each birth brings her closer to "cleaning her house" and "getting ready to stay dead." After "giving Anse" his last child, Vardaman, she declares, "And then I could get ready to die" (176). On her deathbed, as her son is building her coffin, Addie seems to welcome death, "Glad to go," says Cora, "Her mind is set on it," affirms Anse (23, 33).[37] By choosing to die, Addie finally takes control of her life and shows that she alone can control her body, not others.

In "Women's Biological Straightjackets," Ann Digby shows how women remained subordinated to their bodies up until the later part of the twentieth century.[38] Through Temple, Addie, and Dewey Dell, Faulkner depicts the life of women in a culture that deprived them of a real right of refusal to have sex or to bear children, of the medical instruction and support that could have given them control over their fertility, and of any social recognition of their right to make choices. This culture also deprived them of a safe sanctuary. For all three characters, the only refuge, or escape, seems to be death: they end up choosing to die, being partially dead, or obsessed by death.

Since the publication of *Sanctuary* and *As I Lay Dying*, legal and medical advances have given women power in the field of "women trouble," such as open access to divorce, education, justice, employment, contraception, abortion, in-vitro fertilization, surrogate pregnancy, sperm banks, hormonal treatments, homosexuality, etc. These advances have restored women's "authority" over their body and sexuality. Perhaps this is why it is now possible to read Temple, Addie, and Dewey Dell's ordeals as resistance to obvious and hidden forms of patriarchal oppression.

By exposing different degrees of sexual subordination in *Sanctuary* and *As I Lay Dying* and bearing witness to the sexual culture of his time, Faulkner held up a mirror for his contemporaries. However, many of his contemporaries and the generations of readers that followed failed to recognize what Brown calls "the benign mask behind which everyday oppression operates" in *Sanctuary* and *As I Lay Dying*, and therefore to admit "to what is deeply wrong in many sacred social institutions" (105). Decades later, these works still challenge us to question the current status of our sexual culture, at a time when, almost a century later and in spite of positive social change, patriarchal domination continues to plague gender relations and the myth of the willing victim still prevails and silences numerous victims of sexual abuse. Taken together, *Sanctuary* and *As I Lay Dying* urge us to reconsider the essential question: Does sexual assault have to be as sensational as Popeye's rape of Temple to be noticed and taken seriously? Or, as one of the drummers asks at the end of *Sanctuary*, "What does it take to make you folks mad?" (294).

NOTES

1. William Faulkner, *Sanctuary*, 4th ed. (New York: Vintage International, 1993); *As I Lay Dying*, 4th ed. (New York: Vintage International, 1990).

2. Faulkner married Estelle Oldham in 1929 and became a father in 1931. For an account of both novels' genesis, see Joseph Blotner, *Faulkner. A Biography*, vol. 1 (New York: Random House, 1974), 604–20, and his chapter entitled "Husband and Father, 1929–1932," 623–706. In "The Mutual Relevance of Faulkner Studies and Women's Studies: An Interdisciplinary Inquiry," *Faulkner and Women*, ed. Doreen Fowler and Ann Abadie (Jackson: University Press of Mississippi, 1986), Ilse Dusoir Lind notes that Faulkner was clearly preoccupied with matters of marriage, pregnancy, and childbirth at the time he wrote *As I Lay Dying* and *Sanctuary*, which powerfully display his overall "solicitude for young life and for those who nurture it" (36–38). Between the death of his first daughter—Alabama, five days old,

1931—and the birth of Jill, his second daughter, in June 1933, Faulkner also assembled and published the different poems forming *A Green Bough*, including "Pregnancy" and "Marriage," originally written between 1919 and 1924.

3. Frederick L. Gwynn and Joseph Blotner, eds., *Faulkner in the University: Class Conferences at the University of Virginia, 1957–1958* (Charlottesville, Virginia: The University of Virginia Press, 1959), 90; Blotner, 604.

4. The issue of women and trauma in *Sanctuary* and *As I Lay Dying* is developed at length in my doctoral dissertation, "Women and Trauma in William Faulkner's Novels," Emory University, 2002. The theories of trauma that inspired my work on these novels were developed by Cathy Caruth in *Trauma: Explorations in Memory* (Baltimore, Maryland: John Hopkins University Press, 1995) and *Unclaimed Experience. Trauma, Narrative, and History* (Baltimore, Maryland: John Hopkins University Press, 1996).

5. Jane Gallop, *The Daughter's Seduction* (Ithaca, New York: Cornell University Press, 1982), 67.

6. Ruby is surprised by Temple's brothers' threat to beat her. She tells Temple about her own brother: "My brother said he would kill Frank. He didn't say he would give me a whipping if he caught me with him" (58). For more on this idea of patriarchal control of the daughter, see John Duvall, "Faulkner's Critics and Women: The Voice of the Community," in *Faulkner and Women*, ed. Doreen Fowler and Ann J. Abadie (Jackson: University Press of Mississippi, 1986), 41–57; and Robert Moore, "Desire and Despair: Temple Drake's Self-Victimization," in *Faulkner and Women*, 112–27.

7. In fact, in a "benign" way, Gowan practically kidnaps Temple: "You'd better take me back to Oxford," Temple asks him in vain as she gets in his car (37). She explains to Ruby: "It was Gowan. I begged him. We had already missed the ball game, but I begged him if he'd just get me to Starkville before the special started back. . . . But he wouldn't. He said we'd stop here just a minute and get some more whiskey and he was already drunk then. . . . He got drunk again while I was begging him to take me to a town anywhere and let me out . . . and I begged him to just let me out anywhere and lend me enough money for a ticket because I only had two dollars, but he——" (56–57). At the Frenchman's Bend, Gowan is so drunk that he lets the men "pester" Temple under his very eyes, despite her begging for help (48–49). Finally, even sober, Gowan is a selfish coward who flees on his own, abandoning Temple to her sad lot at the Frenchman's Bend (130).

8. Sally R. Page, *Faulkner's Women: Characterization and Meaning* (De Land, Florida: Everett/Edwards, 1972), 78.

9. Kali Tal, *Worlds of Hurt: Reading the Literature of Trauma*, Cambridge Studies in American Literature and Culture, ed. Eric Sundquist (New York: Cambridge University Press, 1996), 155. This omnipresent threat is the reason why Abby Werlock calls *Sanctuary* a "conscious portrayal of the helplessness of the woman in the brutal male world" in "Victims Unvanquished: Temple Drake and Women Characters in William Faulkner's Novels," in *Women and Violence in Literature: An Essay Collection*, ed. Katherine Anne Ackley (New York: Garland, 1990), 9.

10. Laura Brown, "Not Outside the Range: One Feminist Perspective on Psychic Trauma," in *Trauma: Explorations in Memory*, 104.

11. Quoted in Brown, 107. This dissonance parallels the ongoing debate over the inclusion of sexual assault in the list of potentially traumatic events, defined by the American Psychiatric Association since the 1970s as "events outside the range of human experience." Seeing sexual abuse as "unusual" is a "self-deception," says Brown, as in actuality, it concerns all women (108). "American women have nearly a 50 percent chance of being raped at some time in their life," says Charles Figley, and "a third of all girls are sexually abused prior to the age of sixteen," reports Brown (100). Charles Figley, *Trauma and Its Wake*

(New York: Brunner/Mazel, 1984), 8. In fact, considering sexual assault as exceptional prevents us from dealing with it as a common part of a woman's everyday life and dangerously excludes "milder," silenced forms of sexual violence from being taken seriously. For more on the debate over rape and trauma, see medical and psychological reports such as A. W. Burgess and L. Holstrom, "Rape Trauma Syndrome," *American Journal of Psychiatry* 131 (1974): 981–86; and I. T. Bownes, E. C. Gorman, and A. Sayers, "Assault Characteristics and Postraumatic Stress Disorder in Rape Victims," *Acta Psychiatrica Scandinavica* 83 (1991): 27–30.

12. See Joseph Urgo, "Temple Drake's Truthful Perjury: Rethinking Faulkner's *Sanctuary*," *American Literature: A Journal of Literary History, Criticism, and Bibliography* 55.3 (1983): 435–44.

13. John Duvall, *Faulkner's Marginal Couple: Invisible, Outlaw, and Unspeakable Communities* (Austin: University of Texas Press, 1990), 70.

14. "Anybody in Memphis can tell you who Reba Rivers is. Ask any man on the street, cop or not. . . . They all know Reba Rivers" (143). Reba is an outlaw running a whorehouse, but interestingly, as Deborah Clarke comments, "Despite [her] shady legal dealings," she is "not only tolerated but valued." Deborah Clarke, *Robbing the Mother: Women in Faulkner* (Jackson: University Press of Mississippi, 1994), 57. At Miss Reba's, Temple is encouraged to accept her circumstances, and even enjoy them. The prostitutes are envious of Temple for "having gotten" Popeye, and Reba "began to tell Temple how lucky she was": "That blood'll be worth a thousand dollars to you, honey" (145). The brothel's secrecy stems from a male conspiracy: "I've had some of the biggest men in Memphis right here in this house, bankers, lawyers, doctors—all of them. I've had two police captains drinking beer in my dining-room and the commissioner himself upstairs with one of my girls . . . buck-nekkid, dancing the highland fling" (143).

15. The amalgam between father and law is omnipresent in the novel, where Temple ineffectively invokes her father-judge for help and husbands, fathers, and brothers are tied to the law in some way. For more on this, see Duvall's above-mentioned "Faulkner's Critics and Women" and Scott Yarbrough, "The Dark Lady: Temple Drake as Femme Fatale," *Southern Literary Journal* 31.2 (1999): 50–64. In the courtroom, Temple sits "motionless" under the gaze of the onlookers, her hands "palm-up on her lap," just as they are when Popeye and other threatening males approach her throughout the novel: "She lay motionless, her palms lifted, her flesh beneath the envelope of her loins cringing rearward in furious disintegration like frightened people in a crowd" (159, 102). As Duvall suggests, "The courtroom in the texts of William Faulkner . . . foregrounds the silencing of women by patriarchy" (Faulkner's *Marginal Couple* 76). *Sanctuary* reflects the fact that the law is not made for women, and the courtroom is an unwelcoming place for them. Duvall also reminds us that at the time, the courtroom was so male-dominated that women were not allowed to be jurors until 1968 (75–76). In the novel, Snopes sums up a widespread opinion about these male institutions: "The church aint got no place in politics, and women aint got no place in neither one, let alone the law. Let them stay at home and they'll find plenty to do without upsetting a man's law-suit" (186).

16. Patricia A. Cluss, "The Rape Victims: Psychological Correlates of Participating in the Legal Process," *Criminal Justice and Behavior* 10 (1983): 342.

17. Julie A. Allison and Lawrence S. Wrightsman, *Rape: The Misunderstood Crime* (Newbury Park, Calif.: Sage Publications, 1993), 98.

18. As a "cautionary tale," *Sanctuary* could very well be interpreted, as it has often been, as an illustration of the fact that women such as Temple need to be punished for misbehaving (see Diane Roberts, *Faulkner and Southern Womanhood* [Athens: University of Georgia Press, 1994], 110). Early critics such as Lawrence Kubie, Leslie Fiedler, Olga

Vickery, and Sally Page consistently saw Temple as the source of evil in *Sanctuary*. Not only did they argue that she cooperated in her own rape and abduction, but that she actually desired, caused, and even enjoyed these assaults. Since the 1980s, critics such as Elisabeth Mulhenfeld started to look at Temple less ideologically and more humanly, but most critics continued to see Temple as "the epitome of the sexual aggressor," a "trembling, sexless, ferocious bitch," "tak[ing] pride in this adventure, in which she is absolutely important," says Kathreen Lee ("From Narcissist to Masochist: A New Look at Temple Drake," *Journal of Evolutionary Psychology* 5.1–2 [1984]: 27, 30). Many critics still denunciated "her apparently willing (even enthusiastic) collusion with evil at Miss Reba's," like Robert Moore in "Desire and Despair" (112). It is only "In recent readings," says Barbara Ladd, that "Temple has been transformed from a woman who 'embraces corruption' to a victim of repression." Barbara Ladd, "'Philosophers and Other Gynecologists': Women and the Polity in *Requiem for a Nun*," *Mississippi Quarterly: The Journal of Southern Cultures* 52.3 [1999]: 489.

19. Sigmund Freud, "Beyond the Pleasure Principle," trans. James Strachey, *The International Psycho-Analytical Library*, ed. Ernest Jones, vol. 4 (London: Hogarth Press and the Institute of Psycho-Analysis, 1920), 35.

20. Lisa Aronson and Robert Pynoos, "Traumatic Experiences: The Early Organization of Memory in School Age Children and Adolescents," *Memory Overwhelmed: Interdisciplinary Approaches to Trauma*, Emory University School of Public Health, 17–19 October 1997.

21. Yarbrough and others have stressed the presence of incestuous subordination in *Sanctuary*, especially in the trial scene (57). As such, *Sanctuary* is arguably the kind of text that Brown describes as calling us "to look beyond the public and male experiences of trauma to the private, secret experiences that women encounter in the interpersonal realm and at the hands of those we love and depend upon" (102).

22. Lee explains that her upbringing as a coquette has made her the perfect candidate for the objectification Popeye operates on her: "Since she was raised as a narcissistic coquette, she has naturally developed the masochistic tendencies that maintain her in the status of object" (27). She quotes Simone de Beauvoir: "When a woman's self-image is that of an object, not a person, she can expect others to treat her accordingly" (28).

23. Amy Louise Wood, "Feminine Rebellion and Mimicry in Faulkner's *As I Lay Dying*," *Faulkner Journal* 9.1–2 (1993): 99–112. Darl also alludes to this lack of control over bodily functions, imagining his mother trying "to conceal a soiled garment that she could not prevent her body soiling," (97–98) and Moseley the pharmacist concedes that "female trouble" can be abnormal and frightening. He says about Dewey Dell: "I thought maybe she was younger than she looked, and her first one had scared her, or maybe one had been a little abnormal as it will in young women" (200).

24. This lack of information about birth control was in part due to the Comstock Act, which made it illegal to distribute "obscene" material of any kind. The part of the Act that dealt with contraceptive material and health-related documents was declared unconstitutional in 1936, after much public debate, so its implications and precedents must have been on Faulkner's mind as he was writing *As I Lay Dying*.

25. Three of Faulkner's early poems allude to the themes of uncontrolled fertility, sexuality, and problematic pregnancies. The first short poem is "Music dying languidly in darkness," written in 1919. It relates to the premature death of Estelle Oldham's sister, Tochie, as she was pregnant for the first time (qtd. in Blotner, *Faulkner. A Biography* 1: 242). Although Tochie's death might have been the sole incident related to death in childbearing that Faulkner witnessed directly, it apparently made a lasting impact on him. A later poem, "Pregnancy," first written in 1924 as an "exercise" and later published in 1933 in *A Green Bough*, as poem XXIX, with no title, presents an unusually dark vision of pregnancy, which goes against the conventional glorification of motherhood that was prevalent in Faulkner's

time and region. See Susan Snell, *Phil Stone of Oxford: A Vicarious Life* (Athens: University of Georgia Press, 1991), 171. The poem also presents female fertility as a "warm and wet" seed. The third poem related to that theme is "Marriage." Probably written in 1925, it was published in 1933 in *A Green Bough*, as poem III. It is, according to Blotner in his introduction to *Mississippi Poems*, "Full of tension and animosity rather than bliss." *Mississippi Poems by William Faulkner* (Oxford, Miss.: Yoknapatawpha Press, 1979), 7.

26. Nancy Theriot, "Puerperal Insanity," *Diseases of Pregnancy and Childbirth*, ed. Philip Wilson (New York: Garland, 1996), 138.

27. Sheila Kitzinger, "Birth and Violence against Women," *Women's Health Matters*, ed. H. Roberts (London: Routledge, 1992), 74.

28. James Reed, "Doctors, Birth Control, and Social Values, 1839–1970," in *Women and Health in America: Historical Readings*, ed. Judith Walzer Leavitt (Madison: University of Wisconsin Press, 1984), 124–40.

29. Suzanne Lyons, "A Prospective Study of Post Traumatic Stress Symptoms 1 Month Following Childbirth in a Group of 42 First-time Mothers," *Journal of Reproductive and Infant Psychology* 16.1 (1998): 110.

30. In an interview, Dr. Chester McLarty, one of Faulkner's personal physicians, mentioned this new interest of medicine in gynecological and obstetrical matters. He made it clear that giving birth was previously not considered a medical matter. For instance, the main physician of the practice Dr. McLarty came to work with after medical school "despised pediatrics and obstetrics." At that time, most of the obstetrical matters were taken care of at the patient's home, by midwives, and there was no hospital in Oxford before the late teens, related Dr. McLarty, but things were slowly changing. Personal interview. Oxford, Mississippi. 24 October 2000.

31. James Mohr reports, "By the mid-1930s . . . there was one abortion for every four pregnancies in the United States," 90 percent of which "were being performed upon married women." James Mohr, "Patterns of Abortion and the Response of American Physicians, 1790–1930," in *Women and Health in America: Historical Readings*, 122, 124. Abortions were practiced by illegal "abortionists" and were rather common, although they were against the law. In the above-mentioned interview, Dr. McLarty was cautious to specify that there were no abortionists in Oxford and that, even today, he could not reveal the name of the closest abortionist most patients were referred to in Greenwood. He added that someone near the state line performed abortions between Oxford and Memphis and related the case of an Ole Miss graduate student who had had a high fever following one of those "criminal abortions." The case became famous on campus and the issue of abortion widely discussed.

32. Sally McMillen, *Motherhood in the Old South: Pregnancy, Childbirth, and Infant Rearing.* (Baton Rouge: Louisiana State University Press, 1990), 1.

33. Judith Leavitt and Whitney Walton, "'Down to Death's Door': Women's Perceptions of Childbirth in America," in *Women and Health in America: Historical Readings*, 156. The high mortality rates linked to childbearing, for both mother and child, were responsible for the dread entailed by the experience, as Leavitt reports: "During most of American history, an important part of women's experience of childbirth was their anticipation of dying or of being permanently injured during the event." Leavitt, *Brought to Bed: Childbearing in America, 1750 to 1950* (New York: Oxford University Press, 1986), 13.

34. Susan Mendus explains that although "puerperal insanity occurring after childbirth was recognized as both more frequent and more serious an illness than the insanity of pregnancy," Victorian doctors were also concerned with the insanity of pregnancy, "alternatively called 'insanity of reproduction.'" *Sexuality and Subordination: Interdisciplinary Studies of Gender in the 19th Century*, ed. Susan Mendus and Jane Rendall (New York: Routledge, 1989), 205.

35. This connection between pregnancy and death is also present in Faulkner's above-mentioned early poem "Pregnancy," which associates pregnancy with the "rain and fire and death" that form the menace set above the pregnant woman's door. The poem presents pregnancy as a potential threat on selfhood, a demanding and exhausting splitting in which the baby's life has priority over its mother's.

36. Harriet Hustis, "The Tangled Web We Weave: Faulkner Scholarship and the Significance of Addie Bundren's Monologue," *Faulkner Journal* 12.1 (1996): 3–21.

37. Addie has no medical reason to die, and as Dr. Peabody says in the novel, death is "merely a function of the mind" (43–44). She is "brought to death seemingly (from the absence of any explanation, even a medical reason from Peabody) by her own commanding will," says David Williams in *Faulkner's Women: The Myth and the Muse*, 1st ed. (Montreal, Canada: McGill-Queen's University Press, 1977), 4.

38. Ann Digby, "Women's Biological Straightjacket," in *Sexuality and Subordination*, ed. Susan Mendus (New York: Routledge, 1989).

Contributors

John N. Duvall is professor of English at Purdue University and editor of *Modern Fiction Studies*. He is the author of *Faulkner's Marginal Couple: Invisible, Outlaw, and Unspeakable Communities, The Identifying Fictions of Toni Morrison: Modernist Authenticity and Postmodern Blackness, Don DeLillo's "Underworld,"* and *Race and White Identity in Southern Fiction: From Faulkner to Morrison.*

Kristin Fujie is a doctoral candidate in the department of English at the University of California at Berkeley. She is currently writing her doctoral dissertation on the interrelation of race and gender in Faulkner's novels from *Soldiers' Pay* to *Absalom, Absalom!*

Caroline Garnier received her doctorate from Emory University in 2002, with a dissertation on women and trauma in William Faulkner's novels. After teaching at Morehouse College for six years, she moved back to France and created a translation, interpreting, and ESL training company. She recently completed several entries to be published in the forthcoming *Richard Wright Encyclopedia* and is working on the publication of letters to and from five nineteenth-century French authors.

Jaime Harker is associate professor of English at the University of Mississippi. She is the author of *America the Middlebrow: Women's Novels, Progressivism, and Middlebrow Authorship between the Wars* and coeditor of *The Oprah Effect: Critical Essays on Oprah's Book Club.*

Catherine Gunther Kodat, professor at Hamilton College, has published widely in the areas of narrative theory, film, and dance, as well as on such writers as Faulkner, Zora Neale Hurston, Jean Toomer, Allen Tate, and Toni Morrison. She is completing an interdisciplinary study, "Don't Act: Rediscovering Cold War Culture."

Peter Lurie is assistant professor English at the University of Richmond. He is the author of *Vision's Immanence: Faulkner, Film, and the Popular Imagination* as well as essays and reviews on Faulkner, Hart Crane, Cormac McCarthy, and film. His current research project is entitled "American Obscurantism: History and the Visual in American Literature and Film."

Deborah E. McDowell is Alice Griffin Professor of American Literature and director of the Carter G. Woodson Institute at the University of Virginia. She is the author of *"The Changing Same": Studies in Fiction by Black Women* and *Leaving Pipe Shop: Memories of Kin*. A period editor of the *Norton Anthology of African American Literature*, she has also edited or coedited five volumes of fiction and literary study, including *Slavery and the Literary Imagination* and *Nella Larsen: Quicksand and Passing*. She served as founding editor of the Black Women Writers Series, published by Beacon Press.

Gary Richards is assistant professor of English, Linguistics, and Communication at the University of Mary Washington. He is the author of *Lovers and Beloveds: Sexual Otherness in Southern Fiction, 1936–1961*, named a *Choice* Outstanding Academic Title, 2005.

Annette Trefzer is associate professor of English at the University of Mississippi. She is the author of *Disturbing Indians: The Archaeology of Southern Fiction* and coeditor of *Reclaiming Native American Identities*; *Global Faulkner: Faulkner and Yoknapatawpha, 2007*; and "Global Contexts, Local Literatures: The New Southern Studies," a special issue of *American Literature*.

Michael Wainwright received his Ph.D. from Royal Holloway, University of London in 2005, with a dissertation entitled "Faulkner, Evolution, and the American South." He is the author of *Darwin and Faulkner's Novels: Evolution and Southern Literature* and a forthcoming volume entitled *Toward a Dawkinsian Hermeneutic: Essays on Literature and Genetics*. He is currently a visiting lecturer at Staffordshire University.

Michael Zeitlin is associate professor of English at the University of British Columbia and has coedited eight issues of the *Faulkner Journal*. He has published thirty essays in journals and books on such figures as Faulkner, Joyce, Melville, Donald Barthelme, Freud, and Lacan, and is coeditor of the volume *Soldier Talk: The Vietnam War in Oral Narrative*.

Index

www.ingramcontent.com/pod-product-compliance
Lightning Source LLC
Chambersburg PA
CBHW030308060726
47498CB00002BB/543